I0663460

LET THE
PEOPLE DECIDE

Neighborhood Organizing in America

U.

SOCIAL MOVEMENTS PAST AND PRESENT

Irwin T. Sanders, Editor

Abolitionism: A Revolutionary Movement
by Herbert Aptheker

The American Communist Movement: Storming Heaven Itself
by Harvey Klehr and John Earl Haynes

The American Peace Movement: Ideals and Activism
by Charles Chatfield

American Temperance Movements: Cycles of Reform
by Jack S. Blocker Jr.

The Animal Rights Movement: From Compassion to Respect
by Lawrence and Susan Finsen

The Anti-Abortion Movement and the Rise of the Religious Right: From Polite to Fiery Protest
by Dallas A. Blanchard

The Antinuclear Movement, Updated Edition
by Jerome Price

The Charismatic Movement: Is There a New Pentecost?
by Margaret Poloma

The Children's Rights Movement: A History of Advocacy and Protection
by Joseph M. Hawes

Civil Rights: The 1960s Freedom Struggle
by Rhoda Lois Blumberg

The Conservative Movement, Revised Edition
by Paul Gottfried

The Consumer Movement: Guardians of the Marketplace
by Robert N. Mayer

Controversy and Coalition: The New Feminist Movement
by Myra Marx Ferree and Beth B. Hess

The Creationist Movement in Modern America
by Raymond A. Eve and Francis B. Harrold

Family Planning and Population Control: The Challenges of a Successful Movement
by Kurt W. Back

LET THE PEOPLE DECIDE

Neighborhood Organizing in America

Updated Edition

Robert Fisher

TABOR COLLEGE LIBRARY
Hillsboro, Kansas 67063

TWAYNE PUBLISHERS

NEW YORK

Let the People Decide: Neighborhood Organizing in America, Updated Edition
Robert Fisher

Copyright © 1994 by Robert Fisher

All rights reserved. No part of this book may be reproduced or transmitted in any form or by any means, electronic or mechanical, including photocopying, recording, or by any information storage and retrieval system, without permission in writing from the Publisher.

Twayne Publishers

1633 Broadway
New York, NY 10019

Library of Congress Cataloging-in-Publication Data

Fisher, Robert, 1947–
    Let the people decide : neighborhood organizing in America /
Robert Fisher.—Updated ed.
        p. cm.—(Social movements past and present)
    Includes bibliographical references and index.
    ISBN 0-8057-3859-2.—ISBN 0-8057-3860-6 (pbk.)
        1. Radicalism—United States—History. 2. Community organization—United
States—History. 3. Social action—United States—History. 4. Social movements—
United States—History. I. Title. II. Series.
HN90.R3F57   1994
361.8—dc20   94-4261
                                                                              CIP

The paper used in this publication meets the minimum requirements of American National Standard for Information Sciences—Permanence of Paper for Printed Library Materials. ANSI Z3948-1984. ⊚™

10 9 8 7

Printed in the United States of America

Contents

Acknowledgments

I would like to thank some of the people whose criticisms improved this second edition of *Let the People Decide*. My friendship and coauthorship of a number of articles and an anthology with Joe Kling, which began with his reading of the first edition of this volume, has been both a personal delight and an intellectual challenge; our work together is stamped all over the second edition. Mike Miller, Bruce Palmer, and Sam Bass Warner, Jr., provided detailed comments on the new material. I appreciate heartily their taking time away from their own work to read and critique this one. Mike Eichler and Wade Rathke offered insights and gracious support. Harry Boyte challenged me with his own work. To all of their credit, they tried to improve the manuscript more than I was willing or able. Carol Chin, my editor at Twayne, did get me to reorganize some of the materials, and the book is much the better for it.

Earlier portions of this work have appeared in *New Politics* and in *Mobilizing the Community: Local Politics in a Global Era*, respectively coauthored and coedited with Joseph Kling. Grateful acknowledgment is made to the editor of *New Politics* and to Sage Publications, Inc. for permission to reuse this material.

This book is dedicated to the past, present, and future. To my father, Leo, who shouldered me for a long time. To Ace, who, I presume, had the good sense to delay his arrival until the neoconservative ascendancy seemed to be in its final days. And, most of all, to all those activists who continued, against great odds and obstacles, to struggle throughout the 1980s and early 1990s and whose work has planted millions of seeds for a more humane, democratic, and sustainable world.

Introduction

The problem with history is that it's written by college professors about great men. That's not what history is. History's a hell of a lot of little people getting together and deciding they want a better life for themselves and their kids.

—Bill Talcott, community organizer

Across the centuries . . . cities have given shape to and provided a backdrop for the most liberating of political action. . . . Indeed, what remains of public life in cities can be one base upon which a politics of urban rebirth and social transformation might be built.

—Larry Bennett, urban politics commentator

Much has happened in the world since the first edition of this book was published in 1984. The Berlin wall, Soviet Union, and the Cold War are gone. Communism has virtually disappeared as an alternative ideology and economic system. Nations fall apart and emerge overnight. Cities in the United States falter under the weight of unattended problems and displaced priorities. Worldwide political alienation and dissatisfaction mount, resulting in electoral instability, revolts, and repression. Global economic competition pressures even the most powerful multinational corporations and destroys communities, businesses, cities, and nations with sparse resources or less desirable ones. We are in the midst of an epochal global transformation, one comparable with the industrial revolution of the late nine-

teenth century. It is a difficult time to be writing about contemporary
events.

It is, however, an easy time to be cynical and pessimistic about the
prospects for democracy. By almost any standards, for example,
democratic participation has dramatically declined in the past 15
years. Voter turnout has dwindled. Political party identification is rare.
Those with money almost completely dominate electoral politics and
the policy-making process. Elite domination limits access to politics.
Citizens distrust politicians. Most are deeply cynical about and alienated from public life. Civic culture has devolved into a brutish individualism. Only the private—personal and family issues—seem to matter.
These are the themes of a number of recent bestsellers, the titles of
which mirror the concerns: William Greider's *Who Will Tell the People:
The Betrayal of American Democracy* (1992), Kevin Phillips', *The
Politics of Rich and Poor* (1990), James Stewart's *Den of Thieves* (1991),
E. J. Dionne's *Why Americans Hate Politics* (1991).

Countering this vision of despair is one of hope in a democratic
revival. Grounded in and sustained by the proliferation and persistence of grassroots organizing since the 1960s, activists hope that the
1990s will yield a more humane, participatory, grassroots politics.
Such a politics, they propose, has the potential to revive civic culture
at the level of everyday life, to empower previously powerless and mar-
ginalized groups, and to build the capacity of communities to meet
their own needs and advance progressive agendas.[1] Beneath the "trou-
bled view of politics," the Kettering Foundation reported in 1991, lies
"an American public that cares deeply about public life . . . a foundation for building healthy democratic practices and new traditions of
public participation in politics."[2] Contemporary social theorists such as
Alain Touraine, Manuel Castells, Joan Cocks, and Immanuel
Wallerstein see these grassroots efforts as having the greatest potential for challenging elite domination of the emerging "new world
order."[3]

One thing is certain about contemporary community organizing. It
is not restricted to the United States. The first edition of *Let the People
Decide* focused exclusively on the United States, and most of the new
material in this volume does so as well. But it is important, if we are to
understand and effectively respond to the epochal, global transformation underway, that we also view citizen action as an international
response to global changes. Grassroots organizing has become a dominant form of popular resistance and social change worldwide.

Jeff Drumtra in 1991 provided sketches of citizen action in 38 countries.[4] His research emphasizes how recent political reform in 25 countries in Asia, Africa, and Latin America now allows for wide voter participation in free elections with multiple candidates. Alan Durning goes further. In a similar comparative study he argues that people are coming together "in villages, neighborhoods, and shanty-towns around the world," in response to forces that endanger their communities and planet.[5] Karen Paget estimates that 2 million citizen action groups exist in the United States alone.[6] Stuart Lowe sees a similar upsurge of activity in the United Kingdom.[7] The same is true for most of Western Europe. Grassroots organizing and urban protest have been key elements of politics in the West since the late 1960s. But community action is not limited to Western industrial states. What happened in the West is only part of a widespread escalation of urban resistance throughout the world. The picture shows "an expanding laticework covering the globe," Durning continues. "At the local level, particularly among the close to 4 billion humans in developing lands, it appears that the world's people are better organized in 1989 than they have been since European colonialism disrupted traditional societies centuries ago."[8] Community organizing efforts, with hundreds of millions of members, have proliferated in the past 20 years, extending from nations in the West to those in the South, and, most recently, with extraordinary and very mixed results, to the East.[9]

The proliferation of grassroots efforts is in fact a hallmark of the era. Many efforts have come and gone in the past decade, but the view of the 1980s and early 1990s as devoid of continued activism and resistance is political myth. The rule of thumb was that citizen initiatives, like those pioneered by the "Freud of community organizing," Saul Alinsky, discussed in this book, couldn't last more than six years. This is no longer valid. ACORN (Association of Community Organizations for Reform Now) celebrated its 20th anniversary in 1990; National People's Action (NPA) did so two years later. Communities Organized for Public Service (COPS) in San Antonio will soon. Citizen Action, The Metropolitan Organization (TMO) in Houston, the New Jersey Tenants Union (NJTO), and many others, recently passed the 10-year mark, with no signs of declining despite having to organize under adverse conditions. Grassroots efforts tied to such nationwide causes as women's right to choose, gay rights, and the environmental movement not only persist but continue to grow. This was not the case in the mid-1970s, when the break-up of a four-year-old neighborhood organization I was involved with pushed me into writing this book. In the early 1970s I was teaching in Boston and working with a neighborhood organizing effort in Cambridge. In 1973, I had moved to Cambridgeport—a working-class and student-populated neighborhood across the river from Boston University, sandwiched between the Massachusetts Institute of Technology and Harvard University— where I quickly became involved in the founding and development of the Cambridgeport Homeowners and Tenants Association (CHTA), an Alinsky-style neighborhood organization. This was my first opportunity to assume leadership and responsibility in a political organizing effort. Like millions of others, I had been active in the antiwar movement of the late 1960s, but I was not really a "movement person" and my participation was limited mostly to political discussions, leafletting, and protest demonstrations. Organizing at the grassroots level in Cambridgeport in the neighborhood where I lived felt right. Talking politics with the neighbor next door or the grocer across the street, or getting a slumlord's vacant building torn down and replaced with a community-controlled cooperative garden, grew naturally out of everyday experience with friends and neighbors.

CHTA was founded largely by Steve Meacham, who had the original idea to build an insurgent neighborhood organizing effort around the issue of housing. But unlike the more radical tenant organizations in Cambridge, Meacham sought to unite tenants and resident homeowners in a class-based, not single-interest, organization willing to fight as much for just rents for tenants as tax rebates and a stable neighborhood for resident homeowners. From 1973 to 1976 hundreds of meetings were held in people's homes, in churches, and in neighborhood cooperatives. We held actions to protest university expansion into, and destruction of, the neighborhood, picketed City Hall to demand improved services, walked in support of strikers in local labor struggles, blocked evictions, and traveled on weekend mornings to the suburban homes of neighborhood slumlords to hand out leaflets informing residents of how their next-door neighbors exploited poor people.

Unlike new left radicals of the late 1960s, the organizers in CHTA consciously downplayed their radical sentiments and rarely sought to clarify their ideology. The organizers—those neighbors, most often college educated and young, who took a more active role in building the organization—were not leftist "intellectuals." In fact, we consciously sought to get beyond the barriers that radical ideology and rhetoric seemed to foster between activists and workers in the 1960s.

While CHTA won many battles, improved the quality of life in the neighborhood, and raised many people's political consciousness, it ultimately failed to create a working-class neighborhood organization. It remained dominated largely by young, college-educated, white men and women who had been or were still active in the peace and women's movements. The goal of empowering people at the neighborhood level in order to build from the grassroots up a left-oriented, national movement of working people was never approached. Initially most white working-class people in Cambridgeport were suspicious of the politics and motives of CHTA organizers, and the countless hours spent working, playing, and meeting together succeeded in bringing a significant but nevertheless small number of neighborhood natives into the group's leadership. CHTA had even less success with organizing the African-Americans in the neighborhood, who tended to doubt the primarily white organization's long-term dependability. Nevertheless, CHTA's serious commitment to democracy at all steps of the organizing process continued over time to break down resident suspicions. Despite obvious weaknesses, the organization in 1976 was growing, winning battles, broadening its focus by uniting with other efforts in the neighborhood, and continuing to be self-critical but also moderately self-satisfied. Then the "split" occurred.

The split in CHTA was caused by organizers who were more radical and who pointed out the limits and failures of CHTA's "nonideological" approach. They emphasized that a militant, avowedly socialist ideology—a clearly stated view of how the capitalist system works and why working people needed to join together to oppose it—was lacking. CHTA needed a clear and correct "line" to offer working people; then residents would get involved and devote more time and energy to building a multiracial working-class organization.

A few key leaders agreed almost completely with this criticism. They felt that CHTA needed to come out of the closet and openly advance an anticapitalist ideology. Many of the working-class leaders supported this position as well. And while most participants in the organization agreed to strive toward greater ideological clarity and organize people around a socialist vision, the split occurred because most of the more active members did not share the same socialist analysis and vision. The more individualistic and democratic socialist members emphasized the need to place democracy and democratic process at the center of community organizing; they believed that a socialist analysis would emerge from effective leadership and resident involvement. The more communistic members said that was like the tail wagging the dog and that "letting the people decide" was what CHTA and other "neo-Alinskyite" groups had been doing over the years with only limited success. They emphasized the importance of a clear, socialist ideology in attracting working people and the need for a centralized organizational structure that would provide direction and unity from above without sacrificing democracy at the grassroots. The "individualist" segment believed that the "centralists" had no understanding at all of democratic process and were fundamentally authoritarian, doctrinaire, and dogmatic. The Communists saw their opponents as petit-bourgeois reformers. Everyone was forced to take sides.

This type of split was not novel in the history of the left or neighborhood organizing. As the economic and political conditions of the mid-1970s made effective left organizing increasingly difficult and as many found the "nonideological" approach to neighborhood organizing of the early 1970s wanting, people seemed to turn on one another and inward to political theory for explanations and solutions.

The split sent people in all directions. Some activists left CHTA, joined more radical organizations, and went to work in factories to do union organizing. Others remained in Cambridgeport and continue today in their struggle to build a cooperative community that supports and empowers neighborhood residents in conflicts with slumlords, university expansion, and so forth. I got another teaching job and, with a good deal of doubt, left Cambridgeport.

Organizing with CHTA was one of the most powerful learning experiences of my life. But it left as many questions about political and neighborhood organizing as it had provided answers. Why do grassroots groups succeed or fail? How important is ideology and a long-term vision in the organizing process? How do successful groups balance a commitment to democracy with the need for direction and leadership? What were the advantages and limits of organizing at the neighborhood level? Can groups operating at a community level ever achieve any significant degree of success as social change organizations? How can grassroots groups connect up with national movements or organizations? These questions and many others heightened my interest in studying the history of neighborhood organizing.

One of the central themes of this book, that neighborhood organizing movements must be seen and evaluated within the context of national political and economic developments, grew not only out of my experience with CHTA but also out of changes in the historical discipline. For years people had been taught that the historical arena was limited to politicians in Washington or corporate executives in New York City. This led to a distorted view of how history is made, for it assumed that most people—those of the working class, minorities, women—did not have the power to affect history, that they were not historical actors but only objects of the forces set in motion by "historymakers." Historians were the chief proponents of this elite-serving myth. Courses and books in United States history traditionally limited their scope to the history of white, wealthy men. Even when addressing locally initiated efforts, historians wrote history from a national perspective and from "the top down."

In the 1960s a new group of historians emerged, reflecting both the radical spirit of the decade and different class and ethnic backgrounds from their elders in the profession. They began to study the historical roots of contemporary social problems. They wrote urban, ethnic, family, labor, community, and women's history. They consciously explored history "from the bottom up," and as they did the daily life and human relationships of ordinary people became an increasingly important and valuable part of the historical record.

But the "new social history" had a serious limitation. In the effort to uncover and write a "people's history," social historians rejected traditional approaches and thus tended to ignore political and economic developments at the national level that directly affected the lives of working people. The "turning inward" of members of the profession to locally based issues yielded an understanding of the history of working people and how "ordinary people" play a part in shaping history. But there was an absence of analysis of how the overall system functioned and where working people fit into it.

This limitation began to be corrected in the late 1970s as a better integrated social history emerged. Marxist historians have always written social history within the framework of larger political and economic developments. Increasingly their wider view, if not always their methods and conclusions, came to be adopted generally. "The social interpretation of history," a non-Marxist writes, "places ideas, events, and behavior as well as institutions in a larger context of the overall social system."[10]

What I came to learn from the events and literature of the 1970s was that social developments are part of a total economic and political system—a political economy—in which all strands of life, from the national to local level, intertwine. Most problems that contemporary communities face manifest at the neighborhood level but result from city, state, national, and even international factors. What is most striking, however, is how immune we think we are from the penetrations of the national political economy into our daily lives. We live in local communities, neighborhoods, towns, and cities; we participate in neighborhood organizing efforts on a scale of society where decisions of immediate and direct importance occupy our days. We direct our attention to our jobs, to the price of groceries, cars, and housing, to our health and that of our family. The local area is where we live our lives on a small, intimate, comprehensible scale. And rarely do we know or do anything about decisions made in corporate and governmental centers that will determine our course next year and many years after.

But this is not a one-way street where the national political economy exerts its will over a populace preoccupied with daily living. There is a dialectical relationship between the national and local arenas in which working people and their communities are not only acted upon but also cooperate with, resist, and stimulate national developments. For every national decision to expand the rights of workers in a Wagner Act in the 1930s, or to increase federal social services in a War on Poverty in the 1960s, there were militant local strikes and urban rebellions and protests that demanded and initiated these social changes. For every national decision, from declaring war against the Japanese in 1941 to invading Cambodia in 1970, there were the people who lived their lives at the local level who did or did not consent to fight.

The brief history of neighborhood organizing that follows seeks to contribute to the new social history by viewing the subject within the context of changes and developments at the city and national level, with an eye to the interpenetration between the national political economy and neighborhood-based organizing efforts. Accordingly, this study divides the past century into six periods that correspond with shifts in the national political economy and changes in the dominant form of neighborhood organizing. Each section begins with an overview of the political economy of the era and is followed by case studies of the most prominent or significant neighborhood organizing projects of the time. As sketched in Table 1 and discussed more fully in the conclusion, the book breaks down the history of neighborhood organizing into three dominant and distinct approaches: social work, political activist, and neighborhood maintenance. The goal, then, is to describe and assess the history of the dominant strategies of neighborhood organizing used since the 1880s and to provide a general introduction, not a comprehensive history, primarily for students and organizers, which does not artificially isolate the subject at the local level.

Before proceeding further, some terms need clarification. "Let the people decide" was a slogan used specifically in new left neighborhood organizing projects of the 1960s, but its ideal of democratic grassroots decision making captures so well the history of neighborhood organizing, its strengths and weaknesses, that it seemed a most suitable general title. Moreover, this work is a *selected* history of neighborhood organizing movements. Many important organizing projects are not included. The intent has been to focus where possible on the most significant organizations and the dominant strategies of neighborhood organizing. Where there already is a large body of literature on an effort, such as the social settlements, the treatment here tends to be more analytical; where little is known, the case studies tend to be more descriptive.

The terms *neighborhood* and *neighborhood organizing* also require definition. People can usually identify their neighborhood by name; they can give its boundaries; and they know who belongs and who is a newcomer. But because of intrinsic differences "neighborhoods" are sometimes hard to define. Sociologists Rachelle and Donald Warren, for example, identify six major types of neighborhoods based on how much people share a sense of neighborhood consciousness, how often neighbors interact, and what channels exist between the neighborhood and outside groups. Suzanne Keller, another sociologist, offers a comprehensive and a workable definition that better suits my purposes: a neighborhood is a locality with physical boundaries, social networks, concentrated use of area facilities, and special emotional and symbolic connotations for its inhabitants.[11]

This study does not seek to romanticize the value of neighborhoods. The more people turn away from large-scale institutions and corporate and government leaders, the greater the tendency to overstate the virtues of smaller institutions such as the neighborhood unit. But not all neighborhoods are desirable places to live, nor do all residents want to live there. Many people are trapped in neighborhoods by class barriers and racism; others view the neighborhood as

TABLE 1

History of Neighborhood Organizing: Three Dominant Approaches

	Social Work	Political Activist	Neighborhood Maintenance
Concept of community	social organism	political unit power base	neighborhood residence
Problem condition	social disorganization social conflict	powerlessness exploitation neighborhood destruction	threats to property values or neighborhood homogeneity insufficient services
Organized group	working and lower class	working and lower class	upper and middle class
Role of organizer	professional social worker enabler and advocate coordinator and planner	political activist mobilizer educator	elected spokesperson civic leader interest-group broker
Role of neighborhood residents	partners with professional recipients of benefits	fellow activists indigenous leaders mass support	dues-paying members
Strategy	seek consensus pursue gradualist tactics work with power structure promote social reform	engage in conflict mediate challenge power structure	seek consensus apply peer pressure do political lobbying engage in legal action

TABLE 1 (continued)

History of Neighborhood Organizing: Three Dominant Approaches

	Social Work	Political Activist	Neighborhood Maintenance
Goals	form groups achieve social integration deliver services bring about social justice	obtain, maintain, or restructure power develop alternative institutions	improve property value maintain neighborhood deliver services
Examples	social settlements community centers Cincinnati Social Unit Plan community chests United Community Defense Services Community Action Program United Way	Unemployed Councils tenant organizations Alinsky programs Student Nonviolent Coordinating Committee (SNCC) Students for a Democratic Society (SDS) Association of Community Organizations for Reform Now (ACORN)	neighborhood preservation associations neighborhood civic clubs property owners' associations

only a temporary space, a place to live before moving to a better community.[12]

Neighborhood appears at first to be a conservative concept—a place with boundaries to protect, a space where one can be "safe," a site for raising a family, growing up, and going to school. But this should not imply, as many modern sociologists have been quick to do, that neighborhood organizations are fundamentally committed to maintaining the status quo. Sociologist Emile Durkheim saw neighborhood institutions as progressive "mediating institutions" organized by the powerless that could challenge and limit the power of the state.[13] Neighborhood organizations have as much potential to heighten awareness and promote change as they do to maintain the status quo. It depends, in large measure, on the type of neighborhood, the conditions it faces, its class and racial composition, the motives and politics of the organizers, and the national political-economic situation at the time.

Neighborhoods are territorial spaces whose values, goals, and activities are not inherent but rather mirror the class and racial conflicts of the larger system. Poor people facing problems of unemployment, job discrimination, substandard housing, high crime rates, and only slight hope of improvement stand to gain little, if anything, from using the neighborhood as a vehicle to maintain the status quo. Their class position demands social change, and while they might seek to conserve, restore, and improve aspects of their community, their fundamental goal in neighborhood organizing is to change the conditions that keep them poor and powerless. Likewise, organizations in more affluent neighborhoods most often express the conservative and protective needs of their residents. They oppose commercial development, organize neighborhood police watches, and protect real estate values. The issue is more complex than suggested here. Lower-class and working-class neighborhood organizations also seek to defend their turf and can be as conservative and reactionary as their more affluent counterparts, and neighborhood organizations in more affluent areas often advocate social reform and use their organization to challenge authorities. Nevertheless, class and race factors determine to a large degree the direction and tactics of the neighborhood organizing effort and the extent to which goals can be realized.

In general the term *neighborhood organization* refers to an institution in which people who identify themselves as part of a neighborhood promote shared interests based primarily on their living or working in the same residential area.[14] The process in which they engage to achieve their objectives is referred to as neighborhood organizing or, covering a somewhat wider area, community organizing or community organization. Neighborhood organizing is often fueled by a conviction that people must take action themselves to realize their aspirations, by an emphasis on organizational autonomy, and by the subordination of all other activity to the priorities of neighborhood issues and concerns. This study focuses on groups that first and foremost identify themselves as neighborhood organizations. Many neighborhood institutions, interest groups, and voluntary associations, such as churches, fraternal associations, and benefit societies, might seem to qualify as neighborhood organizations but do not fall within these borders. Also not included are the host of racial and ethnic organizations in neighborhoods where residential area was not the primary basis of organization. This comes down to hairsplitting in some cases, as segregation patterns in our cities make it difficult to distinguish an organization based on race or ethnicity as opposed to one based on locality. In some circumstances I have taken the liberty to include organizations that do not fit the mold of a self-defined neighborhood organization in order to describe and assess more fully the variety of neighborhood organizing styles.

The words *reactionary, conservative, liberal, and radical,* used throughout the study, are relative terms that can hide as much as they explain. Until a more appropriate political vocabulary of neighborhood organizing develops, however, they are the best available. I use them in the following general manner: *reactionary* describes efforts to stop social change and decrease the power of lower-class and minority groups; *conservative* describes attempts to maintain the political and class status quo; *liberal* describes efforts to promote social changes that do not challenge the existing class and economic system; and *radical* describes efforts to advance political, economic, and social democracy that often, though not always, see the capitalist system as the cause of problems.

In preparing this second edition I have chosen to keep the first edition much as it was, preserving its spirit, voice, and analysis. The second edition adds this updated introduction, a new chapter on neighborhood organizing in the 1980s and early 1990s (chapter 6), a revised conclusion, and an updated bibliography. Beyond the obvious need to update the first edition, four major influences in the past 10 years serve as a backdrop for and inform my motives for writing this second edition. First, my move to teaching at a graduate school of social work has afforded a much closer look at and better understanding of the "social work model" and its relation to social change. Some of the most impressive activism I have witnessed in the past decade has been done by women employing a "feminist practice" and by gay men delivering social services to persons with AIDS (PWAs) while engaging in a political struggle against homophobia in particular and injustice in general.

Second, my deepening intellectual interest in urban political economy and in political and cultural theory, assisted by my friend and frequent coauthor Joe Kling, has given me a keener appreciation of social theory as a wide-angle lens through which to view the changes of the past generation and specifically the last decade. The new theories afford a better intellectual framing of the practice described herein.

Third, two years in Austria forced upon me an international and comparative perspective. Being abroad made me miss and appreciate the openness, multiculturalism, and creative energy in the United States. But the comparative perspective made me angrier about the deplorable conditions of our cities and the absence of fundamental social rights and services, such as health care, housing, and safety in the United States.

Fourth, conditions in most neighborhoods are much worse than when I wrote the first edition. This is no time to either forget the issues or to temper our involvement. I remember a coalition meeting a few years ago with child advocates, some of whom were concerned about getting angry. It was not professional. It was not rational. It made them personally uncomfortable. Good. We should all be uncomfortable with contemporary conditions. Change demands it. This second edition is designed to keep encouraging that anger. But it is also intended to promote hope, hope that comes from knowledge, perspective, critical analysis, and a collective memory of prior struggles and victories.[15]

Chapter One

Social Welfare Neighborhood Organizing, 1886–1929

Industrialization and Liberal Reform

> *The whole process of modern life, the whole process of modern politics, is a process by which we must exclude misunderstandings, exclude hostilities, exclude deadly rivalries, make men understand other men's interest, bring all men into common counsel, and so discover what is the common interest. That is the problem of modern life which is so specialized that it is almost devitalized, so disconnected that the tides of life will not flow.*

—Woodrow Wilson, governor of New Jersey

Woodrow Wilson was a historian, president of Princeton University, governor of New Jersey, and president of the United States. He was never a neighborhood organizer. His sentiment that the conflicts of modern urban/industrial life could be resolved through education and interclass communication was shared, however, by the first generation of neighborhood organizers. In social settlements, community centers, and neighborhood health clinics, in cities throughout the nation, community workers put into practice their plans for "progressive democracy." Their goal, like Wilson's, was to resolve the conflicts that had emerged in the prior generation of rapid and often traumatic industrialization, and to do so without fundamentally challenging the existing class system. Life in the United States had changed dramatically in the half century after the Civil War. As Henry Adams put it: "In the essentials of life . . . the boy of 1854 stood nearer the year one than to the year 1900." Adams's view that life had changed more in 50 years than in the 1,850 years before was more accurate for the middle class than for the working class. But the dramatic transformation he spoke of affected all segments of the society.

The cause was the industrial revolution, which began in England in the late eighteenth century, took hold in the textile mills of New England in the late 1820s, but did not become a dominant force in the United States until after the Civil War. The speed and magnitude of the changes during the two generations after the war, however, were awesome. Briefly stated, the following fundamental changes occurred: economic relationships expanded from the personal relations of a village community to the impersonal forces of a national market; goods and methods of production were standardized along with many other aspects of life; people were segregated by occupation and task at work and by class, race, and ethnicity in communities; bureaucratic, institutional forms of control were expanded to socialize the workforce and direct people's public and private lives; and material acquisition was exalted as the primary goal in life. It was almost as if a traditional world had been recast into a modern civilization in one generation. Woodrow Wilson and the activists in the first neighborhood organization movement were part of a liberal reform effort after 1900 that sought solutions to the most obvious problems caused by this rapid economic change.

The astounding growth of cities in the generations after the Civil War attests to their importance as the nuclei of the industrial transformation. Between 1870 and 1920, for example, Boston Philadelphia, Pittsburgh, and Washington, D.C., more than tripled their populations. New York City and Brooklyn consolidated in 1898 to form a city of some 3.5 million people. In the next 20 years an additional 2 million people stretched the limits of the Empire City. Chicago, a child of the railroads and the industrial revolution, grew from just under 300,000 in 1870 to 2.7 million in 1920. The South was still largely rural, but major centers like Atlanta, Birmingham, and Houston grew at similar breakneck rates. Ironically, the creation of a national network of major cities signified not the strengthening but rather the disappearance of the city as an autonomous economic, political, and social unit. As the city became the headquarters of a national economic revolution, local concerns mattered less and less to the corporate leaders who ordered and controlled the direction of industrialization and who focused on national and international, not local, markets.

Nevertheless, the internal structure of cities mirrored the economic transformation of industrialization. Prior to rapid industrialization, cities were relatively small, compact, and well integrated. With walking being the major means of transportation, the physical distance between the places where people lived, worked, worshipped, shopped, and played was minimized. Neighborhoods distinguished by class, race, or ethnicity appeared as early as the 1820s, but in general the "pedestrian city" was not spatially segregated or fragmented. Between 1870 and 1920, however, cities like Boston grew from a radius of 2 to 10 miles. The preindustrial walking city was replaced, more or less, by an industrial city that radiated out from a central business district (CBD) in rings of ascending class status, most of which were further segregated by ethnicity or race. This "ring-sector" model of the industrial city is too simplistic to be generalizable to all cities. But the pattern of increasing segregation, fragmentation, and centralized growth occurred in cities as different as Boston, Chicago, and Houston.

The first neighborhood organization movement must be seen as one trend in the national liberal reform movement called progressivism. Progressivism grew out of the industrial relations of the years 1870 to 1895, a period characterized by fierce and unbridled competition among capitalists and between capitalists, on the one hand, and workers and farmers, on the other, over who would control and benefit from industrialization. The decade from 1895 to 1905 was a watershed in the transition from the industrial capitalism of 1870–95 to the finance capitalism and liberal reforms of the generation that followed. Around 1895 bankers like J. P. Morgan of Morgan Guaranty and Trust purchased controlling interest in corporations as diverse as the newly formed U.S. Steel and General Electric from industrial capitalists like Andrew Carnegie and Thomas Edison. Control of key industries began to be consolidated among an elite group of financiers. The period 1895–1905, for example, saw the merger of some 300 separate firms each year into highly centralized and powerful industrial conglomerates.[1]

This economic transformation profoundly affected all relations in the society. Many representatives of small and middle-sized firms in the business world continued to support the logic of laissez-faire industrial capitalism. Led by organizations like the National Association of Manufacturers, they supported unbridled competition and the quick dispatch of insurgent worker movements that threatened their ability to compete and grow. But a new strategy among more "progressive" corporate leaders of large corporations like General Electric and International Harvester emerged after 1895 to profit from the changing economic situation. The new economic situation encouraged stability, not competition. This new strategy, since labeled "corporate liberalism," sought, of course, to maximize profits, but it emphasized the shortsightedness of earlier repressive tactics and the need to develop more liberal mechanisms and attitudes that would ameliorate conflict and disorder and promote industrial harmony.[2] Corporate leaders could better achieve their objectives, the corporate liberals argued, by promoting a fundamentally unaltered but peaceful economic, social, and political climate.

As economic power became more centralized, many corporate leaders concluded that the social order, too, should be stabilized by supporting programs of social concern and responsibility. At the state and national level government regulations were passed to curb grossly excessive corporate practices, practices corporate liberals believed bred unnecessary conflict and disorder, and corporate liberals supported ameliorative social and health programs to address, at least superficially, the social byproducts of rapid industrialization. In short, corporate liberal leaders of big business and government sought to demonstrate that capitalism worked in the interests of all the people, not simply the wealthy, that businessmen were not robber barons, and that politicians were not insensitive to the difficulties of life in the urban/industrial order.

Of course, businessmen and their political voices had always preferred harmony and stability to conflict and disorder. In the past, however, in part because of labor militancy, the cost of stability had been too high. With finance capitalism, however, the increased concentration of control in some industries, especially the ability to control prices, coupled with the intervention of the federal government to promote economic stability, made the strategy feasible. The new progressive relations between government, business, and the people did not end industrial conflict and insurgency. But, as a historian of progressive reform succinctly summarized, the nationwide progressive movement in the years 1900 to 1920 did "achieve order, stability, and control, while preserving the existing class system and distribution of wealth."[3] In these years liberal corporate leaders and public officials replaced repressive measures with reform programs and replaced the social Darwinist ideology of laissez-faire capitalism, which had dominated the Gilded Age, with a new rhetoric of building a people's democracy through private and public social engineering.

This new political economy was worked out in the decade before World War I by corporate and government officials, sometimes in cooperation with conservative union leaders. It was neither a conspiracy in the sense that it was planned nor an instantaneous stroke of corporate genius. The initial proponents of social change were workers and their advocates, those at or near the bottom of society, who were benefiting least from industrialization. The corporate liberal vision, which has dominated economic relations in most of the decades since 1900, emerged from liberal experiments initiated by corporate and public officials at the local level to capitalize on the shifting economic situation and to defuse more radical demands for change made by workers, farmers, and even some segments of the middle class. As the strategy proved successful, corporate and government leaders increasingly adopted it.

Liberal reformism became a nationwide political movement in 1900 with the succession of Theodore Roosevelt to the presidency, but it began in the 1880s with reform experiments at the local level. Some of the earliest reform efforts were initiated in cities like New York and Chicago by "communitarian" reformers. Unlike most of their liberal contemporaries in the civic-commercial elite, who emphasized the need for concentrated, centralized, and corporate forms of organization to promote social order, the first social welfare activists sought to address local problems by working at the neighborhood level in face-to-face relations with the urban working class. These communitarian reformers were among the first to draw attention to the serious poverty, health, housing, recreation, and labor conditions in immigrant and working-class areas of industrial cities. And they were among the first to warn of the need to ameliorate conditions of industrial capitalism lest class warfare result in a cataclysmic revolution. They worked in social settlements, community centers, adult education schools, and neighborhood health clinics located in or near neighborhood slums. These "decentralizers" were ultimately more democratic and open-minded and less tied to corporate economic objectives than their liberal counterparts in business and government. But they shared with them the underlying perceptions, ideology, and objectives of the larger reform impulse, and it was not until after 1900, when progressivism took root at the national level, that such local neighborhood reform efforts like the settlement movement found prestige and a sound footing.

To be sure, there were many faces and shades of progressivism—from suffragettes and temperance advocates to Woodrow Wilson and the members of the influential National Civic Federation, an association of representatives from the corporate, government, and labor sectors. Of course social reformers did not approach the problems of the era exactly as did their corporate counterparts. But it was ultimately corporate leaders and national political figures, the most conservative elements in the reform movement, who set the tone and parameters of reform activity in the years 1900 to 1920. And it was within the limits of the emerging political economy of corporate liberalism that urban communitarian reformers formalized the first neighborhood organization movement in American history.

The Social Settlement Movement

Like the medieval monasteries, the university settlements, facing the worst results of the industrial revolution, of a new migration, and of the unmanageable growth of cities, may at first fill a strange variety of functions; but their deep and abiding use lies in direct effort toward scattering the social confusion and reestablishing social order.

—Robert Woods, settlement worker

The settlement house movement began in the slum neighborhood of the East End of London, when two Oxford University students spent Christmas Eve, 1884, in the half-completed Toynbee Hall. Toynbee Hall was established primarily to ameliorate the problems of poverty and "bridge the class gap" between rich and poor. The method was simple if not completely successful: put college students into working- and lower-class neighborhoods, have them serve neighborhood resident needs as much as possible, and have them offer programs that introduced the poor to the student's upper-class world. Earlier efforts at charity had failed, settlement workers in England believed, because of condescending and hostile attitudes toward the poor. What was needed was a "new approach to poverty." By working and living directly in the poverty neighborhood, settlement workers hoped to address problems more sensitively and more effectively than charity workers and, most significantly, they hoped to work with, not for, residents.

Less than two years later, Stanton Coit, a graduate of Amherst College in Massachusetts with a Ph.D. from the University of Berlin, spent three months at Toynbee Hall and returned to the United States in 1886 eager to establish similar "neighborhood guilds" throughout America. In late summer Coit moved to the Lower East Side of New York City, an immigrant enclave, where he organized a workingmen's club that first met in his apartment and then in a small building he purchased. Begun with the support of reformers, labor leaders, and ministers, Coit named this initial American settlement house Neighborhood Guild. Befitting the optimism of contemporary social activists, Coit declared that within 10 years neighborhood guilds would "be the foundation of a civic renaissance in America," a civic renaissance based in neighborhoods and committed to facing the wide range of problems that beset America's immigrant and native working-class communities.

Of course Coit overestimated the impact of the guild and neighborhood self-help programs in general, but the idea did catch on. Independent of his effort, college women from the upper-class schools of Smith, Wellesley, Vassar, Bryn Mawr, and Radcliffe founded College Settlement in 1898, not far from Neighborhood Guild. A week later Jane Addams and Ellen Gates Starr, roommates at Rockford College in Illinois, initiated what became the most famous settlement, Hull House, in an inner-city, working-class neighborhood in Chicago, not far from where Mrs. O'Leary's cow was said to have performed its act of arson almost two decades before.

The settlement workers were in large measure the college-educated daughters and, to a lesser extent, sons of "old wealth," families of "substance" but not great wealth or power. For example, the fathers of Jane Addams and Julia Lathrop, a coworker at Hull House, were successful lawyers and Republican senators in the Illinois legislature. Many, especially the men, were children of ministers or members themselves of the social-reform-minded clergy of the day that developed in response to the gross inequities of industrial capitalism in the Gilded Age. Like Coit, many of these social reformers found their inspiration in trips to Toynbee Hall. But the "alarming" conditions in America's slum neighborhoods provided more than enough fuel for the settlement movement to spread and grow rapidly. In 1891 there were 6 settlements in the United States; by 1900 over 100; five years later more than 200; and by 1911 more than 400. As early as 1907, less than a decade after its founding, Hull House had expanded from a single, roomy mansion to 13 buildings covering more than a large city block.

Settlement workers got involved in neighborhood organizations out of a mixed bag of sympathy, fear, guilt, social concern, and a desire to give purpose to their own lives. The latter was especially true for the women, whose career opportunities were limited to teaching, nursing, library science, and the emerging field of social work, of which settlement work was the most progressive branch. Depending on the individual settlement, settlement workers sought to "uplift" and "Americanize" the immigrant poor, improve health and social conditions, and espouse the virtues of Protestantism, Catholicism, Judaism, or some variant of secular humanism. But all settlements shared an objective: to promote social order by serving as class mediators between the rich and poor, between capitalists and workers. They hoped to inform the upper class about the existence and needs of the "other half" and to instruct the poor that the capitalist class were businesspeople who, like all people, belonged to "the one great brotherhood of humanity." To be sure, settlement workers had more immediate objectives and each leader had his or her priorities. But it would be difficult to overemphasize the perception of liberals of this era that society was coming apart at the class and ethnic seams and that anarchy was imminent if "capital" did not mend its ways and if reformers did not go into the slum neighborhoods and ameliorate the "festering conditions" of ghetto life.[4]

To achieve their goals of class cooperation and social harmony, settlement houses offered a wide variety of programs. Some settlements were more vigilant in their commitment to social justice, and their activities reflected it. Others were more conservative, especially the religious-affiliated settlements, which were generally more interested in controlling, not advocating for, the poor. Individual differences apart, however, settlements offered classes in English, civics, literature, art, cooking, sewing, dressmaking, and wood and sheet-metal working; provided services such as legal aid, employment assistance, laundry facilities, health care, nutritional counseling, day and night nurseries for working mothers, and public baths; and sponsored recreational and athletic programs, neighborhood vegetable gardens, and concerts and theater productions to acquaint neighborhood residents with what they called their "higher life" culture. The more progressive settlements permitted and sometimes encouraged neighborhood groups, labor unions, and even radicals to use the house for discussions on contemporary issues.

Settlement workers chose to organize at the neighborhood level because for them the local community was the appropriate base for reform activity. Robert Woods, the founder of South End House in Boston, described why:

The neighborhood is large enough to include in essence all the problems of the city, the State, and the Nation and in a constantly increasing number of instances in this country it includes all the fundamental international issues. It is large enough to present these problems in a recognizable community form, with some beginnings of social sentiment and social action with regard to them. It is large enough to make some provision for the whole variety of extra-family interests and attachments. . . . On the other hand, it is small enough to be a comprehensible and manageable community unit. It is in fact the only one that is comprehensible and manageable; the true reason why city administration breaks down is that the conception of the city breaks down. The neighborhood is concretely conceivable; the city is not, and will not be except as it is organically integrated through its neighborhoods.[5]

Well-organized neighborhoods, advised by enlightened settlement leaders and furnished with rudimentary social services, would serve as the counterforce to what social reformers saw as the "inchoate anarchy" and greed of nineteenth-century industrial capitalism. But the neighborhood was not to be the culmination of settlement work. Workers disdained excessive localism, especially that practiced by their opposition, the ward politicians. Settlement activity was intended to transcend neighborhood borders. The more progressive settlements, for example, were active at the city, state, and national level lobbying for tenement reform, kindergartens, school nurses, child labor laws, playgrounds, workers' rights, progressive education, and city planning. Settlements were conceived as the locally based "spearheads" of a nationwide liberal reform movement, not simply as neighborhood-based social service centers.[6] The history of the settlements has been ably detailed elsewhere. What is important to underscore here is that their social welfare style of neighborhood organizing did not visibly improve ghetto conditions, increase the power of neighborhood residents, or alter significantly the elitist practices and biases of traditional organized charities. For example, instead of addressing political and economic problems that undermined ghetto neighborhoods they chose to concern themselves primarily with social issues. In their own neighborhoods, settlements limited their political activity to gathering information on tenement, health, and recreation conditions. When the more adventurous settlements did venture into local electoral battles to take on a ward boss, they almost always lost. They were successful in local politics only in the rare circumstance when the proportion of middle- and upper-class voters in their district outweighed immigrant support for local machine candidates.

Likewise neighborhood residents turned elsewhere—to themselves, their families, their institutions—for economic support. The problems of slum life that neighborhood residents faced were, after all, the result of a lack of economic power to alter their conditions. Working people needed better wages; they needed job security; they needed more control over their economic life so that they, too, like the upper and middle classes, could live more comfortably and healthfully; they needed to share more equitably in the profits of industrialization. The settlement's sponsorship of social programs that sought social harmony within a framework of economic inequality reflects the unwillingness of liberal reformers to challenge the economic causes of the poverty that surrounded them. Preferring not to take sides in the class conflict or address the economic roots of problems meant that the settlements served the interests of the class in power by, as Robert Woods said, "scattering the social confusion and reestablishing social order." To have taken the side of workers would have been inconsistent with liberal goals of order and harmony because it would have heightened, not ameliorated, class tensions. Such a position would also have jeopardized settlement funding from philanthropic capitalists. Therefore, settlements focused on social issues, not political or economic ones. Community, not class, was the keyword in the new liberal state.[7]

Where they did address economic problems, as on the tenement issue, settlements pursued a strategy of working with those in power—in government and in the housing industry—rather than working with tenement dwellers. Tenement reform legislation was planned, passed, and, of course, applauded in reform circles without the assistance or participation of those most affected, the neighborhood residents. Settlement reformers failed to address the serious undersupply of decent, affordable, low-cost housing. Tenement reformers urged successfully that old tenements be torn down and replaced with parks and playgrounds. Between 1900 and 1917 the city of Chicago alone built 90 new parks and 100 new playgrounds. Code enforcement legislation sponsored by reformers improved housing conditions but also displaced tenants as rents increased to unaffordable levels. Without participation from the poor and without a commitment to serving the needs of the working class, such neighborhood renewal efforts often hurt working people rather than helped them.[8]

Moreover, the settlements' social welfare style of neighborhood organizing remained elitist, despite the fact that every progressive settlement from Toynbee Hall and Neighborhood Guild to Hull House professed to work with, not for, the people. And without citizen participation, as on the tenement issue, settlement programs were often part of the problem, not the solution, for working-class people. John Daniels, the author of a book in 1920 on neighborhood organizing and an advocate of neighborhood democracy, tried to explain the settlements' "top down" approach.

The reasons for proceeding in this way, instead of in a way which actually enlists the neighborhood, are quite understandable. The settlements general motive, to promote the local welfare, is good. The specific object in view, as for instance a playground, is good. The need is believed to be urgent. Therefore the quickest way to obtain the desired object appears to be the best way. To attempt to secure an organized demand on the part of the people of the neighborhood would take a lot of time. Besides, some element in the neighborhood might not agree with the settlement as to the urgency of the need and the best way of meeting it. So, the settlement workers argue, as long as they have the situation in hand and really represent the neighborhood, their best plan is to do the thing themselves, "for" the neighborhood, rather than to take the longer and slower route of having it done "by" the neighborhood.[9]

But this elitist decision-making process derived from more than the magnitude and exigency of the task. The very idea of settlement work to "elevate" the masses to "an appreciation of the higher life" defined the class relationship between "uplifters" and those needing uplifting. When Mary McDowell established the University of Chicago settlement in the Back of the Yards neighborhood no one asked the residents whether they wanted one. Settlement workers in Back of the Yards and elsewhere did not seek to work through existing immigrant neighborhood associations or to organize the existing indigenous leadership. Rather McDowell and other settlement workers moved into a neighborhood, developed a settlement in their own image, furnished it in upper-class style, imposed moral values such as no swearing or drinking wine or beer at the settlement house, and then went out knocking on doors and talking with people in the streets, inviting them to come and take part in settlement activities.[10]

The typical response of most neighborhood residents was to stay away. John Daniels offered why. If community organization is "the local vitalization of democracy, so that the neighborhood truly functions in ways which are 'of' the people, 'by' the people, and 'for' the people," Daniels said, "the reason why most schemes of community organization are not accomplishing much is that they are attempts from without, and usually from above, in which the neighborhood itself has little or no part and to which therefore it fails to make any substantial response."[11] While as early as 1894 Hull House, perhaps the most successful settlement, attracted some 2,000 visitors per week, more than 70,000 people lived in only a six block radius of the settlement. Once settlements were established institutions in the neighborhood most immigrant leaders expressed a good-natured friendliness and willingness to cooperate with them. Community leaders knew that settlements provided valuable social services, especially for women and children. But settlements did not represent the neighborhood or its residents. "They're like the rest," one immigrant community leader noted, "a bunch of people planning for us and deciding what is good for us without consulting us or taking us into their confidence."[12] Settlements were even less of a force in nonwhite neighborhoods. As one African-American commentator put it: "The influence of the settlements in our life is negligible. If they were to disappear overnight, the life, the growth, and development of my people and their assimilation into American life would go on just the same."[13]

Instead of turning to settlements organized and run by outsiders, working-class people relied on themselves, their families, and their own self-help ethnic and religious institutions. Reformers were wrong, not to mention ethnocentric, in assuming that urban slums were "disorganized" and that neighborhood residents needed externally initiated efforts to organize their community. Industrialization, immigration, and slum life did not destroy people's need for or ability to create supportive community networks. Instead of relying on settlements organized by upper-class outsiders, neighborhood residents preferred to use their own churches, synagogues, mutual benefit associations, and ethnic, labor, and political organizations, not to mention informal networks of support, to advance their collective and personal interests.[14]

Settlement founders and leaders were correct in their assessment about the extent of class and ethnic segregation that divided people in the modern metropolis. Mistrust, antagonism, and chauvinism dominated most interclass relations. Settlement leaders came from the other side of the tracks, a world of privilege, devoid of hard physical work and material discomfort. Their new neighbors in the inner-city slums knew keenly the problems of poverty and industrial labor and viewed "uplifters" with a healthy suspicion. Given this situation, settlement efforts to legitimize their work and their existence by encouraging resident participation in decision making should have been of paramount importance. This is a first principle of neighborhood organizing. The absence of such efforts merely underscores the extraordinary extent of class mistrust and ethnic division in the industrial metropolis. At Hull House the board of directors was composed of wealthy residents of Chicago and its suburbs, never people who lived in the Near West Side neighborhood, except Jane Addams. When Graham Taylor, the founder of Chicago Commons, relinquished his position as head resident, his daughter Lea succeeded him. Taylor believed that neighborhood people lacked the necessary skills to be settlement workers because they only understood the working-class world of their community and were ill prepared to interpret the slum neighborhood to the upper classes.[15] The same was true of ethnic-initiated settlements. At the Harlem (New York) Federation Jewish settlement, founded in 1905 by upper-class German Jews and East European Jews to mold the values of the newly arrived, proletarian immigrants from Eastern Europe, old-guard German Jews permitted no workers and only one member of the Eastern European elite on the board of directors.[16]

Class elitism, not democratic selection, determined who participated in and decided on the objectives and programs at Hull House, Chicago Commons, and the Harlem Federation, three of the more liberal settlements. Most settlements were not as progressive or as sensitive to immigrant and working-class culture; programs of most Catholic and Protestant settlements, for example, were often a direct assault on the Old World heritage and self-image of workers. In general, reformers sought an association with the working class in which they provided the direction and in which fundamental class and power relationships remained unaltered. It is testament to the hard work and zeal of these settlement workers and to the severe conditions of neighborhood slum life that the settlements' services were used even as much as they were.

In sum, there is no question about the sincerity or commitment to social reform of those who made the settlement their life's work. They lived and worked in slum areas. They braved small-pox epidemics to inspect tenement and sweatshop conditions. They faced the frustration of door-to-door neighborhood work in communities where they were clearly outsiders. They even got shot at when, on the rare occasion, they supported factory workers engaged in labor disputes. Overall, they played a positive role in delivering needed services, raising public consciousness about slum conditions, and calling for collective action to ameliorate selected problems. What they did not do is address the causes of these ills. Their vision of *one* community, of *one* democracy consciously avoided the different interests and objectives of the segregated and divided groups in America's cities; they acted as if the assumption of a classless, united society would make it so. They wanted neighborhood residents to have faith that social workers could successfully determine and meet the needs of the poor, and ultimately offered social service solutions to economic and political problems. In response, working-class people took what they needed from the neighborhood services. Neighborhood people knew, though they may not have said it this way, that liberal neighborhood programs primarily served the interests of stability and order by providing only modest reform programs within the framework of deep economic and political inequities. They knew that such social welfare neighborhood organizations served the interests of those in power more than they did the needs of working people.

The Community Center Movement

I am more interested in what you are doing [with social centers] than anything else in the world. You are witnessing the foundations of DEMOCRACY.

—Charles Evans Hughes, governor of New York

By the second decade of the twentieth century, other liberal reformers also interested in neighborhood organizing saw the need for something more effective and widespread than the settlements. Settlements, it was plain, were not fulfilling their stated objective of participatory democracy and, even if they were, 400 settlements were far fewer than Stanton Coit's dream of one in every neighborhood. Moreover, settlements cost money to establish and run, and the interest of corporate benefactors in settlements was seriously limited. In fact, the more officials at the national, state, and local levels supported reform programs to maintain class harmony, the less need there was to fund such private enterprises as social settlements.

In an effort to give their work greater legitimacy, to make it more systematic, more efficient, and more attractive to funding sources, neighborhood workers in the years preceding World War I began to transform their vocation into the profession of "community organization." Professionalization came earlier to most other white-collar occupations; by this time doctors, lawyers, and professors had raised themselves to the level of "experts." In neighborhood work professionalization began almost imperceptibly before 1914, accelerated during the war, and was formalized in the 1920s when community organization, along with case work and group work, became subfields of the newly emerged profession of social work. In the process, the focus of neighborhood work shifted from social reform to the coordination of social welfare agencies and activities. This led to programs not only devoid of citizen involvement but also without any interest in democratic participation. In fact, the more community organization emphasized "expertise," the more neighborhood residents were seen as passive "clients" and "recipients" of social services. Nowhere is the effect of professionalization on social welfare neighborhood organizing more vivid than in the early history of the community center movement.

Social reformers active in settlements, recreation, and adult education banded together as early as 1907 to lobby for the use of school buildings after school hours as neighborhood social centers. The effort began in Rochester, New York, where public funding enabled Edward Ward to establish a neighborhood-based civic association in a public school. This was not the first time schools were used after hours as recreation centers. Since the 1890s boards of education in major cities had offered free adult education classes and recreation activities in public schools in the hope of speeding up the process of Americanization. The new social centers were to be different, however, because they were not limited to recreational activities, and, most important, because "socialized schools," their organizers argued, could act as magnets attracting citizens whose segregation into class and ethnic groups had obscured their common bonds, loyalties, and responsibilities. Like the social settlements before them, social centers would lend harmony and foster cooperation among the working-class and immigrant elements and at the same time ease some of the difficulty of slum life.

Despite the reluctance of public officials to support a program that might develop into an independent and alternative political machine, the idea of using schools as neighborhood centers caught on as readily in the decade after 1910 as settlements had in the decade before. Schools were used as centers for voting, employment information, recreation, education, health services, and Americanization programs. Attendance at the social center in P.S. (Public School) 63—the first center in New York City, located on the Lower East Side—was nearly 130,000 in 1911–12, its first year of operation. In 1912 the national campaign platforms of the Democratic, Republican, and Progressive parties all endorsed the social center idea. By 1918–19 community centers—the name changed from social centers around 1915—were operating in 107 cities. Five years later the number of centers more than doubled to 240, and by 1930 New York City alone had almost 500 centers with an annual aggregate attendance of more than 4 million. By 1930 community centers had clearly met the objective of reformers for widely accessible neighborhood public spaces.

The first centers, begun during the heyday of progressivism, between 1907 and 1915, emphasized neighborhood self-help and cooperation. Clinton Childs, the organizer at P.S. 63, saw them as centers of neighborhood democracy:

A community clubhouse and Acropolis in one; this is the Social Center. A Community organized about some center for its own political and social welfare and expression; to peer into its own mind and life, to discover its own social needs and then to meet them, whether they concern the political field, the field of health, of recreation, of education, or of industry; such community organization is necessary if democratic society is to succeed and endure.[17]

The organization of centers nationwide followed a pattern similar to the one at P.S. 63. The People's Institute, a private, multifaceted reform organization working primarily in the neighborhoods of the Lower East Side of Manhattan, sponsored Childs's efforts at P.S. 63. The institute organized a committee of professional reformers, academics, and businessmen, which identified the neighborhood project area and secured permission from the Board of Education to use the neighborhood school if residents were interested in the idea. Childs, an organizer employed by the People's Institute, went to live in the immigrant neighborhood, where he identified groups that might support the social center idea and enlisted their help and participation. With the assistance of local organizations, Childs organized a mass meeting at the school to discuss the projected center. The meeting established a social center committee and formed a neighborhood group, composed primarily of representatives from neighborhood clubs, to govern the center. Childs was elected director of the neighborhood group.

Word spread quickly in the neighborhood that the school was open for after-hours use and people responded avidly. The People's Institute and other groups sponsored concerts, weekly civic forums, a child welfare exhibit, and various entertainment activities. An orchestra of some 30 workers and students calling themselves the Beethoven Musical Society, under the direction of a neighborhood resident, gave 10 concerts at the center. Political meetings to discuss workers' problems and contemporary issues were held and union representatives as well as those from the Progressive, Democratic, and Socialist parties all participated.

Programs varied from center to center and from city to city, reflecting organizers' interests as well as the local political situation. Rochester social centers emphasized civic and political forums. New York City programs ranged from service activities to entertainment and recreational programs, political forums, and club meetings. In general, however, entertainment and recreational programs, not activities focusing on political issues or social change, predominated at most centers. Public officials discouraged political programs. In Rochester, for example, where centers focused on contemporary political concerns, local officials attacked them as "socialistic" and cut off funds. Ideally, social centers were to be governed "from the bottom up." But from the outset, citizen involvement, as in the social settlements, was limited to membership in clubs and participation in center activities. While club and organization leaders sometimes participated in the initial neighborhood groups, planning and supervision was left primarily to the professional organizers who initiated and directed the centers. The initial ideal of having professionals serve as advisers to neighborhood residents swiftly degenerated into an elitist relationship in which social welfare professionals made all important decisions without the assistance of community people.

As a result, social centers were not much more successful than settlements in transcending the limits of liberal, social welfare neighborhood organizing. Center organizers should have had an easier time of neighborhood organizing than their predecessors. By 1910 residents in many neighborhoods were accustomed to "do gooders" and the more sensitive and progressive social reformers had won some degree of acceptance based on the services they provided. By the second decade of the twentieth century social reform was a permanent feature of the urban landscape and social center activists had a tradition and a historical experience on which to build. The settlement experience should have indicated that institutional longevity could ease tensions with neighborhood people but not resolve class and ethnic suspicions by itself. The paternalism and elitism of liberal neighborhood organizers on the one hand, and the antagonism and mistrust characteristic of most interclass and interethnic relations on the other, required more than time or good intentions.

Overcoming such barriers was not impossible, but doing so required vastly different organizing objectives and methods than the settlement experience provided. It required meeting the needs of working-class people as they defined those needs. To begin with, people in neighborhood groups at social centers had to be assured that they could run the centers, that the space was *theirs.* Such a people's organization never developed. The public school was not controlled by the residents, and the school boards and organizers were not about to give them control. Organizers improved on settlement practice by asking neighborhood residents what the area needed and what they wanted and by contacting and enlisting the support of community leaders and organizations. But given the class bias of social center organizers and the restraints imposed by using public facilities in cities where local officials feared resident control could lead to independent working-class political organizations, citizen participation in social centers remained largely advisory and token. Without legitimacy as neighborhood organizations run by neighborhood people, organizing practice in the social center movement quickly developed into a professionalized form of neighborhood work characteristic of much social work community organization before and since that time.

Throughout the liberal reform movement of the early twentieth century, there existed a tendency toward professionalization, bureaucratization, and centralization. Corporate liberals put this into practice first in their businesses; "good government" advocates of such municipal reforms as the city manager plan followed. In the emerging field of social welfare, community work became increasingly professionalized after 1915, and community centers were no exception. Increasingly center organizers became less concerned with fostering class cooperation and more so with coordinating social welfare programs and developing professional associations that could guide neighborhood efforts "expertly" and systematically. In 1916, for example, they founded a professional organization, the National Community Center Association (NCCA). The NCCA published a weekly newspaper, the *Community Center,* which offered current news on what organizers were doing in their neighborhoods, what methods seemed to work and which did not, and generally how the profession was developing. Professional conferences sponsored by the NCCA enabled community workers to get together, share experiences, and develop a supportive network out of which a better sense of professional identity could arise.

At the local level, many center organizers grew increasingly interested in providing comprehensive planning and professional programs in neighborhoods. In one district in New York City, the Gramercy area, neighborhood workers set up not only a community center but also a training school for community workers and a community information clearing house. The training center was the first to offer academic and experiential training to those interested in the new career of community work. The clearing house was a professionally administered service that provided employment, health, housing, and reform movement information for neighborhood residents. Like the NCCA, these local programs provided a source of identity, instruction, and experience for professional community workers.

Reflecting this new direction, even the rhetoric of citizen participation was rewritten in new professional terms that emphasized the importance of "scientific expertise." When Clinton Childs founded the first social center in New York City in 1911, for example, he saw it as a "community clubhouse and acropolis." John Collier, a leading organizer in New York City who would become the director of the Bureau of Indian Affairs in the 1930s, saw the community center in 1917 as a neighborhood place where "experts" would be based. In his words, "Democracy needs science, and the community movement aims to put science—which means experts—into the people's hands . . . [so that] the laity share the enthusiasm of the expert and the expert becomes in a true local sense the adviser and servant of the citizen."[18]

But that was the ideal, not the practice. Increasingly, the centers belonged to the professionals who ran them, not to the neighborhood residents. Collier's staff were supervisors, not advisers. By 1915 in many centers the neighborhood groups that initially consisted of elected representatives from neighborhood organizations were now composed of appointed professionals from local social service organizations and city bureaus. Because of the new emphasis on professional and efficient service delivery, the neighborhood group came to serve not as a vehicle of citizen participation but rather as a coordinating board of service delivery representatives from hospitals, recreation associations, and the like. Community centers began to look more and more like a neighborhood-based, professional social service bureaucracy rather than a community acropolis.

Professionalism, in and of itself, is not a major drawback. Support networks, communication links, training centers, and programs to create a more effective and systematic practice of neighborhood organizing were important and natural developments. But whose interests did the new emphasis on professionalism serve? As historians have shown, the emphasis on "expertise" in most elements of the liberal reform movement made activities significantly undemocratic. The growing professional orientation in the social center and settlement movements reflected liberal reform objectives that degenerated into a preoccupation with competence, peer approval, and the technical aspects of community work. Without a truly democratic theory of citizen involvement and without a history of developing neighborhood-run organizations, professionalism resulted in increasing insulation from the residents. And as professional objectives and concerns became paramount, the initial ideal of neighborhood self-determination became no more than a memory of the social center movement's infancy.

The entry of the United States into World War I sealed this trend. In late 1917 the federal Council of National Defense and local subsidiaries at the state and city levels organized a highly bureaucratic and centralized program to "nationalize neighborhoods" in support of domestic war mobilization efforts. Community center professionals, seeing the program as an endorsement of their neighborhood organizing efforts, wholeheartedly promoted the use of community centers to coordinate grassroots support for programs developed in Washington. In their support of the war "to make the world safe for democracy," center organizers and local social welfare and political leaders transformed community centers into neighborhood-based arms of the state.

Increased supervision and surveillance of activities accompanied wartime bureaucratization. Representatives from the public and private sector were appointed to the neighborhood groups by the city officials and social workers, among others, who sat on local Councils of National Defense. Center programs soon reflected the demands of the war and the new special interest groups represented on their governing boards. Recreation became less important. Forums were watched more closely for subversive activities by community center workers who were under pressure from local authorities. Some programs, for example, were canceled because they were conducted in a foreign language that city officials could not understand and did not trust. Patriotic propaganda dominated civic and social club activity and motion pictures were censored to conform to war objectives. Centers became sites for coordinating Americanization classes, Red Cross relief, Liberty Loan drives, and food austerity programs.

As before, but even more so now, citizen participation was limited to programs sponsored by center professionals. Centers were the sites where residents could enlist to become involved, provide support, and make sacrifices in the war effort. To this end all residents using the centers had to sign a pledge, which read:

I promise to continue within my ability for the period of the war to conserve food as the Food Administration orders, conserve fuel as the Fuel Administration prompts, subscribe to Liberty Loans or buy War Saving's

Stamps according to my income, help worthy organizations with books, clothing or funds, give personal labor when time permits.[19]

In a sense, centers prospered during the war years. Activities multiplied, funding increased, and in the end 107 cities in the nation had community centers. The whole "community movement" achieved widespread recognition and prestige during the war. But the bureaucratization, centralization, and professionalization of community work that brought such success also promoted values and goals very different from those first announced by social center organizers a decade earlier. Reform goals of increasing citizen participation, easing class tensions, and providing valuable services devolved under the pressures of war mobilization into outright social control, professional and governmental domination, and repression of dissent. Some neighborhood workers, like John Collier, grew anxious about the increasing centralization and bureaucratization. Most, however, regarded the war-related programs as the conscious application of democratic social engineering, which, if successful, would establish a neighborhood-based, postwar reconstruction program. But all supported the war and the use of centers in war mobilization.

The trend toward professionally controlled and bureaucratic neighborhood work continued in the 1920s. Not only did the 1920s fail to spawn a postwar reconstruction program as reformers had hoped, it produced a conservative reaction that blamed liberal "do goodism" for getting the United States into the war. During the decade neighborhood service programs devoid of citizen participation and administered by professionals became the accepted norm. Leroy Bowman, a leading theoretician of community organization in the 1920s, went so far as to disparage earlier efforts as "the community religion of a few years ago when the drive was on to go out and get people into community organizations, democratic in the extreme and supposedly dominated by neighborly sentiments."[20] The hard-headed realism of professional community work in the 1920s was supposed to be focused on meeting people's social welfare needs, not the "romantic" ideals of democratic community organizing.

Bowman was wrong on two counts. First, prior community organization had not been democratic. The only thing "extreme" about it was the gap between the stated goal of citizen involvement and the actual practice of elite professional control. Second, programs of the 1920s did not meet neighborhood needs any more than did prewar efforts.

Community workers in the 1920s may have spent more time studying and analyzing community problems, whereas their predecessors spoke of the virtues of democracy, but the results of liberal community work in both decades were similar. Recreation programs dominated community centers in the 1920s as they had prior to the founding of the first social centers in 1907. In the 1920s local officials accepted community centers as part of local government's responsibility and implemented a highly bureaucratic, and centralized, system of well-attended community schools run by school officials and social welfare and recreation professionals.

Although Bowman's remarks reflect social work's break in the 1920s with the ideal of democratic citizen participation, the practice and impact of neighborhood organizing remained fundamentally the same. Community work continued to focus on professional concerns and the efficient delivery of services. Partnership between "experts" and "the people" was no more or less a reality in the 1920s than it had been before. And if the conditions of urban poverty had improved at all, it was not because of the ameliorative recreational services that community center professionals offered as their solution to the conditions of slum life. In neither the social settlements nor the community centers had liberal reformers built neighborhood organizations that were either democratic or effective in combatting the causes of poverty.

The Cincinnati Social Unit Plan

We see democracy not merely as government by the people, or as representative government, but as an organization of us—of ALL of us—through which we ourselves can come together to study for ourselves our common needs; to decide for ourselves which of these needs comes first; to employ the highest technical skill the nation affords in formulating plans for meeting those needs; to study such plans in advance of their operation; and finally to carry out those plans ourselves, not only because we desire them for ourselves but because their nature is such that they cannot be carried out by anyone except ourselves. The aim, the purpose, of such an organization is not the good of some of us to the hurt of the rest, but the good of all of us, as well as of each.

—Wilbur Phillips, community organizer

The plan[s] of Mr. and Mrs. Wilbur Phillips for community organization are, I believe, the best signs we have that democracy is yet possible for America.

—Mary Follett, settlement worker

The most ambitious, acclaimed, and widely advertised single experiment in neighborhood organizing in the years before the Great Depression was the Cincinnati Social Unit Organization. Wilbur and Elsie Phillips were the architects and chief organizers of the "social unit plan," which they tested first in St. Cyril's parish in Milwaukee and then in the Mohawk-Brighton neighborhood of Cincinnati. Like their predecessors in the settlement and social center movements, the Phillipses were dismayed by the increasing segregation of life in urban America. They too initiated neighborhood-based experiments they hoped would transcend class barriers and get working people to participate in progressive political efforts. They too held great hope in the potential of "experts" to solve America's problems. The social unit plan hinged on the premise that "experts" should serve the needs of the people and that consumers of social services ought to share joint responsibility with professionals in determining, in a democratic manner, what those local needs were. But unlike settlement and community center leaders who shared a similar vision, Wilbur and Elsie Phillips laid out and implemented an elaborate neighborhood-oriented health care plan that practiced what they preached. In the process, however, their effort to deemphasize the political nature of their neighborhood organizing backfired. To the chagrin of Wilbur and Elsie Phillips, their project in Cincinnati to organize a social unit, address social problems, and forge social harmony soon became embroiled in a political conflict that destroyed the organization.

Wilbur Phillips began his social service career in 1906, when after graduating from Harvard he went to work for the New York Milk Committee. The New York Association for Improving the Condition of the Poor, a long-standing charity organization, set up the committee to investigate the quality of milk available in poor neighborhoods and the infant health problems that seemed to result from "impure" milk. There was a heated controversy at the time among health care professionals over whether pasteurized milk and bottle feeding contributed to infant mortality and childhood disease. The results of the free milk program that Phillips organized in neighborhood milk stations did not resolve this nutritional debate. But it did demonstrate to Phillips that poverty, not the quality of milk, was the chief cause in poor neighborhoods of the high infant mortality of one out of every six babies.

Phillips's marriage shortly thereafter to Elsie LaGrange Cole helped him decide to leave the Milk Committee. Cole, the Vassar-educated daughter of the superintendent of schools in Albany, New York, was working with women's trade unions and was a member of the Socialist party when she met Phillips. Wilbur joined Elsie in matrimony and party membership. As members of its more conservative wing, the Phillipses, like many of their fellow neighborhood workers, thought that class divisions were largely a product of misunderstanding. A capitalist like John D. Rockefeller, whom Wilbur had met once, was for them merely "a thoroughly good man who hasn't the steady stink of poverty under his nose."[21] They believed in the need for a system of production and distribution that was organized, as Phillips put it, for human use, not for profit. For them, the Socialist party articulated best the ideals of brotherhood, human solidarity, and a peaceful transition to a cooperative democracy.

The Phillipses left New York and moved to Milwaukee in 1911 to join the first elected socialist municipal government. Wilbur convinced the new administration to support an experimental, community-based, democratically organized child welfare program that would put into practice some of his Milk Committee experience. As coexecutives of the Child Welfare Commission, a semiprivate organization under the supervision of the city government, the Phillipses set up a child health center in one neighborhood—St. Cyril's Parish. They brought doctors, nurses, and midwives into the center and put them in a working partnership with a committee of neighborhood women who gathered data on infant health problems in the neighborhood and who encouraged residents to use the new neighborhood health service. Based on the positive results of the project and the supportive response of neighborhood residents, Wilbur and Elsie sought to expand the program throughout the city. Now more than ever before they were convinced that a cooperative commonwealth was possible if residents and experts worked together in a mutually helpful and democratic manner.[22]

But socialist control of Milwaukee's city government was interrupted by the electoral victory of an antisocialist fusion effort, and the new administration, amid a full-scale attack on socialist programs, phased out the Child Welfare Commission. The Phillipses returned East, temporarily out of work, convinced of the correctness of their approach and scarred by the harsh realities of urban politics. If democracy were to become a reality, they now believed, government had to be restructured along nonpartisan lines from the neighborhood block on up. They called this idea the "social unit plan," and in 1915 they assembled a temporary organizing committee to gather support for their program. At a committee meeting in Washington that year the Phillipses brought together an impressive contingent of progressives. Prominent philanthropists like the Guggenheim and Tiffany families rubbed elbows with socialists Helen Phelps Stokes and John Spargo, industrialists Adolph Lewisohn and William Loeb, Jr., intellectual and political leaders Gifford Pinchot, Felix Frankfurter, and Herbert Croly. These people were among the most influential and acknowledged leaders and supporters of reform prior to the 1930s. The meeting raised $100,000 in support of what was to become in 1916 the National Social Unit Organization (NSUO), and Pinchot, Harriman, and Tiffany, as well as prominent community workers, accepted committee directorships.

The central components of the social unit plan were a block council, citizen's council, occupational council, and general council. The entire plan rested on the block councils, which were composed of block residents; here neighborhood people were to determine their needs and priorities and pass them on to the citizen's council for consideration. Each block group elected a block worker, who represented them on the citizen's council. Occupational groups of professionals functioned as block groups, each electing a representative to an occupational council. The general council, which served as a governing board, was composed of the members of the citizen and occupational councils. In sum, a simple democratic structure, applicable for many types of neighborhood-based programs, would ensure meaningful participation from residents and specialists.

When the Phillipses and the NSUO went looking for a neighborhood in which to base an experimental child health care center, they chose Cincinnati because social and medical workers there proved to be especially enthusiastic about the social unit plan. Wilbur Phillips spent most of 1917 laying the groundwork for the project. He gave informational lectures throughout Cincinnati and organized support from key professional sectors. In March 1917 some 600 Cincinnatians voted the Cincinnati Social Unit Organization (CSUO) into existence and established committees to administer the competition among various neighborhoods vying to be the demonstration project site. The five neighborhoods that emerged as leading contenders, including the eventual winner, Mohawk-Brighton, came from that section of the "ring-sector" city that settlement workers called the "Zone of Emergence." The "zone" was situated just outside the slum core, and its residents were "old immigrant" Irish or German workers who "had emerged from the slum into the mainstream of American life."[23] The zone neighborhoods, and especially Mohawk-Brighton, were more attractive to the Phillipses than the "new immigrant" slum neighborhoods of the inner city because, while the inner city slums were in greater need of health care services, the "zone" neighborhoods exhibited more interest and were less difficult to organize.[24]

The social unit structure was quickly set in place. Mohawk-Brighton was divided into 31 blocks, each with approximately 500 people. The CSUO then contacted known supporters in each block area and asked them to initiate a block council. Each block council then elected a block worker to represent and serve them. Voter turnout in the block worker election was 71 percent, far beyond voter participation levels in local elections. All the block workers were unemployed women, as women tended to be more interested in and knowledgeable about infant health care. The Phillipses explained the concept of the social unit plan to the block workers and instructed them in the methods and duties of block organizing. Each worker was paid $8 per week to collect data, develop citizen participation in the block group, disseminate information, and offer services to the block as would a social service advocate. The Phillipses and a temporary organizing committee also set up occupational groups of doctors, nurses, and social workers, who elected representatives to the occupational council. The physicians council of 26 doctors, for example, elected 9 representatives to the occupational council. Teachers, businesspeople, and members of the clergy were also asked to participate but exhibited little interest. Only six months after establishing the CSUO the Phillipses had formed the Mohawk-Brighton Social Unit Organization (MBSUO) with a budget of some $35,000 raised through private contributions and a $15,000 grant from various Cincinnati social and health organizations.[25]

The first project, a child health care center, succeeded remarkably. The nursing staff and block workers made some 5,388 visits to 576 babies, of whom over two-thirds received full medical examinations. This postnatal care program led the organization into other preventative and prenatal health projects. By 1920, in response to the demand for increased services, the MBSUO was sponsoring prenatal care, medical examinations for preschool children, bedside nursing, supervision of local tubercular cases, epidemic disease prevention, and postnatal examinations.[26] In two short years the Cincinnati Social Unit Organization had established one of the most comprehensive, effective, and cooperative public health programs in the nation.

In March 1919, Franklin K. Lane, secretary of the interior in the Democratic Wilson administration, became the honorary national chairman of the National Social Unit Organization and took the opportunity to announce the organization's plan to set up other demonstration projects around the nation. The social unit plan of Wilbur and Elsie Phillips looked like it was about to achieve widespread success and renown. On that same day in March, however, Mayor John Galvin of the very Republican city of Cincinnati took the opportunity to dampen Lane's optimism by charging the CSUO with being but "one step away from Bolshevism." "It aims at establishing a government within a government," he warned.[27] The Cincinnati baseball team, who would win the World Series that year, were the only Reds Galvin was going to tolerate in his town, especially if they had the potential to build an alternative political force in the city. One year later the CSUO was but a memory. The lessons of its quick demise are instructive.

The Phillipses had defused a similar charge in 1918. Jimmie White, the director of the Department of Public Welfare and the head of Union Bethel Settlement, who had been invited, given his prominent position, to participate in the social work occupational group, was shocked by the "socialistic ideas" he heard expressed among the social unit leaders, most of whom were politically liberal, not socialist. But Jimmie White was a conservative Cincinnatian, and the progressive ideas of the CSUO sounded dangerous to him. White was a close friend of the ultraconservative Charles P. Taft, the multimillionaire owner of the *Times-Star* and the brother of William Howard Taft, former president of the United States. When White resigned because, he said, the CSUO was really a national political party with socialistic tendencies, Taft made sure that all charges were displayed on the front page of the *Times-Star*. The Phillipses, in a nation preoccupied with World War I, were able to weather this first storm.

One year later, however, Mayor Galvin's charge occurred amid the "Red Scare," a nationwide purge of radicals orchestrated by the politically opportunist attorney general, A. Mitchell Palmer. The success of the revolutionary Bolshevik faction in the Soviet Union provided the excuse for political repression throughout the United States. Under concerted attack by the elite in Cincinnati, support for the CSUO dwindled fast. The Council of Social Agencies in Cincinnati, a prime funding source controlled by conservative business and political interests, withdrew all financial support, including money already promised. The council further threatened to cut off funding to any agency that continued to support the social unit. In response, the Phillipses and their liberal supporters organized a plebiscite on the social unit. More than 4,000 out of an estimated 7,000 eligible voters in Mohawk-Brighton declared in favor of the plan; only 120 voted against it. It was an impressive show of support, but the neighborhood referendum was not enough to keep the plan alive.[28] The CSUO closed its doors shortly thereafter, and the social unit idea was defunct nationwide by mid-1921.

Part of the social unit's problem was the antiradical, antireform, postwar political situation. Neighborhood-based efforts are often affected deeply by national programs over which they have little control, and the Red Scare and the "return to normalcy" of the decade after 1919 destroyed many liberal and radical programs. But part of the cause of the CSUO's quick collapse and failure to withstand, even minimally, the attacks of reactionary forces rests with some serious errors in neighborhood organizing practiced by the Phillipses and their progressive cohorts. Some years later Wilbur Phillips summarized the failure of the CSUO as the result of a lack of independent, economic self-support. But this was in reality only part of the problem. Depending on elite support does, most often, doom social change efforts to either a short life or co-optation. But the CSUO failed because it never sank political roots in the district of Mohawk-Brighton, roots that would have supported and nourished it in turbulent times.

The social unit plan succeeded largely because of the impressive support of wealthy, prominent, and influential liberal backers at the national level. Securing such support formed an important aspect of the Phillipses' organizing strategy; they put much energy into this activity, and they did it well. They were much less successful, however, getting neighborhood people to participate in the block groups. To its credit, the Mohawk-Brighton experiment attracted and developed indigenous neighborhood leaders; the block workers were active, hard working, and effective intermediaries and advocates. Certainly the social settlements and community centers never approached this level of indigenous leadership in their neighborhood organizing projects. But the block groups rested on these block workers. Most residents saw no need to get involved.

True, the Phillipses and the block workers never had much time to develop indigenous support at the block level and sink the potentially sustaining grassroots. But their style of nonpolitical organizing compounded the problem of failing to attract neighborhood people as active participants. The issue of child health care successfully attracted widespread liberal support and convinced the city's elite to permit the demonstration project. But the need for decent health care could have mobilized militant neighborhood support as well. The Phillipses' "post-Milwaukee" brand of politics sought consensus and cooperation with the existing powers, so they never presented health care in the neighborhoods as a political right that neighborhood people might some day have to defend. The Phillipses organized around a conservative strategy. They never emphasized the real need for citizen involvement, never emphasized that without resident participation and a willingness to fight for the program, opponents or liberal benefactors could take away health care services as easily as they had permitted or supported them. Without militant grassroots support, the Social Unit Organization lost battles where its liberal elite support was less powerful than local interests.

The Cincinnati Social Unit experiment reveals that regardless of what some organizers say, neighborhood organizing is a political act with political consequences. Organizing for a more cooperative and more equitable democracy is a highly political act. Mayor Galvin stretched the point when he accused the Phillipses of trying to establish a "government within a government," but he came closer to the truth than Wilbur or Elsie, who thought after Milwaukee that they were "through with politics."[29] The Phillipses saw their community work as being above politics. They saw the social unit as a plan that in its universality would transcend politics and win adherents from all "reasonable" segments of the population. But without a political analysis of the situation they faced and without a good understanding of class and power interests in Cincinnati, the Phillipses and the CSUO were doomed to defeat by more powerful and more politically astute opponents.

The Phillipses should have known better. Their experience in Milwaukee demonstrated the fragility of reform programs. Ironically, the Phillipses became more conservative after their experience in

Milwaukee, seeking to depoliticize their program and appealing to the lowest common political denominator. But this "pragmatic approach" only helped to get the project started. They were on thin ice from the outset. After all, the Phillipses were outsiders, ex socialists at the least, with a large following of nationally prominent reformers, who did not necessarily have the same immediate interests as the local Cincinnati elite. Without the potentially militant support of the neighborhood residents in Mohawk-Brighton and without political power at the local level, when suspicion turned to opposition in Cincinnati the Phillipses and the social unit plan had nothing to stand on.

Chapter Two

Radical Neighborhood Organizing, 1929–1946

Depression and New Deal

Landlord, landlord,
My roof has sprung a leak.
Don't you 'member I told you about it
Way last week?

Landlord, landlord,
These steps is broken down.
When you come up yourself
It's a wonder you don't fall down.

Ten bucks you say I owe you?
Ten bucks you say is due?
Well, that's ten bucks more'n I'll pay you
Till you fix this house up new.

What? You gonna get eviction orders?
You gonna cut off my heat?
You gonna take my furniture and
Throw it in the street?

Um-huh! You talking high and mighty.
Talk on—till you get through.
You ain't gonna be able to say a word
If I land my fist on you.

Police! Police!
Come and get this man!
He's trying to ruin the government
And overturn the land!

Copper's whistle!
Patrol bell!
Arrest.

Precinct Station.
Iron Cell.
Headlines in Press:

MAN THREATENS LANDLORD
TENANT HELD NO BAIL
JUDGE GIVES NEGRO 90 DAYS IN COUNTY JAIL
                    —Langston Hughes, "Ballad of the Landlord"

The corporate liberal strategy of progressive reform depended on a sound and prosperous economy. Because programs were expensive, they were only instituted when corporate profits were large enough to both satisfy investors and cover the costs of increased wages, improved working conditions, and ameliorative social reform programs. In general the period 1900 to 1929 was one such period of corporate growth and sizable profits. But that era ended with the stock market crash in 1929 and the decade-long economic depression the crash initiated. The plans of corporate liberals, not to mention those of working people, were dashed on the rocks of the nationwide depression.

As the depression deepened, frustration with evictions, unemployment, and inadequate relief programs resulted in individual acts of defiance, like the one Langston Hughes described in the "Ballad of the Landlord." Insurgent groups organized from the neighborhood up to the national level to harness and maximize this energy. Most notably for the history of neighborhood organizing, Communists, Socialists, and independent radicals organized the unemployed in neighborhoods throughout the nation. Tenant unions opposed the unilateral power of landlords. Activist Saul Alinsky began his lifelong work of developing "people's organizations" at the neighborhood level. While such neighborhood organizing projects differed, they all shared the spirit of militancy and radicalism that dominated neighborhood organizing in the years 1929–46.[1]

Cities, the geographic centers of the economic system, were devastated by the depression. Some southern and western cities, which were less integrated into and therefore less dependent on the national economy, were not hurt as badly as the northern industrial centers. Cities devoted more to finance than industrial production tended to fare better. But in general, people could not pay taxes, so many cities simply went bankrupt. State and city officials were helpless. At the neighborhood level, community workers in the settlements, community centers, and the social work profession had few ideas about how to stem the tide. They did, however, turn away from neighborhood organizing as a solution to the economic depression and looked to the national capital for answers. Because, they reasoned, the economy of the nation, not to mention the industrial world, was far more integrated in 1930 than it had been in 1900, a well-coordinated, centralized national plan of action, most likely issued from the White House and similar to domestic efforts during World War I, seemed the only salvation. Decentralized, local responses were viewed by most progressives as an anachronism with little utility in the current national economic crisis.

The White House responded slowly and conservatively. At first President Hoover suggested that the depression was largely a psychological problem. If business leaders would think and act more positively and invest new capital, then prosperity would be "just around the corner." Business leaders, however, foresaw no imminent economic upturn. The demand for products did not exist to warrant chancing capital investments. Better to sit tight. So, as the depression deepened and demand declined further, business laid off more workers and continued to cut costs. The wealthy could wait until the economy bottomed out or until more favorable incentives for investment appeared. It was the workers who had little to fall back on. In the latter part of his administration Hoover replaced his unsuccessful plan of "think positively" with a strategy of federal intervention best labeled "pump priming from the top." According to this plan, profit incentives to business, initiated by the federal government, would encourage investment and stimulate the economy. Hoover's Reconstruction Finance Corporation (RFC) offered loans to banks and other businesses, and as an afterthought to local government agencies, in the hope of stabilizing these sectors and allowing recovery to filter down through the society. But the program was too hesitant and too limited and had little impact.

When Franklin Delano Roosevelt succeeded Hoover he offered little more than the psychological and trickle-down approach of his predecessor. FDR's inaugural message that "we have nothing to fear but fear itself" was no sounder than Hoover's "prosperity is just around the corner." The initial programs of FDR's New Deal, especially the National Industrial Recovery Act (NIRA), the Agricultural Adjustment Act (AAA), and the first Banking and Securities Acts, represented only a more creative form of pump priming from the top. The NIRA, for example, organized committees to maintain wages and employment but also sought to stimulate investment by waiving all antitrust action against corporations involved in NIRA planning, thereby giving them virtual license to consolidate. The first AAA developed a plan of agricultural subsidies that paid farmers to keep land out of production. The AAA used the power of the federal government to maintain agricultural prices by reducing production at the very time consumers lacked food and could not pay the old, declining prices, let alone the new, subsidized ones. Moreover, most of the AAA money went to large-scale operations, not the tenant farmers and sharecroppers in the South who needed it most. The thinking behind these business-designed plans maintained that if federal programs could stimulate profits and investment (the "supply side" of the cycle) then purchasing power and demand too would be heightened, and a cyclical upturn would be forthcoming.

Roosevelt used this conservative approach without success from 1933 to 1935, a period often referred to as the First New Deal. Business accepted the benefits of the programs but remained unconvinced that the economy was ripe for investment. In 1935 unemployment and purchasing power were little better than they had been in 1933. During the First New Deal, FDR initiated a number of relief activities, among them the Federal Emergency Relief Administration (FERA), Public Works Administration (PWA), Civilian Conservation Corps (CCC), and Civil Works Administration (CWA), which provided some benefits and jobs. But, in essence, little trickled down to the bottom half of society except continued hard times.

By 1935, however, with a presidential election just around the corner, Roosevelt had more to fear than fear itself. In the early years of his administration, Roosevelt was able to portray himself as the defender of the common man and woman against the interests of big business. "Mr. Roosevelt is the only man we ever had in the White House who would understand that my boss is a sonufabitch," was how one worker put it. And in the beginning of his first term most workers accepted their bad fortune with courage, fortitude, and patience, choosing to stick it out while Mr. Roosevelt did his best to improve the situation. But by 1935 patience was growing thin. The New Deal looked pretty much like the usual practice: government helping business and asking workers to make continued sacrifices. Always the shrewd politician, FDR shifted to a Second New Deal around 1935, which emphasized the "demand side" of the economic ledger. This approach sought to "prime the pump from the bottom" by encouraging employment, thus raising purchasing power and increasing demand. The greater demand for products, the administration figured, ought to stimulate capital investment. Programs like the Works Progress Administration (WPA), Unemployment Insurance, Social Security, Aid to Families with Dependent Children (AFDC), and the National Labor Relations Act ("Wagner Act") gave workers jobs, direct relief benefits, and improved bargaining positions with management. FDR was not a fan of the deficit spending ideas of the English economist John Maynard Keynes. But given the dismal political and economic situation in 1935–36 and the fact that big business had failed to get in line and support Roosevelt's fiscally conservative program from 1933 to 1935, FDR had few other alternatives if he wanted to ensure his reelection.

The growing discontent and protests of the destitute elderly, workers, farmers, and the unemployed also demanded change. Some 5 million elderly joined Townshend clubs, a movement begun by Dr. Charles E. Townshend, an elderly physician in California who promoted a plan to secure a federal pension of $200 a month for everyone over 60. Senator Huey Long of Louisiana mustered a considerable following nationally and launched a powerful attack on the New Deal with his "Share Our Wealth" program. Townshend, Long, and others commanded a considerable number of votes and represented an important electoral threat to FDR and the Democratic party. James Farley, a New Deal tactician, estimated in 1935 that Long alone could receive 3 or 4 million votes if he ran on a third-party ticket, which could hand the 1936 election to the Republicans. The more Roosevelt saw a rising tide of discontent taking electoral form, the more he moved left to undermine its taking hold.[2]

But it was not only these electoral threats that forced the New Deal into an economic program of deficit spending and social welfare capitalism. Locally based, direct action movements of radicals and workers also pushed Roosevelt and the New Deal further left than they cared to venture. The Unemployed Councils of the Communist Party of the United States of America, Upton Sinclair's End Poverty in California (EPIC) campaign, Farmer-Labor parties, Socialists, Musteites (the followers of pacifist A. J. Muste), and independent radicals organized mass protests in workplaces and communities that demonstrated the growing militancy and dissatisfaction of working-class people. These activities, unlike those of Huey Long, for example, were viewed less as challenges to Roosevelt's reelection and more as threats to the social order and system of capitalism in general.

But the relationship between local organizing and White House policies was not a one-way street from the local to the national level. FDR's Second New Deal did more than respond to workers' protests; it also encouraged, sometimes unintentionally and reluctantly, future direct actions at the local level. New Deal programs like the Wagner Act, for example, which lent federal support to union organizing efforts, led to the formation, growth, and success of the Congress of Industrial Organizations (CIO). The industrial union movement, in turn, created a mass base for worker-initiated reform throughout the nation and spawned a political climate that was both conducive to and supportive of left-oriented neighborhood organizing programs. These ranged from unemployed councils to tenant movements and the initial efforts of Saul Alinsky in Chicago. Those begun before 1935 were the direct product of depression-era conditions at the local level. Those begun after 1935 essentially owed their impetus and direction to the CIO organizing campaigns. In sum, the interaction of depression conditions, radical local organizing, federal policies, and a vibrant national labor movement created a dynamic decade in the history of insurgent neighborhood organizing.

While protest groups developed first and best at the local level where their work was rooted in day-to-day industrial and community struggles, most, like the Socialists and Communists, saw local organizing, whether in the factory or the neighborhood, as essentially the best means for forming a national party or nationwide insurgent movement that could effectively address the failures of a "collapsing capitalist economy." Even Saul Alinsky, who above all thought of neighborhood organizing as a possible end itself, knew that the success of what he called a "people's organization" depended on the coordination of local efforts into a larger, national movement—a community-based, national organization comparable with the CIO.

Neighborhood organizing in the 1930s was characterized not only by its radicalism but by this dual concern of building an insurgent movement at both the national and local levels.

The Communist Party Organizes the Unemployed

The communists brought misery out of hiding in the worker's neighborhoods. . . . Sometimes I'd hear a communist speaker say something so bitter and extreme, I'd feel embarrassed. Then I'd look around at the unemployed audience—shabby clothes, expressions worried and sour. Faces would start to glow, heads to nod, hands to clap.

—Len de Caux, labor activist

The Negro neither fears the communist nor leans over backward in admiration. He (the communist organizer) is just another human being to be judged individually on one basis—is he fighting for the full and complete equality of opportunity for black people.

—Adam Clayton Powell, Jr., Congressman

FIGHT DON'T STARVE

—Communist Party Banner

Almost all Americans in the early years of the depression of the 1930s, and some for its entire course, experienced economic hardship quietly and relatively alone. Families used up all their savings, borrowed, and pawned their belongings. Some blamed themselves. The responses ran the gamut from depending on established communal networks of assistance to individual and group looting of grocery stores. As the depression wore on, however, many workers grew to suspect that their unemployment and poverty were the result not of a personal failing but rather a collapsed economy, and they began to think about the need for some fundamental changes in the economic system.[3]

Radical organizations were quick to promote their vision of a non-capitalist society and their strategy of how to achieve it. Even before the stock market crash, for example, Socialists had formulated a national approach to the problems faced by the jobless. But by far the most influential and novel approach to radical community organizing in the 1930s was that of the Communist Party of the United States of America (CPUSA). The importance of the Communist party's neighborhood organizing did not rest on its ability to resolve depression-era problems. At the time other leftist groups, such as the Socialist party, had organized community efforts of equal magnitude that had more impact on the passage of remedial New Deal legislation. The CPUSA's contribution to the history of neighborhood organizing, however, was in its unique approach and its influence on the radical movements of the 1930s. Most activists now see the primary goal of neighborhood organizing as awakening people to a sense of their own power. The Communists saw neighborhood work as a means of recruiting people into a national organization. Building the national party, not neighborhood organizing, they believed, would best advance the interests of the working class and racial minorities in the United States. To build a national revolutionary organization they advanced a strategy of "internationalism" in their neighborhood work that, however flawed, was impressive in its class consciousness, range of protest, and breadth of concerns.[4]

On the eve of the depression the Communist party was limited to some 7,500 members. The Red Scare of 1919 had decimated their ranks and the political climate of repression in the 1920s continued to keep the party weak, on the defensive, and underground for much of the decade. Nevertheless, the party anticipated the "impending collapse of capitalism" and was surprisingly well prepared, certainly more so than any other group, to address the crisis and mobilize their forces around it. The Sixth World Congress of the Communist International (Comintern), the Moscow-based, policy-making body for Communist parties worldwide, predicted in 1928 the imminent economic collapse and ordered Communist parties to initiate more openly revolutionary actions. Concerned about "the Negro Question," the congress also insisted that the CPUSA make the organization of African-Americans a preeminent priority. Accordingly the organizing offensive of the CPUSA to mobilize the unemployed along interracial lines began even before the depression.

Two months before the stock market crash, in August 1929, the Communist party, now operating above ground, organized a new labor federation, the Trade Union Unity League (TUUL), which sought to build an alternative union to the AFL and to set up councils of the unemployed. Communist party community organizers went into impoverished, working-class neighborhoods in the nation's largest cities to build the Unemployed Council movement.[5] Within four months after Black Thursday on Wall Street, the combination of skillful organizing by communist radicals and the spontaneous dissent growing among the jobless produced an aggressive and vital, Communist-led, community-based movement. As early as February 1930, 2,000 workers in Cleveland and 3,000 in Los Angeles stormed their respective city halls demanding relief benefits. It took police wielding nightsticks and lobbing tear gas cannisters to disperse them. In March, the party organized an International Unemployment Day, with protests across the country from coast to coast. The marches were orderly and peaceful, except where local officials and police grew anxious and tried to stop them. In New York City, police attacks transformed some 35,000 orderly demonstrators into an angry, fighting mob. Bloodied workers, men and women, tried to flee once it was clear they were unprepared to sustain a police assault. But the police prohibited the retreat, throwing people to the ground and pummeling them. Thirty-seven people were arrested and 130 were injured.[6]

As the depression deepened and as authorities grew more alarmed by the insurgent activity of the unemployed, conflict escalated. In October 1930, a CPUSA protest at the national convention of the American Federation of Labor in Boston brought out 200 police, including a special "Flying Squadron" equipped with machine guns, bulletproof vests, and tear gas bombs. Mayhem ensued. The protesters were badly beaten, and Mayor James Michael Curley, the son of Irish immigrants, demanded that the demonstrators, by no means all aliens or Russian, be deported to the Soviet Union. One year later Curley stepped up the repression with arrests for "carrying a placard," "making loud outcries in the park," and public "speaking without a permit."[7] Imprisonment of communist organizers, attacks on demonstrators, and repressive local ordinances isolated Communists from most of the unemployed who, afraid of the official brutality, stayed clear of radical protest organizations. For some, however, it had the opposite effect. The assaults served to radicalize them and steel their resolve to fight a political system that preached democracy but denied dissent when it challenged the system of capitalism.

The success of the protests rested on the extraordinary commitment and fearless leadership of Communist party organizers. Communist organizers worked hard and seemingly all the time. They organized the unemployed at factory gates, on breadlines, in flop houses, relief centers, and neighborhood street corners. They attended meeting after meeting with workers and party members. They wrote leaflets and articles, songs and banner slogans. They planned and participated in demonstrations, and they led these protests in a most courageous and impressive way. The estimated 4,000 demonstrators arrested in the summer and fall of 1930 while participating in Communist-led actions throughout the nation indicated the intense level of activity generated by a relatively small group of committed, radical organizers.[8]

These initial efforts were impressive for their militancy and for their ability to win concessions from local officials and relief bureaus, but they had a purely ad hoc quality about them. Spontaneity had its virtues; more people could be mobilized for a protest than could be attracted to become members of an ongoing organization. Demonstrations were often exciting and cathartic, while organizations tended to be dull and to require a lot of hard work. Nevertheless, the goal of the CPUSA was not simply to politicize people at demonstrations or to give people a sense of their own power through protest victories. The fundamental goal of the party was to build an effective communist organization that could lead a working-class revolution in the United States. The councils were planned to be the mass protest organizations of the party, designed as "transmission belts" for the recruitment of members into the party and as community-based organizations that could supplement the party's union organizing efforts in factories.

When organizing Unemployed Councils the party would begin by dividing a city or rural area into sections and branches. Organizers who "knew what was going on in the factories and neighborhoods" were assigned by the party to each section. In places where the party was already well established, as in Chicago or New York City, it supervised the initial organization and direction of the council. In areas somewhat removed from the nation's big cities, organizers had greater freedom but also less party support. Organizers did not go into a community "cold." They always had "contacts," contacts who might be old party members or progressive sympathizers active in ethnic and fraternal associations. After agitating, sometimes for weeks, "against capitalism" and talking about the "need for socialism," a local council would be formed. While membership in the council only entailed having to sign up at a council-sponsored event and while most members did not attend meetings and could not be counted on to participate in demonstrations, councils usually had an active core among the membership who would attend meetings and conferences and participate regularly in demonstrations. It was from among this core group that party members would be recruited.

Despite the obvious tension of a reform-oriented, community-based effort seeking primarily to recruit members for a national communist movement, local councils did become real neighborhood organizations. Local conditions demanded, and communist organizers recognized, the need for each council to be grounded in the traditions and institutions of the local community. "We made every effort to make the councils part of their neighborhoods," Steve Nelson, a leading party activist, recalled. "For fund raising we tried to stage events that fit into the cultural life of the community. Most councils relied on bingo, raffles, picnics, and block parties. [In Chicago] since the Catholic church was always sponsoring such affairs, they were part of the natural way of life."[9] In the anthracite region of Pennsylvania, council meetings opened with "Hail Marys and Our Fathers." In Harlem, given the local importance of the black church in community activities, it became common practice to begin council meetings with a prayer. Despite their avowed atheism, party organizers in the United States accepted religious practices and encouraged the participation of progressive religious and community leaders because of their influence in the local community.

Communist organizers also accepted and encouraged local decision making on important organizational issues, such as where to picket, what hall to use, who should give the speech at a rally, and when and how to hold an upcoming meeting. These were critical organizing concerns that consumed much of the time and energies of council organizers and members. In this respect, as well as the acceptance by local councils of certain community traditions and institutions, councils were administered from the grassroots far more than would be expected given the autocratic organizing strategy and hostility to the local parochialism of the CPUSA.

Like most mass movements of the 1930s, and especially those organizing the unemployed, the councils were extremely unstable. Membership in councils was very fluid, for people often left after their particular grievance had been addressed. The party felt that it was impossible to organize a mass movement of the unemployed without effective party organization, without a core of committed and focused activists to do much of the daily work and to spread the movement.

Accordingly, despite the neighborhood character of councils and despite the creative adaptations of Comintern policy, the party organized, directed, and controlled the local councils. Continuity in the local councils was provided by paid functionaries—local leaders who were given a stipend by the party for their work and who were most often, but not always, party members. The bone and sinews—and money—that made the councils work were provided by the party.[10]

In essence there was never much real autonomy for the local councils. The party came to neighborhood people with a prearranged ideology, program, and strategy—a "line" they called it—that provided an analysis of current problems and their solutions. They had less interest than later radical organizers in "letting the people decide." The Comintern determined the goals and platform of the party and, ipso facto, the local councils. It was the Comintern that decided, for example, to bring the CPUSA out from underground in the late 1920s, to tackle the issue of organizing the unemployed and racial minorities, and to support a Popular Front strategy in 1935. "Colonization" of white working-class and black communities was fundamental, they reasoned, in order to provide the leadership and direction necessary to build the party and a revolutionary working-class movement. Most important, the councils often developed into highly effectual mass-protest organizations because of the leadership of party organizers, who drew their strength and direction from the party apparatus.[11]

The party line to build the Unemployed Council movement developed as early as 1930. The four-pronged "bread and butter" strategy focused on relief, housing, race, and "translocal" issues, the latter being issues outside the community which would concern neighborhood residents. At the outset of the depression people accepted relief reluctantly. But most unemployed workers soon came to see local relief benefits not only as a necessity but as a right. Local welfare offices, however, lacked the funds to furnish all unemployed workers with relief funds, and these bureaus often relied on intimidation or harassment to keep relief requests down. Communist organizers fought for relief funds by representing workers at welfare offices and, if that were not sufficient, by staging protests to ensure relief payments. While their goal was to build the party organization, not simply to win benefits, and while Communists were revolutionaries, not social workers, they nevertheless saw service delivery as one way to win support and members. In Harlem, for example, organizers would take a large group of unemployed to a relief station and demand benefits. If they were refused, they camped in the offices until they received benefits or were removed by the police. The greater the resistance of local officials, the more violent the response of the protesters. Incidents varied from council members breaking down the doors of a Harlem relief bureau and overturning furniture to bloody struggles between police and demonstrators. Communist organizers viewed such protests as one of the best methods for winning benefits and educating participants in the fundamentally repressive nature of the capitalist system.[12]

The second part of the Communists' strategy to build the council movement focused on fighting housing evictions. Tenants often could not pay their rent because they were out of work, but this did not deter many landlords from evicting them. This was an openly callous act and the party made the most of it. From August to October 1931, 2,185 eviction cases came before the Chicago Renters Court, 38 percent of which involved black families. Communist community organizers accompanied neighborhood people to eviction hearings and staged mass actions to block evictions physically. Not uncommonly members of an Unemployed Council grabbed furniture being brought out the front door during an eviction and took it back into the apartment through the rear entrance. On one occasion in Chicago, for example, several thousand people marched to a house to block an eviction. When the police arrived, the 5,000 people already there refused to disperse. Scuffling broke out, guns blazed, and before it was over police had killed three protesters. By nightfall the party spread leaflets throughout the neighborhood demanding the death penalty for the murderers. Chicago's elite grew fearful that the city was on the brink of revolution; the Renters Court immediately suspended all evictions and the city expanded its relief program. The same kinds of situations led to the same results in other northern industrial centers. By 1931 the Unemployed Councils in Detroit also had stopped practically all evictions.[13]

A third element in the council-building strategy was to organize the African-American community around a platform of interracial cooperation and equality. "Black and White Unite to Fight" was a prominent communist slogan. As far back as the 1920s, small groups of Communists were working in African-American neighborhoods, especially in New York and Chicago, sponsoring interracial dances and leading protests against slum housing and high rents. Alone among primarily white political organizations in the 1930s, Communists demanded complete unity and complete equality between black and white workers. They emphasized that the struggle of white workers could never succeed unless workers of all races were included as equal participants. (It was common practice for industrialists to keep wages down by using black workers as a surplus labor force and as strike breakers.) A Comintern directive on the "race question" in 1930 emphasized that white workers were to "march at the head of the struggle" against Jim Crowism and segregation. This emphasis on black and white unity, one historian writes, "had a catalytic effect on the black community."[14]

No group in the United States had more reason to join a revolutionary organization committed to altering an oppressive system than did African-Americans. As bad as the depression was for white workers, it devastated the black community. Unemployment figures for workers in some key industries throughout the nation reached 40 percent, but in Harlem, for example, unemployment was 80 percent in 1935. African-Americans joined the Unemployed Councils to fight unemployment and discrimination and to gain greater control over their communities. Equally important, the councils provided a supportive and racially integrated political and cultural movement that was an exciting and challenging, if essentially culturally "white," experience. Most of all, African-Americans joined because the party and the councils supported their winning relief benefits, stopping evictions, and "taking up black issues," such as antilynching legislation or the case of the Scottsboro Nine (in which nine young black men were accused of raping two white Georgia women). At a time when little other support existed outside the black community, African-Americans did not discard allies simply because they were called "reds." No other organization composed primarily of white workers was willing to struggle along side of, on behalf of, and, most important, under the leadership of African-Americans.

A fourth tactic for organizational building was to address issues that transcended local boundaries but could galvanize and politicize the local community. Community and neighborhood-based organizing was for Communists largely a question of tactics and strategy; it represented no belief in the intrinsic value of the neighborhood unit. Councils were based in neighborhoods hit hardest by the depression, especially black slum areas, because community-based organizing was seen by the party as the best way of reaching African-Americans, unemployed housewives, and others who did not work in factories where party organizing was most active. But limiting campaigns or issues to a neighborhood ran counter to the party's goal of building an international organization. Any organizing that did not transcend local boundaries and make connections with national and international issues the party considered parochial and potentially reactionary, pitting neighborhood against neighborhood. Three of the most effective organizing issues in Harlem were support of antilynching legislation, defense of the Scottsboro Nine, and opposition to the Italian invasion of Ethiopia, then the only independent African nation. None of these issues affected Harlem residents directly. But community people saw them as important campaigns in the struggle for racial equality, and they held meetings, demonstrations, and direct actions in support of their brethren in the South and in Africa. In one year, for example, communist organizers held some 40 street meetings in Harlem solely on the antilynching issue.

From 1931 through 1935 the Unemployed Councils concentrated on this "bread and butter" strategy of organizing militant protests around neighborhood and translocal issues. Most of the protest was directed at government agencies and officials. In 1935, a switch in party line issued from Moscow called for a Popular Front in which Communists would align themselves with all "progressive forces," including New Deal liberals, in the struggle against the rising menace of fascism. Hitler, the Comintern realistically decided, presented a greater threat to the Soviet people and the international socialist movement than the depression-straddled ruling groups in the United States and Western Europe. Comintern required, therefore, that all Communist efforts, no matter where they occurred, be oriented toward building a popular front against fascism. The new line transformed the CPUSA and the councils from opponents into critical supporters of the social welfare programs of FDR and the Second New Deal.

In the spirit of the Popular Front, for example, the CPUSA and the councils joined with socialist and independent radical efforts in 1935 in a national and unified organization of the unemployed known as the Workers Alliance of America. By the end of 1936 this "national poor people's organization" claimed 1,600 locals and a total membership of 600,000 people distributed among 43 states. The new organization focused on lobbying for national relief and unemployment insurance benefits in Washington and accepted the terms of the Popular Front to work with all progressive groups in the New Deal coalition and within the parameters of New Deal liberalism. Calls for reform and opposition to fascism replaced demands for revolution and socialism.

The Popular Front line also sought to respond to organizing problems facing communist activists. Despite the near complete collapse of the economy in the United States and despite vigorous and militant work by Communists from 1929 to 1935, party membership and support remained small. Harlem, a key center for communist community organizing, had only 100 party members in late 1933. While thousands in Harlem were members of its Unemployed Councils, the national unemployed organization led by the CPUSA could claim no more than 100,000. This was fewer than 1 percent of the total number of unemployed workers. But the change in line after 1935 made the party more acceptable. Party leaders deemphasized the need for revolution, developed alliances with local and national progressive organizations, and generally pursued a more "Americanized" organizing strategy. The more they fought for democracy and equality rather than communism, and the more the depression continued unabated, the greater the party's community support and popularity among workers. The party in Harlem, for example, grew from 100 members in 1933 to 800 by 1936.[15]

But it was not only the Comintern policy decision and the desire for more influence that caused the party and its councils to take new directions. The passage of progressive, worker-oriented legislation like the Social Security and Wagner Acts in 1935 posed a dilemma for radical community organizers. While the legislation was a victory for grassroots insurgent groups, at the same time it presented the threat of both cooptation and "ultraleft" isolation. The Social Security Act, for example, offered not only benefits but a means of draining radical protest into a bureaucratic relief structure. Welfare bureaus were now more responsive to applicants, setting up relief complaint offices and even establishing procedures that recognized unemployed organizations as the legitimate representatives of relief recipients. According to Herbert Benjamin, a communist leader of the Unemployed Council movement, "No one could long maintain leadership of the unemployed who would direct the struggle of the unemployed against progressive officials supported by organized labor and progressive forces."[16] Party organizers now emphasized transforming the system not by attacking it from the outside but rather by "boring from within." They hoped that by gaining greater influence in official, labor, and community activities they could continue to make demands on the system and build the party more effectively.

As late as 1937 the party remained a militant voice at the neighborhood level for the rights of workers and the unemployed. Its members continued to lead protest activities on rent strikes, campaigns to improve local schools, and efforts to reduce milk and meat prices. They fought cutbacks in national social welfare programs, cutbacks that began just a few months after FDR's successful reelection in 1936. In cooperation with the Workers Alliance, in 1937 they helped organize a hunger march on Washington that received wide support from progressives and radicals. But in general the party toned down its militancy and began to publicly support liberals as well as liberal programs. Most notably, in 1937 the CPUSA publicly supported Franklin Roosevelt, and the following year the Workers Alliance campaigned actively for New Deal candidates. Not surprisingly, militant community organizing by Communists began to be reduced substantially.[17]

Two elements of the Popular Front strategy especially undermined local community organizing after 1937. First was the emphasis on the fascist threat. For the party, the international struggle always took precedence over local community concerns, and this was certainly so as the threat of the Axis powers mounted. Second was the party's increasing emphasis on union organizing. The party had always judged union organizing to be the most effective means of expanding its influence and the power of working people. With the CIO experiencing extraordinary growth after 1936, partially through the work of communist organizers, the CPUSA put almost all its energies into factory organizing rather than community work, so that by 1938 the almost singular concern of party organizers was working with the union. In a few places, such as Harlem, where the "color line" kept most urban blacks out of factory work and labor unions, Communists continued to focus attention on neighborhood-based work. The only way to reach urban blacks was through community organizing. But even in these communities, union efforts, not "black concerns," became paramount. Generally the party abandoned its vigorous defense of black rights when this defense conflicted with CIO organizing objectives.[18]

By 1938, therefore, Communists played an increasingly conservative role in community struggles. As they sought to appease CIO progressives and to work within the New Deal coalition at the local and national level, their community-based organizing became less successful. Local activists in Harlem began to criticize the party for sacrificing black and white workers in order to protect its good relationship with liberals like FDR, New York City Mayor Fiorello LaGuardia, and the city's black elite. When members of the African-American community asked Communists to support a bill in the New York legislature that sought to limit the bargaining rights of unions that discriminated against African-Americans, the party refused to do so on the grounds that it was unnecessary. The party said the unions could police themselves. While this paralleled the position of CIO leaders, it opposed that of black activists and workers. One year later the local Workers Alliance did little in response to cutbacks in the Harlem WPA program. Ultimately, the party was unwilling to defend the "special needs" of African-Americans and the relief benefits it and the councils had fought so hard to create. By 1939 the community work of the CPUSA and the unemployed movement had lost not only its support but also much of its credibility.

Although the party's neighborhood-based efforts were short-lived, they were impressive in many ways. Most visibly, their skillful and courageous use of direct action tactics, most of which were directed at the public sector, helped force those in power to adopt more progressive positions and programs. But the effectiveness of party organizers stemmed from more than their militancy and courage. Community organizing as practiced by the CPUSA was successful because it emphasized organizational discipline, defined local issues in a national and international context, linked community struggles with those in the workplace, developed alliances between black and white workers, and offered a thorough political analysis of the problems community people faced. Such accomplishments by radicals had rarely been seen before in this country. In general, militant, disciplined, and ideological communist organizing gave the people who participated in the Unemployed Councils, and perhaps even people in the neighborhoods who watched from their apartment windows, a confidence in and a sense of their own power to change the political system. It offered a community organizing experience that provided council activists with an important theoretical and practical grassroots political education.

On the other hand, the obvious organizing errors of the CPUSA deeply affected neighborhood work as well. The party's political opportunism, its interest in the needs of the Soviet Union over those of American workers, and its autocratic organizational structure, which quashed the type of criticism necessary to prevent ideological and tactical errors, were serious mistakes. The party's abandonment of African-Americans was a shortsighted and major error. The party ultimately refused even to support progressive protests against social discrimination, such as that of A. Phillip Randolph's threatened march on

Washington in early 1941. The single-minded commitment to the CIO and the Popular Front strategy prevented effective criticism of a New Deal that was intellectually and programatically stagnant after 1937. More specifically, in its neighborhood organizing work the sources of communist organizing strength—its internationalism, autocratic discipline, and emphasis on the workplace—proved to be weaknesses as well. The desire to build a mass working-class organization brought the realization that local issues needed a national and even international context. The same goal, however, led to the party and Comintern's misjudging the value of autonomous, community-based organizing. The party's goal was to organize a worker's movement in support of socialism, not to build community organizations. Therefore, classwide concerns always took precedence over local needs in the communist organizing model. The party knew that building a socialist movement in the United States was no easy task and that organizing the unemployed was not the way to do it. The unemployed and local communities in general, they felt, were too unstable and too disconnected to form the base of a revolutionary movement.

The party had always seen neighborhood work as a secondary aspect of the class struggle, subordinate in importance and effectiveness to international concerns and workplace organizing. But it overemphasized the distinction between factory and community work. In the early 1930s, when union organizing had little promise, the party put energy into neighborhood organizing. Later, with the emergence of the CIO, the party not surprisingly focused more and more on union organizing. By 1939, however, when the growing fascist menace abroad demanded the undivided attention of Communists, the party completely sacrificed its community organizing and with it its unequivocal support of black rights. These were serious errors produced in part by communist theory and strategy that saw little value in community-based organizing in and of itself.

Neighborhood organizing cannot and need not be the only concern of a national working-class organization. In the case of the CPUSA, organizing workers in factories and addressing international issues complemented and empowered their community organizing efforts. But if local groups belonging to a national or international organization are to have any chance of success in the long run, they must have some degree of independence. Of course, democratic mechanisms must be established whereby communities with competing interests can resolve problems in the interests of both the local and larger group. This type of integrated, federated democratic structure that both respects the integrity of local community organizing *and* provides for coordinated national leadership was not to be found in the theory or structure of the CPUSA. Communists understood that effective party building developed first and best at the local level, where it was rooted in day-to-day community and industrial struggles. But their ultimate mistrust of decentralized, neighborhood organizing denied the long-term contribution that such grassroots community organizations can make in sustaining a national organization.

Saul Alinsky and the Back of the Yards Neighborhood Council

If I were asked to choose a single agency which most admirably represented all that our democracy stands for, I would select the Back of the Yards Council. All that you have done for the health, the social welfare, the economic advancement, and the happiness of the people in your community is to me one of the most heartening accomplishments of our time.

—Adlai Stevenson, governor of Illinois

The New Deal did not resolve the economic problems occasioned by the depression. For a time in 1936 the social welfare programs of the Second New Deal stimulated the economy, lowered unemployment, and increased purchasing power. But Roosevelt was essentially conservative in economic matters and preferred not to use deficit spending to maintain the economy. He feared the inflationary effect of federal expenditures that gave people money but did not stimulate investment and production. Accordingly, with the election of 1936 behind him, retrenchment began. Old programs were cut. New programs died on the planning table. Without the stimulus of federal funds, the economy declined again. In 1937 unemployment was almost as high as it had been in 1933. Four years of New Deal had not solved the economic crisis. Only preparation for and participation in World War II would do that.

The New Deal addressed more successfully the political crisis caused by the depression. FDR was unwilling to implement programs to halt the economic slide, but he eagerly promoted efforts that stopped the drift to political disorder and possible revolution. The "achievement" of the New Deal was that despite its failure to halt the depression it did prevent radical changes in the economic and political system. FDR's Second New Deal, for example, consciously stole the thunder of reform from left groups offering an alternative to liberal capitalism. But not without ironic consequences. Radicals, community activists, labor leaders, and workers had fought hard for social security and labor programs in the years before 1935. But they did so in relative isolation. Roosevelt sought to defuse and coopt this nascent movement with the passage of Second New Deal social welfare legislation, and he was able to win workers to the Democratic party in 1936 on a platform that responded to the grassroots demands first raised by radical groups like the Unemployed Councils. But, most important, this legislation and the new climate in Washington also helped initiate a nationwide progressive social movement. In the years after 1936 workers and organizers forged in the CIO the largest and most militant workers' movement the nation had seen since the late nineteenth century.

There is a complementary relationship between social movements and community organizing. Local organizing oriented to social change can exist without a movement, but it will not thrive for very long. When a movement develops, however, community organizations often ride the wave of mass support. In the context of the 1930s, local organizing before 1935 pushed politics in Washington to the left, Second New Deal programs in Washington helped stimulate a national industrial workers movement, and, in turn, the workers movement of the late 1930s and early 1940s spawned and stimulated a host of community organizing projects in working-class neighborhoods. These organizations functioned independently of the labor movement but took their impetus, militant spirit, and democratic direction from it. The effort of Saul Alinsky in Back of the Yards is the best known and most significant of the CIO "community spin-offs."

Saul Alinsky was not the sort to leave folks impartial. They either loved or hated him. He was abrasive, forceful, witty, antagonistic, irreverent, and not above shocking people or lying to them. Some saw him as a menace. Corporations hired detectives to watch him. The Oakland, California, city council banned him. Kansas City police jailed him. The right wing saw him as a Bolshevik agitator, the left as a "system confirming populist." One influential supporter, Charles

Silberman, a prominent writer on race relations in the 1960s, saw Alinsky as the hope of democracy. What people were really responding to, however, was less frequently Saul Alinsky the person than the method of community organizing that came to be associated with him. Succinctly stated, if overly simplified, the Alinsky method of community organizing, "Alinskyism," has five essential elements:

1. *The professional organizer is the catalyst for social change.* Alinsky emphasized the need for well-trained organizers. While he was seen as an apostle of democratic decision making and indigenous leadership, his method places a premium on the creative organizer "who can do it all." Because community organizing is perceived to be difficult, and because groups face constant pressures and crises that demand critical and correct decisions, Alinskyism stresses that a well-trained professional organizer is the most likely person to make the right choices. Democracy is important; the organizer is even more so.

2. *The task is to build a democratic community-based organization.* In theory, community-based democracy is the essence of Alinsky organizing. Democracy is defined as the process of self-determination, in which ordinary people make the decisions about things that affect them. For Alinsky, truly democratic organizations can develop only within small spatial units, like a neighborhood, where there are natural bonds of unity and identification. Unlike most other leftist approaches to neighborhood organizing, Alinsky emphasizes gathering the support of traditional community leaders and institutions, people who already have local influence and a wide audience. The organizer is thus regarded as a catalyst, not a leader. Organizers are supposed to work from behind the scenes and work themselves out of a job by training "indigenous leaders" in the skills of community organizing. The people's organization is open to all members of the community—workers, merchants, and union and church leaders—for the broader and more representative the neighborhood coalition, Alinsky believed, the stronger the organization.

3. *The goal is to win power.* Power is the sine qua non of Alinsky organizing. Only by organizing people to struggle for power can democracy be realized; only then can the "have nots" gain control of their communities and their lives. Neighborhood organizations are seen as the interest groups of the powerless and the unorganized. As unions represent factory workers in the labor market, so neighborhood organizations, Alinsky said, represent workers and their fami-

lies outside the factory. The more power the neighborhood organization secures, the better it serves the interests of its members. Alinsky emphasized that since people act from self-interest rather than altruism, it is self-interest rather than exalted ideals that should motivate a "people's organization."

4. *Any tactics necessary should be used.* This element of the Alinsky method achieved widest acclaim and criticism. He argued that people built organizations and won power by winning victories. He saw the traditional, conservative tactics used by most interest groups as inappropriate for neighborhood organizations of working-class people, who, without money or political influence, could achieve power only by using all types of creative and militant tactics. Negotiation, arbitration, protests, and demonstrations; boycotts, strikes, and mass meetings; picketing, raising hell, being diplomatic, and being willing to use anything that might work were key elements of Alinskyism. The end justifies the means, Alinsky counseled. Don't let tactics become predictable; don't be afraid to try something outrageous; keep the "enemy" off guard. On one occasion Alinsky advocated tying up all the bathrooms in Chicago's O'Hare airport; the first "shit-in," he called it. The more disturbing the tactic to those in power, the better the results. After all, he argued, working people will not get power, dignity, freedom, or equality as gifts or as acts of charity. They only win them through struggle. The organizer's role is to give people a sense of their potential power and "rub raw their resentments," so that they will be willing to take on those who keep them powerless. "Controversy was the seed of creation," Alinsky liked to say. "Life is conflict and in conflict you are alive." Through struggle people learn.

5. *A people's organization must be pragmatic and nonideological.* Above all, Alinskyism advises that organizations must be practical if they are to be successful. A program should not be imposed on the neighborhood. All strategies should be considered. Nothing is more successful in organization building than successful actions. Again, the end, not the means, is most important. Alinsky believed that all revolutionary movements are generated from spiritual values and a belief in justice, equality, peace, and fellowship. But he vehemently opposed "ideological" organizations. In his opinion they were undemocratic because their organizers came with preconceived ideals, goals, and strategies; they did not let neighborhood people make decisions. To let the people decide, Alinsky advocated, no matter what they decide,

is the essence of democracy. Imposing a progressive ideology on the neighborhood is counterproductive and unnecessary. Only the progressive ideology that people developed themselves would last. Alinsky believed that democratic processes would yield democratic ideals and goals, and that, most important, organizers must have faith in democracy, in people and their traditions.

Alinsky grounded his pragmatism in the promise of pluralism. He believed that the economic and political system could work for working-class people if they could reach the bargaining tables of power. Once they got there, they could make those in power, whether government officials or corporate executives, responsive to their needs. Ideology would only limit the organization's ability to get to the bargaining table. In sum, the central premise of Alinskyism is that skillful, nonideological, democratic organizations willing to use any and all means can ultimately obtain more power and be more effective than ideological radical groups.[19]

The Alinsky method is usually presented, incorrectly, as a timeless approach developed outside of a specific historical context. The reverse is true. It grew out of his experiences in Chicago in the 1930s as a community worker, his efforts with the CIO, and his coming of age amid the Communist party's Popular Front organizing campaigns. Alinsky was born in 1909 in Chicago, the son of orthodox, working-class, Jewish parents, and went to public schools and college there. It was at the University of Chicago, where he did undergraduate work in archaeology and graduate work in criminology, that he became interested in social welfare issues. From 1931 to 1940 he was employed as a research sociologist at the Institute for Juvenile Research, an organization that was investigating more effective and more democratic methods of curbing juvenile delinquency in Chicago. From this experience Alinsky came to value community-based organizing, learn the importance of professional organizers, and understand the need for democratic, indigenous participation in community work.

Of equal import was Alinsky's experience with the CIO. The extent of his actual association is unclear, but it seems he was a volunteer CIO organizer for about a year in 1937 and 1938. This experience, brief as it was, impressed him deeply. From his work with the CIO Alinsky learned the importance of struggling for power, of being willing to use a variety of tactics, especially conflict and confrontation, and of needing creative, dynamic, skilled, and committed organizers to mobilize working people. He said he learned that what he wanted to do most was apply the techniques he had "mastered" while working with the CIO to "the worst slums and ghettos, so that the most oppressed and exploited elements in the country could take control of their own communities and their own destinies." The early neighborhood efforts of Alinsky were therefore a kind of "trade union in the social factory"—an instrument at the neighborhood level through which people could bargain, struggle, strike, and advance their interests, just as they did in the CIO.[20]

Significant as well was his coming of political age in the early 1930s amid the radical ferment and growing antifascist movement in Chicago. Alinsky may have played down the role of ideology in the neighborhood organizations he helped develop, but that does not mean that he acted without a worldview. All neighborhood organizing is based on certain political, social, and economic assumptions. Otherwise people would not become organizers. In his later years Alinsky saw himself as an "urban populist," but in the 1930s, when he first started out, he saw himself, in typical Popular Front terms, as a "professional antifascist." As a student he spent much of his time involved in Communist party and antifascist related activities, such as stopping evictions, fighting for public housing, and raising money for the International Brigade in the Spanish Civil War and for sharecroppers in the South.

While Alinsky claimed he never joined the Communist party, he seems to have been a "fellow traveler" who borrowed heavily from party protest tactics and antifascist ideology without direct involvement in the party or acceptance of Comintern line and discipline. His association with the party taught him that radical organizers, by organizing people for power in grassroots organizations, could counteract the cynicism and despair that led to fascist movements. Ever since the days of the American Revolution, he liked to recall, "radicals" had always served in the forefront of support for democracy and opposition to dictatorship. Moreover, the Popular Front strategy of antifascism brought home to Alinsky the importance of uniting with all potential allies in the community, a sort of neighborhood-based united front. Alinsky never sought to impose or even offer in a systematic way his ideology of antifascism to neighborhood groups. He always objected strongly to communist autocratic methods. "Pragmatic pluralism" was more in keeping, Alinsky believed, with the process of neighborhood organizing. But his formative experiences with left-wing groups and causes in the 1930s laid the foundation for and fueled his work. He first put the organizing method into practice in the Back of the Yards neighborhood of Chicago. This was the same neighborhood, 30 blocks south of the Loop and just west of the stockyards from which it got its name, that served as the locale for Upton Sinclair's *The Jungle*. In 1938 there were some 90,000 people living in this four-square-mile community. It was an old, stable, white, ethnic, working-class neighborhood, not uncommon to Chicago or northern industrial cities. Back of the Yards was 95 percent Catholic, mostly second and third generation Poles, Lithuanians, Czechs, and Ukranians. "This was not the slum across the tracks. This was the slum across the tracks from across the tracks," Alinsky said. "It was the nadir of all the slums of America, worse than Harlem is today [1970]. You had this dingy gray mile-by-two-miles of track, south of the big slaughter-houses. Clapboard frame houses, one behind the other. Many of them with outhouses. The neighborhood was practically all Catholic. You never saw so many churches. It made Rome look like a Protestant Gothic town."[21]

Ethnic national rivalry was as much a part of Back of the Yards as were its churches. Irish fought Poles, who fought Lithuanians, who fought Mexicans, all of whom fought African-Americans. The neighborhood had a militant labor heritage, but ethnic groups were so busy defending their small turfs against invaders they were unable to make gains as a class against the Swift and Armour meat-packing corporations. As the depression deepened, impoverished workers in Back of the Yards increasingly found scapegoats in African-Americans, Jews, and Communists. Like most such neighborhoods in the 1930s, Back of the Yards had more than its share of fascist groups trying to get a following.[22] But for Alinsky and the CIO there was a more serious difficulty than fascist organizing in Back of the Yards, namely, the many priests, and the Catholic church in general, who vehemently opposed the CIO because of its association with "atheistic communists."

Alinsky became involved in the neighborhood through his work with the Chicago Area Project (CAP). The CAP created an experimental program to test whether a democratic, grassroots program to curb juvenile delinquency would be more effective than traditional, authoritarian, and externally imposed approaches. Sponsored by the project, Alinsky was sent into Back of the Yards in 1938 to organize neighborhood youth committees and encourage the kids to develop their own programs. Instead, Alinsky followed his own inclinations and in early 1939 organized a multi-issue neighborhood organization, the Back of the Yards Neighborhood Council, composed primarily of adults. The CIO was trying to form a Packers Union in the slaughterhouses, and Alinsky believed that communitywide support in Back of the Yards for this organizing drive was more important than the juvenile delinquency project.[23]

Alinsky envisioned Back of the Yards as a first step in building a chain of progressive "people's organizations" nationwide. These community organizations would be led by neighborhood people, usually church and union leaders, and, Alinsky hoped, dedicated like the radicals in the CIO to an eternal war with the forces of injustice.[24] Alinsky recruited Joseph Meegan, a recreation director in the neighborhood, to help organize the council. As it turned out, Meegan was a key contact, the indigenous leader Alinsky sought, a man of perpetual energy with a keen sense for the neighborhood and grassroots politics. Meegan and Alinsky set out to build a broad-based coalition in the neighborhood, which by its breadth and strength would be a force that officials and corporate leaders in Chicago would have to reckon with.

The first hurdle was getting the priests to unite with radical labor organizers. Alinsky realized that the Catholic church was the most important institution in the community and that no neighborhood-wide organization in Back of the Yards could succeed without it. But the Catholic church possessed a long history of opposing radicals, and Herb March, the president of the packinghouse workers local in the area, was a Communist. Alinsky's forthright, populist style of organizing and his antifascist, noncommunist politics won the support of the liberal, auxiliary bishop of the Catholic Archdiocese of Chicago, Bernard J. Sheil, the founder of the Catholic Youth Organization and a public advocate of the CIO. Sheil proclaimed, for example, that "Catholics could not be in opposition to something that was so obviously for the benefit of all the people."[25]

But most clergymen were not as sympathetic. As Alinsky told the story, he conned other priests who were opposed to the CIO into joining his alliance of church and labor by playing on their pride, asking some if they were afraid to join an organization with Herb March in it, and telling others that Herb March "thought the world of them." There is little reason to believe that Alinsky duped the priests. Alinsky often fabricated stories in person and in his writings to make a point—in this instance, that organizers need to be "creative" and pragmatic. Some years later Alinsky described his organizing of the priests in Back of the Yards more realistically.

I'd go in to see this Catholic priest. I'd say, "I heard your sermon denouncing the union, calling it Communist. You know something, Father? Your people nodded and then walked out and joined the union. Know why? They're unemployed, their families are shot to hell and you're not doing a God damn thing about it. You sit on your ass in the sacristy, and you're no longer a shepherd of your flock. Everybody is disregarding you. You want to be a leader? Get back with your people, get out in the streets and fight for the union. The enemy is the meat packer; the enemy is low wages." So he'd do it.[26]

The priests who attended those first meetings of the council acted out of informed self-interest. Neighborhood instability presented as serious a problem to the church as it did to neighborhood residents. Back of the Yards was in a state of rapid deterioration, and neighborhood improvements could only enhance neighborhood stability and strengthen the local churches.

Joseph Meegan organized the first meeting in February 1939. By mid-April, Meegan was acting as temporary chairman of the Back of the Yards Neighborhood Council (BYNC), which included Communists, priests, merchants, and other neighborhood residents. In May the temporary organizing committee drew up a set of by-laws that established a democratic structure with provisions for an executive committee, regular meetings, and an active, participatory membership. Five months after Meegan and Alinsky began their work, the BYNC held its first "Community Congress." The date was 14 July 1939, Bastille Day. Alinsky, Meegan, Bishop Sheil, Herb March, local priests, merchants, and 300 to 350 others attended, representing some 50 groups and organizations. "Its sole reason for coming into existence," Alinsky declared, "was to wage war against all evils which cause suffering and unhappiness." Ambiguous rhetoric, to say the least. But people knew what he was talking about. They knew that two days later the CIO packinghouse local was scheduled to go out on strike, and so the Congress passed a resolution in support of the union and its demands.

Alinsky and Meegan had done an impressive job of organizing support for the "neighborhood people's organization" and the United

Packinghouse Workers union prior to the community meeting. Once the congress began, the work was largely completed. In the Alinsky tradition a well-organized meeting should hold few surprises for the organizer. This is not exactly "democratic," but it gave the appearance of being so, and it was effective and efficient. The first Community Congress in Back of the Yards went smoothly as planned. It developed a rudimentary program for the BYNC, which emphasized that on issues like labor, health, housing, and juvenile delinquency, the people in the neighborhood, regardless of their national background or political preferences, would unite for common ends. And it beckoned the "beginning of a new solidarity" between unions, churches, and the community.

The motives for this unity were clear to Alinsky. "I'm going around organizing, agitating, making trouble [in the Back of the Yards neighborhood]. At the end of three months, I had the Catholic Church, the CIO and the Communist Party working together. . . . I even got the American Legion involved, because they didn't have a goddam thing to do. They all had one thing in common: misery. Powerlessness."[27] Two days later they had something else in common: a victory. Faced with a united front of labor, community, and church opposition, the packinghouse industry caved in to the demands of the union and the next day raised wages in the stockyards from 39 cents to 55 cents an hour, a 41 percent increase.[28] This was quite a sterling beginning for the Back of the Yards Neighborhood Council. A newly formed community organization allied closely with church and union leaders had strengthened the bargaining position and helped win a major victory for stockyard workers.

Build the organization by winning victories, Alinsky emphasized. From 1939 to the close of World War II this strategy took form in Back of the Yards in an emphasis on service delivery. The BYNC, under the direction of Joseph Meegan, set up an infant welfare station in Davis Park Square, where the city employed Meegan as a recreation director. The BYNC held a carnival to raise money, got people jobs in projects of the Works Progress Administration and National Youth Administration (NYA), lobbied successfully for hot lunch and milk programs in the public and private schools, set up a floodlit baseball field on land leased from the railroads for $1 a year, and founded a credit union to provide low-interest loans for neighborhood development projects. The council also managed to involve teenagers in plan-

ning activities in the neighborhood, one of the results of which was a
noticeable decline in juvenile delinquency rates.[29]

While service delivery demonstrated that the council, with the
active support of neighborhood people, could win concessions from
the city and from business, social change was Alinsky's foremost goal
and social action programs his primary interest. In 1944 the BYNC
hired a social worker to deal with social service issues in the neighborhood, so that Joseph Meegan could devote more attention to political
and social action. It was in the council's social action work that Alinsky
cultivated his "conflict" approach to community organizing, which
raised strategy and tactics to paramount importance in community
organizing, above and beyond questions of ideology, goals, and even
democratic structure. Curiously, the use of militant conflict tactics was
also what distinguished the Communist party's neighborhood work
from most other groups in the 1930s. The "nonideological" Alinsky
shrewdly mirrored communist tactics without adopting communism
or party structure.

The BYNC took on corporations, the Chicago political machine, and
even the federal government. In 1941 the council supported a strike
against one of the largest department stores in Chicago. The corporation was trying to break up a warehouse union to which many residents in Back of the Yards belonged. The BYNC set up a soup line to
feed picketers, threatened a citywide boycott of the store, and held a
public, mock trial at which the department store owner was portrayed
as an un-American fascist who refused to recognize the rights of the
workers to form a union. None of these tactics sufficed. The threat of
bad publicity, however, finally pushed the business to settle with its
workers. The council drew a simple lesson from this struggle. Conflict
tactics, simply threatening confrontation, worked.[30]

In subsequent years the BYNC used conflict tactics to force
Chicago's Nash-Kelly political machine to cooperate with it. In
1943–44 the machine attempted to destroy the council by firing
Meegan from his city recreation job and evicting the council from its
park office. The council, with CIO and church support, responded
with a citywide campaign to oppose Mayor Kelly's reelection. In a
meeting with four Chicago aldermen just before the election, however,
the BYNC agreed to stop its campaign. In return Meegan got back his
job and the BYNC got back its park office while showing the political
machine it was a force to be reckoned with. That same year the coun-

cil successfully used conflict tactics in a protest in Washington, D.C. Members went to the capital, inundated the congress with demands to save a threatened milk and lunch program in the public schools, and came away with the program intact. Actions like these gave the council and the Alinsky method the appearance of radicalism and the reputation for being conflict-oriented and effective.

The BYNC's accomplishments were impressive. From 1939 through World War II and thereafter the council developed into a powerful neighborhood organization capable of winning victories and demanding concessions from public and private power brokers alike. As early as 1941 Alinsky was able to list 17 tangible victories won by the council, among them funding from the city's community chest agency, the Community Fund of Chicago. More important, however, the council's linking of radical union leaders with priests, small businesspeople, and neighborhood residents formed a novel and powerful community-based coalition that gave the white, working-class people in Back of the Yards a sense of their ability and power to effect change and restore a sense of dignity and pride in their neighborhood and themselves.

These successes were ultimately overshadowed, however, by the drift of the BYNC to reaction and racism. If judged by Alinsky's own standards, the council was a success in every aspect but one: it failed to counteract the antidemocratic sympathies in Back of the Yards that had led Alinsky in 1939 to call the neighborhood a "hell hole of hate." While in the early 1950s, more than a dozen years after the council began, the white ethnic groups in the neighborhood no longer engaged in mortal combat with one another, they had rediscovered an old scapegoat for personal and community problems: African-Americans. Initially the BYNC attempted to deal positively with the issue of racial conflict. Taking its lead from the CIO experience, the council sought to manage racial tensions, control rumors, discourage discrimination in neighborhood stores, and encourage priests to oppose racial prejudice in their sermons. But this interest in defusing racism did not last for long. By the early 1950s the council had developed not into a force for social change but rather into a racist and conservative neighborhood protection organization. To say the least, what happened in Back of the Yards surprised and badly disappointed Alinsky.[31]

The goals of racial equality and democracy were important to Alinsky. When he was starting out in the Back of the Yards he thought of himself as a professional antifascist fighting the widespread hatreds that existed among working people and eliminating the powerlessness he felt bred this hatred and potentially fascist orientation. But in Back of the Yards, Alinsky consciously deemphasized ideology, antifascist or otherwise. Process was elevated in importance over goals, and the organizing process was guided by pragmatism. The only political education that occurred focused on tactical questions, such as how to build the organization or what was winnable.

The approach backfired in Back of the Yards. The BYNC was able to win victories and achieve power. But no one put forth a clear antiracist ideology for members to respond to. Neither the organizers nor the leaders saw the importance of political education, especially on issues like racism. Nor did they build concrete coalitions with black organizations, coalitions that could teach through practical experience the folly and destructiveness of racism to all working- and middle-class people. The council chose the path of least resistance and ignored all potentially divisive alliances or issues. Conflict between "us" and "them" was encouraged; "in conflict you are alive," Alinsky advocated. But conflict among members of the organization or among residents of the neighborhood over difficult issues like race, Alinsky regarded as destructive. Because the BYNC was community based, not class based like the Communist party, community unity and local objectives, not those of the multiracial working class, guided its direction.

Accordingly, Back of the Yards remained a white, ethnic enclave, even though the neighborhood was in a direct line of expansion of blacks from Chicago's Near Southside slum, and even though the labor force in the meat packing plants after 1945 was increasingly composed of black workers. The council was never avowedly racist. "We don't have time for race hatreds," Joe Meegan said. He suggested that African-Americans did not live in the neighborhood because they had little in common with the white ethnic residents there.[32] But Meegan was avoiding the issue. A study of the neighborhood undertaken in the early 1950s made clear that the churches and most community leaders opposed racial integration. The BYNC avoided an issue like integration for fear that it would cause dissension among its members and alienate its major supporter, the Catholic church. Alinsky claimed that his organizing method represented the whole neighborhood. But given the emphasis on working with established institutions, finding already established indigenous leaders, and winning immediate victories, the neighborhood elites—priests, small businesspeople, and homeowners—became council leaders and defined the goals and programs of the organization. Over time these elements tended to be the most conservative in the neighborhood.

Ultimately Alinsky's "populist" brand of community organizing in Back of the Yards supported rather than challenged the status quo, and Back of the Yards was not an isolated case. Much of Alinsky-style organizing in the 1960s and thereafter has taken on a parochial and nationalistic cast. This occurs in part because the organizing method offers little critique of the economic system inside or outside the neighborhood, little explanation, other than "powerlessness," of what causes and perpetuates poverty in the neighborhood. Alinsky ultimately possessed a strong faith in the ability of liberal capitalism to resolve these problems. FDR was as much his hero as was John L. Lewis. "I think he thought the system, properly greased and oiled, worked," one Alinsky organizer put it.[33] Because Alinsky organizing does not question the economic foundation of the existing order or seek to replace the political system that maintains that order, his approach overlooks the possibility that capitalism is not set up to serve the poor and working class and that it is ultimately undemocratic. The Alinsky approach accepts an interest-group model of democracy in which organizations compete for resources and pressure the system.

The BYNC did succeed better than most working-class neighborhood organizations because Alinsky was a most effective mobilizer, fund-raiser, and mentor trainer. His shrewd political instincts enabled him to select skillfully from his experience with professional social work, the CIO, and left-wing organizations to fashion a populist organizing style more militant, democratic, and effective than the social welfare approach of the settlements but less threatening to established powers than that of the Communist party. In addition, the backing of the Catholic church and CIO unions contributed to the BYNC's limited success as a neighborhood-based interest group. Ultimately, the council grew in power and stature to become a recognized part of the establishment in Chicago. But while the council did become a recognized political unit in the city—both benefiting from and being manipulated by the political machine—it did not alter the economic causes that kept the neighborhood blighted, its residents poor, fundamentally powerless, and unable to compete successfully—as could people with money and power—in an interest-group style of politics.

The path of the BYNC mirrored in many instances that of the CIO, the initial stimulus to Alinsky's political work. Use all tactics, especially the threat of direct action, to force the opposition to the bargaining table. Use communist tactics (the CIO even used communist organizers), but offer no anticapitalist critique of problems. Downplay ideology. Fight to get into the system. Not surprisingly, the CIO, like the BYNC, moved rightward until by the early 1950s it was indistinguishable from the conservative, racist, and antiradical American Federation of Labor (AFL).

To be effective, community organizing had to be more than the pragmatic trade union in the social factory that Alinsky envisioned.[34] Alinsky's method was on the mark in some respects. Working people do need experience with democratic process. They do need power. They do need victories to build strong organizations and give them a sense of their own power. But in poor and working-class neighborhoods like Back of the Yards they also need political education. The people in the BYNC needed a means of addressing issues of class, race, and democratic values as well as tactics and power. This is not to suggest that they would be made to swallow a particular platform without question or thought, but rather that there be built into the organizing process an opportunity for discussion of important issues, a critique to learn from, respond to, struggle with, change, and use. Of course, the downfall of the Back of the Yards Neighborhood Council, like that of the CIO, derived from many factors inside and outside the organization. It did not fail simply because Alinsky chose to pursue an ultimately unsuccessful interest-group, nonideological style of neighborhood organizing. But as events in Back of the Yards were to prove, relying on the skills of an organizer and the influence of traditional community leaders was often not very democratic, and the programs that nonideological, populist-style organizations like the Back of the Yards Neighborhood Council pursued were sometimes not only undemocratic and ineffective in addressing economic problems, they could be racist and reactionary as well.

Chapter Three

Conservative Neighborhood Organizing, 1946–1960

The Cold War and Antiradical Repression

During those McCarthy days anyone who organized or worked for civil rights was called a Communist. Anyone who talked about police brutality was called a Communist. Everywhere I went to organize they would bluntly ask, "Are you a Communist?" . . . It was fantastic how people were frightened. This was the McCarthy era and they were afraid of their shadows.

—Cesar Chavez, organizer

They cry communism but their real fear is democracy.

—Henry Wallace, secretary of commerce

In the post–World War II decade neighborhood organizing developed, as before, within a specific historical context that profoundly determined its nature and success. The dialectical relation between developments at the neighborhood level and those in the larger national arena was as evident in the postwar decade as it was in the 1930s. But the highly conservative and vehemently anticommunist political climate in the decade after the war was dramatically different from its prewar predecessor. After the war, radical organizers such as those in the Communist and Socialist parties increasingly found themselves isolated from what seemed like almost all segments of society. As radical organizing weakened under intense pressure, conservative efforts at building support for the Cold War and "protecting" middle- and upper-class communities became the dominant forms of neighborhood organizing. Of course, such efforts were not limited to the postwar decade. But the events of these years created an economic and political climate especially conducive to conservative programs and, more important, one so hostile to progressive social change as to give the period a decidedly conservative cast.

The fundamental problem that corporate and government leaders faced directly after World War II was how to avoid another depression during peacetime. The United States emerged in 1945 the premier international power. Britain, France, and, most of all, the Soviet Union had experienced vast physical destruction as well as loss of life during the war. The United States, on the other hand, had increased its industrial and military might and did not experience any physical destruction to its homeland. But despite this comfortable position as the world's leading power, business and government leaders remained fearful of another depression. After all, in 1945 a wartime economy, stimulated and directed from Washington, was the country's only tried-and-proved solution to economic depression. At first their worries were allayed, as the vast reservoir of personal savings built up during the war—some $37 billion—fueled the economy from 1945 to 1947. People purchased all the consumer durables they had wanted but were unable to buy during the war. By 1947, however, personal savings were down to $5 billion. The financial fat stored during the war years had been quickly consumed.

To make matters more troublesome, the leaders of the United States did not find themselves undisputed kingpins of the international economy. The victory of World War II had to be shared with our allies, among them the Soviet Union. The Soviet Union could not compete successfully in economic matters with the United States, but it did offer an ideological alternative to capitalism that proved attractive to leaders in colonial areas. This meant that after the war U.S. economic expansion abroad—in Africa, Asia, Europe, Latin America, and the Middle East—might not go unchallenged. Without dependable and continuous supplies of raw materials, cheap labor, and new markets for U.S. consumer durables, corporate profits would recede. In the late 1940s, amid fear of another depression and the related Soviet challenge, business and government leaders also found themselves faced with inflation, labor strikes, and protests against racial discrimination, all of which presented additional threats to the internal economic and social order.

The prescription to these ills favored by most corporate leaders reflected their preference for a "free market" solution: resolve these problems at home and abroad through peacetime economic growth. This meant out-competing the Soviets abroad and buying social order and economic progress at home with a booming economy rooted in overseas expansion, time-payment purchases of consumer durables, and growth industries such as petrochemicals, electronic technology, and suburban development. But supporters of this vision never got the opportunity to test their plan.

Instead, beginning with the Truman Doctrine in 1947, defense spending served as the cornerstone of U.S. economic growth. The political economy of the emerging Cold War, which emphasized the necessity of containing communism and Soviet imperialism, demanded large allocations for the military and for "foreign aid." With the Cold War serving as its rationale, federal expenditures, especially military allocations, laid a foundation for almost uninterrupted growth from 1947 to 1973 and resolved for some two and a half decades the question of how to prevent another economic collapse. According to one historian,

The military budget . . . became the sponge which absorbed much, if not always all, excess industrial capacity, thereby putting a floor under the capitalist economy. The Pentagon's annual 8 to 10 percent of the GNP provided that critical break-even point of economic stimulus which made much of the rest of the economy viable and far less perturbed by a crisis of demand. . . . As a multiplier in stimulating business it greatly exceeded virtually all others. Until other difficulties arose—as they inevitably would—capitalism could at least resolve the problem of insufficient demand so troublesome during the interwar years.[1]

Of course, "military Keynesianism" was not the only basis of prosperity. New industries, new technologies, suburbanization, the advertising business, the proliferation of automobiles, and highway development, to name a few, also fueled the economy of the 1950s and 1960s. But the "military-industrial complex," as Dwight Eisenhower called it, was the rock upon which all else rested. By the time of the Korean War, the Cold War, economic prosperity, and the resolution of domestic problems had become inextricably linked.

Cold War prosperity eliminated many of the domestic problems faced during the depression of the 1930s. Social disorder, mass discontent, and rebellion were put to rest in the 1950s by an economic growth rooted in U.S. expansion abroad and military expenditures at home. But this solution raised other problems that had to be resolved if the Cold War society were to function efficiently without disruption and with a minimum of overt coercion. First, how were people to be mobilized to support unpopular foreign interventions, such as that in Korea? Second, given that welfare expenditures had to be cut back or held constant to allow funds to be allocated for defense without taxes skyrocketing, how were segments of the population who did not share in the prosperity to be pacified? Third, how were government and business leaders to overcome the serious shortage of workers and yet keep the lid on labor militancy at a time when demand for labor exceeded supply? Fourth, how could the economy meet the "rising expectations" of affluence now shared by racial minorities as well as those in less industrialized regions of the nation, most notably the South?

To meet these problems called for more than military Keynesianism. Prosperity and a continuous stream of "free world" propaganda was sufficient to ensure the support of most Americans for the Cold War. The promise of economic mobility, as represented in increasing opportunities to move from blue- to white-collar jobs, to go to college, and to move out of the city into the suburbs, sufficed to keep most people in the nation content and united in support of "us" and opposed to "the Red menace." But not everyone could be counted on to be so agreeable or quiescent. So the velvet glove of prosperity was accompanied by the iron fist of political repression. Anticommunism at home, called "McCarthyism" by those who considered the phenomenon limited to only one man and a few years in the early 1950s, branded all radical critics of the war economy as traitors, liberals as communist symphatizers, and opposition to the Cold War as skirting treason. This repression, unpopular with many Americans, was intended to mute class and race tensions and prevent any challenges to the political economy of the Cold War by eliminating all leftist and progressive criticism. Prosperity and repression formed a powerful recipe for halting dissent, and few did not fall in behind the cold warriors. The CIO purged its radical affiliates, merged with the conservative AFL in 1955, joined the ranks of cold warriors, and offered up a stable and less militant work force that supported military expenditures and the Cold War. Former radicals and liberals joined the crusade against communism, often calling for America to close ranks and fortify the bastions of democracy throughout the world. Most liberals found the tactics of repression upsetting, but remained silent, partially out of fear, and supported the goals and programs of the Cold War. Some activists tried to sidestep the repression. The Community Political Organization (CPO), a left-oriented organization formed in the Chicano community of East Los Angeles in the late 1940s, changed its name in 1947 to Community Service Organization (CSO) so that it would not be confused with the Communist party (CP). David Rosenstein, the president of the National Federation of Settlements, said it even more succinctly in 1953, at the height of the repression: "People in the neighborhoods are afraid to join anything."[2]

In the highly centralized, conservative, Cold War economy there seemed to be little place or encouragement for neighborhood organizing. The roots of the "affluent society" were in economic and military expansion at the national and international level, not in local developments. A contemporary political science text declared in 1953 that "As yet, it is too early to say with assurance that neighborhood groups and practices are disappearing from American cities, but such evidence as we possess indicates that they have been declining and may be expected to diminish further."[3] The burial, however, was premature. Some social workers, for example, believed that community-based, self-help projects remained an important and viable part of American urban life, and they emphasized that community development activities were a far more positive approach to winning the Cold War than repression and fear. For them, the best way to advance U.S. interests was through community programs at home and abroad, such as the United Community Defense Services and the vast number of community development projects sponsored by the United States and the United Nations throughout the world. These efforts would attest, they felt, to the practice and success of democratic capitalism. Such programs, along with the thousands of neighborhood improvement associations that organized in the nation's new suburbs, best suited the conditions of prosperity and the conservative political climate of the era and became, therefore, the dominant forms of neighborhood organizing in the years 1946 to 1960.

Community Development and the Cold War

Never before on so vast a scale has any nation attempted to build military strength and at the same time expand its consumer goods, and assist in the arming of allies throughout the world. It is a very bold and challenging program . . . [that] calls for a large measure of devotion and unity among our people.

—Charles E. Wilson, former head of General Electric, director of
Defense Mobilization

It is becoming ever more clear that our communities hold in their hands significant power to aid or hinder mankind's struggle for a free world and peace. The unsung job of the community's schools, homes, and factories are the "home work" of American patriots. The call to sane, unflagging, high-visioned community effort is the Call to the Colors.

—Harold Buttenheim, chair, American Council for the Community

During the winter of 1950–51 the NBC network broadcast a radio program, "The People Act," Saturday evenings at 7:00 P.M. (EST). Hosted by narrator Ben Grauer and field reporter Elmore McKee, the show's 13 broadcasts reported "real life stories" of Americans who organized together to solve everyday problems in "typically American communities" like New York City; Baltimore; Toledo; Decatur, Alabama; and Sylvania, Arkansas. These stories told of locally initiated efforts to build a community hospital, ease labor tensions, promote better schools, form a conservation district, clean up a slum area, and enforce local housing codes. Some of these efforts, the program noted, were successful; others were not. But it was the manifestation of the process of democracy, not the results of community action, that most interested Elmore McKee.

The idea for the series took shape, McKee said, in 1947, when he worked with the American Friends Service Committee in European postwar reconstruction efforts. He was assigned to develop self-help neighborhood centers in the badly damaged areas of Berlin and Frankfurt. Through his work McKee concluded that the roots of fascism rested in the German people's dependence on experts and authority figures, but he wondered whether America was any less authoritarian. How healthy, after all, was direct democracy in the United States amid the anticommunist atmosphere after the war? Upon his return to the United States he toured 15,000 miles and discovered that there were people who were doing things for themselves in hundreds of communities.

These examples of American neighborhood democracy clearly had meaning beyond U.S. borders, McKee noted. The 13 case studies chosen from his travels for the NBC broadcasts were aired throughout the United States and beamed overseas by Voice of America and the Armed Forces Network to Americans and "friends of democracy" abroad. NBC advertised them as good examples of freedom and cooperation in the United States, "democracy in action." A second series, covering 26 additional community self-help projects, followed in 1952, supported by a grant from the Ford Foundation and aired this time by CBS. Community organizing had a place in the Cold War, and liberal proponents of democracy like McKee, philanthropic associations like the Ford Foundation, and propaganda outlets like Voice of America appreciated its ideological value.

But McKee was also a sincere advocate of neighborhood organizing and grassroots democracy. A Quaker, he believed that citizen participation in decision making should be the basis of democratic society. He reported in a book, *The People Act* (1955), which chronicled 10 case studies from the radio show, that what he had found in the United States was less rosy than the radio programs made it seem. He had found a general lack of faith in people, the same uncertainty about democracy he had encountered in Germany. He had come home to an America involved in a witch-hunt for subversives, hardly the stuff of which democracy was made. The community efforts described in the book and on the radio programs, McKee wrote, were not so much examples of widespread "real democracy" as important bulwarks of a "democracy on trial."[4]

McKee saw America's weakest link as well as the hope for a "free world" in the practice of democracy at the grassroots level. For him as well as other liberal proponents of decentralization, community development projects at home and abroad could strengthen democracy and in turn strengthen efforts of the United States in the Cold War. A group called the American Council for the Community (ACC), composed of distinguished liberals such as John Dewey, Stuart Chase, and Frank P. Graham, organized a North American Conference on the Community in the spring of 1950 because, they said, "the North American democracies have the vital job of demonstrating the workability of responsible freedom in the modern world. . . . The heart of the job lies in the local community units. These are the masonry blocks with which free nations and a peaceful world are built." One year later the ACC proclaimed that all communities in America needed to be strengthened and integrated "to meet any eventuality—whether it be cold war, hot war, or no war."[5]

The practice of community organizing in the postwar era was deeply affected by the economic policies and political climate of the Cold War. Most of the community work of radicals either came to a halt or took a more conservative approach. For Saul Alinsky, the anticommunism of the early 1950s made a wasteland of his community organizing. People were afraid to stick their necks out and get involved. Radical activity atrophied. Social welfare community work, on the other hand, adjusted itself to the new political realities and enlisted in the crusade against communism. Not all liberal community workers joined the cause, of course, but for those who did, the goals, programs, clients, sites of projects, and available funding for neighborhood work were determined by Cold War objectives.

Of course, the major community development projects of this period sponsored by the United States took place in Third World nations, not within our borders. Community development abroad was not simply a process to create conditions of economic and social progress for the whole community and with its active participation, as the United Nations defined it in 1955. It was also intended to "prevent the spread of Communism" and "to build customers for an ever expanding [U.S.] economy," as Phillip Ryan of the National Social Welfare Assembly frankly noted.[6] The subject of community organizing projects abroad is fascinating and instructive, but one, unfortunately, beyond the bounds of this study.

The primary community organization project within the boundaries of the United States in the decade after World War II began with discussions in the fall of 1950 to establish the United Community

Defense Services (UCDS). UCDS was the joint effort of the National Social Welfare Assembly (the leading professional council of social work agencies) and the Community Chests and Councils of America (the leading funding source for voluntary social welfare activities). These two agencies brought together 15 social welfare organizations to organize communities "destabilized" by military-related projects.[7] The United Community Defense Service was one element of the United Defense Fund (UDF), a social welfare program subsidized by local Community Chests to address the "emergency" defense situation in Korea and Southeast Asia. Most UDF funds during the heyday of the organization from 1950 to 1955 went to its best-known program, the United Servicemen's Organization (USO).

UCDS was charged with easing social problems that accompanied defense mobilization in "critical defense areas." Most of these communities were located outside of large cities. The 227 critical defense areas cited by the federal government in 1951 included 740 separate communities and towns, 86 percent of which had populations of under 25,000 before "defense impact." After "defense impact" more than 20 million people lived in these areas, more than one sixth of the nation's population. Critical defense areas housed armed forces bases, defense-related production plants, and hydrogen bomb development projects. Many critical defense area communities were located in the West and the South, reflecting the flow of defense contracts and corporate capital after the war to more rural areas with lower labor costs, lower taxes, fewer unions, and members of congress with seniority in Washington.

Not all critical defense areas were "destabilized" by the installation of a new defense industry or army base. UCDS estimated that one quarter were "overwhelmed" and one third needed outside assistance. At the Savannah River site, on the border of South Carolina and Georgia, the H-bomb project there urbanized and industrialized this rural area with "a force almost comparable to the bomb itself," reported the president of the UCDS:

Everyone living on the plant site—a tract of land 20 miles long and 15 miles wide—was forced to move out. Even the dead could not rest in peace. 100 cemeteries were to be moved outside the restricted area. People began flooding in, until perhaps 300,000 new people were added. The population of Augusta [Georgia] doubled. Some of the small South Carolina towns increased as much as ten times. . . . Something close to chaos resulted.[8]

Insufficient housing was the major problem in most defense areas. Police protection, health care, hospitals, schools, sewage disposal, and water supply were also usually insufficient or nonexistent. The demand for services grew with the population. In China Lake, California, the site of a newly developed naval ordnance testing station, the population boomed from 100 in 1944 to more than 20,000 ten years later. But inadequate services were not the only problem. Prostitution, gambling, night clubs, and transient trailer camps sprang up on the strips leading to and from the army bases and plants in defense areas. And racial discrimination and conflict made conditions more difficult in critical defense communities in the South. In Savannah River, housing for African-Americans in nearby Augusta had been severely overcrowded before the advent of the atomic energy project. To make matters worse, two housing developments built with government funds and intended for African-Americans were taken over by Du Pont and rented instead to their white employees. At the AEC site in Paducah, Kentucky, guards denied access to the premises to black applicants for jobs. In Savannah River, Du Pont did not hire black workers until pressure from the National Urban League and a need for workers forced them to do so.[9]

Few community residents—black or white—opposed the defense projects. Local officials, landowners, and businesspeople stood to make a good deal of money from the boom; workers stood to improve their standard of living and secure stable, permanent employment. Many local residents, however, were bitter about the extent and intensity of the transformation of their area and the concomitant social problems that the community was left to handle. A community worker described the situation in Paducah:

The people are resentful. They feel they did not want the H-bomb installation but that it was put there by the Federal Government and so it should take the responsibility for military problems relating to it such as housing, etc. There is a lot of bitter feeling in the community and marked cleavage between the former leaders and the new labor leaders. Finally there is much resentment toward outsiders coming into the community and telling them what to do.[10]

In the military spirit of the day, the United Community Defense Services labeled its efforts to resolve social problems in critical defense areas "Operation Community Organization: National." Time and time again, UCDS leaders declared that community organizing was critical to the defense of the United States, that community organizers could be used as domestic "trouble-shooters" and could assist in the Cold War struggle against communism. This interest in international issues was relatively novel for community workers. But their goals and methods were traditional.

UCDS organizers usually went into a community alone and uninvited. They visited the local chamber of commerce or welfare office, familiarizing themselves with local problems and resources. After this initial "reconnaissance" and reports back to UCDS central headquarters in New York City, organizers tried to gather support for social welfare projects. Projects ranged from establishing health investigations, day camps, and immunization clinics to developing permanent social welfare institutions and planning councils. The type of project usually depended on which member group in UCDS sent in a community worker. The American Social Hygiene Association organizer usually addressed problems of prostitution and gambling. Community workers from the National Recreation Association focused on recreational programming. All organizers in UCDS, however, emphasized the importance of getting the backing of influential leaders in the business, political, and social life of the community.

Securing the support of local elites was especially important because UCDS was largely ignored by federal and corporate funding sources. This was not because UCDS was out of step with the Cold War politics of the era. In their appeals for support, UCDS always underscored the role that professional community work played in supporting the Cold War. In 1954 and 1955 UCDS hired Elizabeth Wickenden, a leader in the field of social work and a consultant with contacts in Washington, to draft funding proposals. Her analysis, overwhelmingly approved by UCDS leaders, emphasized the symbiotic nature between social welfare expenditures and national security. In a democracy, she stated, voters and their elected representatives determine national policy. Military defense protected these common policies and our common institutions. The report continued:

Once a democratic nation commits itself to the need for an expanded program of military defense such a program must be considered to exist for the benefit of all its people. No sharp distinctions can properly be made in this situation between considerations affecting people's "welfare" and those affecting their "defense," for defense has become an accepted safeguard to their welfare.[11]

What was good for the military, the government, and defense-related industries not only was good for the people but reflected their democratic will.

The role of social welfare community organizers, accordingly, was to "lubricate" the total social machine. In this connection social welfare programs would take the place of repression. "Facilitating social services substitutes in a democracy for the terror and compulsion used by totalitarian nations in forcing their citizens to adapt to defense objectives." Wickenden wrote. People in a democracy had to be willing to sacrifice immediate benefits, including their own freedom of action, she said, in the service of the national interest.[12] In a class-stratified society, where some made immense profits and others struggled to make monthly payments, it was the role of government and community work to equalize the burden as much as possible and to convince people of the need to sacrifice for national objectives. Community workers in UCDS, like most social welfare predecessors, fundamentally accepted the existing system and sought, within the limits of that system, to ameliorate social inequalities in support of the objectives of those in power.

But the 1950s differed from the early twentieth century. Arguments like Wickenden's on the critical importance of social welfare fell on ears more attuned to other concerns. Unlike the atomic energy sites developed during World War II, where the federal government constructed and operated whole defense communities, Atomic Energy Commission sites and critical defense areas in the 1950s received little, if any, federal support. The Federal Security Agency, which supervised the defense community mobilization, received about $4 million annually during the height of the Korean War. Most of these funds went to finance water and sewer projects, and Congress made sure to legislate that none of it could be used for health, day care, recreation, or other social welfare services.

Corporate support for social projects was little better, and then only because they could not afford to be as aloof as the federal government. In Savannah River, Du Pont sent representatives to community meetings, built approximately 7,500 barracks, bought two housing projects for white personnel, and hired a recreational worker for programs in the trailer courts. They also paid higher wages than local businesses. From their point of view that was a sufficient contribution to the community. The policy of Du Pont, one field worker reported, was "to avoid entanglements that would result in their operating any type of community project or pertaining thereto."[13] A similar pattern was evident in other critical defense communities. In Arkadelphia, Arkansas, a center of bauxite production, the element critical to the production of aluminum, Reynolds Aluminum said they were interested in the social welfare programs of UCDS only "in the event problems develop."[14] The contribution of government and corporate sources to local community welfare programs was marginal at best because it did not have to be otherwise.

In places and times of economic crisis or social turmoil, professional social welfare community workers find support for their efforts. This was true in the period 1900–1920 and the 1930s, and would again be so in the 1960s. It was not the case in the prosperous 1950s, when a large percentage of the population improved their socioeconomic position. But prosperity alone does not explain the period's conservatism and lack of concern for social welfare programs. The decades before World War I and the 1960s were periods of prosperity that nonetheless evidenced much interest in social reform programs as a means of addressing problems of social disorder and insurgency. The 1950s, however, had a more effective means of maintaining social control and unity. Massive doses of propaganda promoting united opposition to communism were reinforced by a campaign of national and local repression.

The combined effect of prosperity, propaganda, and repression was profound. No one in the nation remained unaffected, certainly not community workers. In critical defense communities, organized labor strongly supported the Cold War consensus. At the same time, loyalty oaths and tight security measures made dissent treasonous. In many of these communities, and especially in the South, something akin to a police state existed for blacks and radicals. Even liberal critics kept quiet. There was little threat of insurgency or opposition. In such places and periods of history, social welfare community workers are isolated and ignored. They are left to perform minimal tasks in an unsympathetic, unsupportive environment. They are simply not needed to ameliorate social problems or maintain social order.

Such was the situation facing community workers in the early 1950s. Member organizations and organizers for UCDS openly supported Cold War objectives, nevertheless, because they believed in them and because support for the Cold War was the best method to secure at least minimal funds to keep social welfare programs alive.

But community workers would have to wait until the 1960s for large-scale funding. Then, when the federal government was faced with urban rebellions throughout the nation, a new set of political leaders began to realize again the function liberal community work could play in the political economy.

Neighborhood Improvement Associations, 1880–1948

> *Mr. Speaker, there must have been a celebration in Moscow last night; for the Communists won their greatest victory in the Supreme Court of the United States on yesterday when that once august body proceeded to destroy the value of property owned by tens of thousands of loyal Americans in every state in the Union by their anti-covenants decision [Shelley v. Kraemer].*
>
> —John Rankin, representative from Mississippi, 4 May 1948

The most prominent form of neighborhood organizing in the 1950s were the neighborhood improvement associations that proliferated throughout the nation, most notably in new, affluent suburban areas. No matter what their title—civic clubs, homeowners or property owners associations, or neighborhood protection organizations—all shared common objectives, organizing styles, and structures. The improvement approach to neighborhood organizing is distinct from the two more widely known methods discussed this far, the liberal social welfare and radical activist approaches. In improvement associations the goal is twofold: enhancement and protection. Enhancement includes efforts to secure public services, promote uniform and homogenous development, control taxes, provide neighborhood-based self-help programs or services, and, in general, oversee the development of the community. Most important, however, the association serves to protect property values and community homogeneity by opposing commercial development and excluding members of lower classes and racial minorities.

Moreover, neighborhood improvement associations do not, as a rule, use protest or confrontation tactics to advance their objectives. On an intraneighborhood issue they generally rely on peer pressure. In relations with other neighborhoods or city officials, the leaders of improvement associations work quietly and cooperatively behind the scenes as interest-group "brokers" for their neighborhood. While membership is quite high, in many communities running as much as 100 percent, membership activity is usually quite low. At such times when a neighborhood is "threatened," people will come to meetings and get involved in the association. Generally, however, a handful of lawyers, businesspeople, realtors, developers, or politicians living in the neighborhood organize the association and play the leading and only active roles. There usually are no paid staff and no external professional organizers. The organization funds itself privately through fees and collections within the neighborhood, and rarely does affiliation or activity extend beyond neighborhood or city limits.

Neighborhood improvement associations are not usually considered by either social scientists or activists to be a part of the history of community organizing. Their constituency is very different from that of the social work and political activist types of neighborhood organizing. Until most recently, neighborhood improvement associations were generally not found in working-class and minority neighborhoods. Moreover, in the improvement association approach to neighborhood organizing, organizers are usually indigenous leaders, whereas in social welfare and radical activist approaches the distinction between organizers and leaders is critical. Most significant, the improvement association is fundamentally conservative; usually it can be found resisting, rather than joining, progressive social change efforts. This conservative form of community organizing, however, predates the other approaches to neighborhood organizing, and, according to one historian, is more common, lasts longer, and can exhibit more pressure in local politics than can organizing efforts in working-class and slum neighborhoods. This is to be expected, given the fact that people in these neighborhoods are more affluent and generally more able to join formal organizations than are people in slum communities.[15]

Like most forms of neighborhood organizing, this type has changed little since its inception. The first neighborhood improvement associations developed along with the first suburban neighborhoods in the 1880s. As the industrial city grew and as trolley lines made it possible for the more affluent to live farther from the central business district, "streetcar suburbs" developed in cities as diverse as Boston, Chicago, and Houston. Often these new communities were part of the city proper, or in the process of being annexed. They were not autonomous localities, nor did they want to be. The costs of lighting, drainage, schools, and police and fire protection were too much even for upper-class communities. It was cheapest and most expedient to secure these amenities by remaining part of the city and using political influence to get the city to provide them.

In the generation after 1880, neighborhood improvement associations, especially those in more affluent communities, organized successfully to put pressure on city officials to bring basic urban services to their neighborhoods. Baltimore, for example, had more than 30 neighborhood associations within the city and its suburbs by 1900. The Federated Improvement Association, an organization of neighborhood improvement associations in Cincinnati, included 36 neighborhood affiliates and 8,000 members in 1913.[16] A path-breaking sociological study of neighborhood and local life in Columbus, Ohio, in the early twentieth century captured in its description of neighborhood organization in an affluent suburb there the essence of these early improvement associations.

It was promoted by a number of the most enterprising citizens of the community including one of the city's most prominent councilmen. No local organization of the city has been more active in the promotion of local interests, or has achieved more for the territory served than the Hilltop Improvement Association. Its field of activities included negotiations with the city council for the procuring of local satisfactions, such as a recreation building, streetcar accommodations, city deliveries, etc. It has also stimulated local pride in the care of property and in the repulsion of undesirable commercial encroachments, and at the same time has done much to engender a feeling of neighborliness and sociability among the people.[17]

Likewise, neighborhood improvement associations sprouted throughout Chicago's suburbs. The Woodlawn Improvement Association organized in the affluent Woodlawn neighborhood in 1882 to keep the sidewalks in this large and then sparsely settled district free of snow. In 1903 the Neighborhood Center Committee of the Woman's Club of Chicago organized a Neighborhood Improvement League of Cook County, with some 30 participating neighborhood organizations. By 1909 there were 55 member associations in the league. Almost all of them represented newly developed suburban communities. They focused on securing public services from the city or providing their own basic necessities. The Fine Arts Society of Oak Park, initially the Oak Park Improvement Association, expanded its art criticism to "conducting spring cleaning campaigns, making public inspection of the entire village, and photographing all property not cleaned up, for publication."[18]

Certainly not all neighborhood associations were based in peripheral communities as affluent as the Hilltop in Columbus or those noted in Chicago. Nor were all as successful. As with most transactions in interest-group politics, the extent to which neighborhood improvement associations secured public services or supplied their own neighborhood needs was directly proportional to the economic and political power held by individual members of the association. What makes people with less power less effective in city politics also explains what makes inner-city and working-class neighborhood organizations less effective as neighborhood interest groups. Because the people moving to the urban periphery in the years before World War I were from the more affluent and influential segments of the urban population, their neighborhood associations commanded a disproportionate amount of political and economic resources for improvement efforts.

The initial concerns of the first improvement associations were community enhancement and development, although in the South neighborhood protection practices accompanied enhancement from the outset. William Wilson, the developer of the Woodland Heights neighborhood in Houston, advertised in 1909 that the neighborhood deed included "protective restrictions" that preserved "the original beauty of the property," banned commercial development, forbade the sale of liquor in the subdivision, and detailed architectural restrictions for new homes and home improvements. "You are also protected from colored neighbors, as the lots are sold to white people only," Wilson assured.[19] While deed restrictions were common in suburban neighborhoods throughout the nation at this time, race and ethnic restriction clauses appeared more prominently in the South where a legalized and official system of segregation was thoroughly enforced.

The black population was relatively small in most northern cities prior to 1914, and the system of de facto segregation by class and race served to keep African-Americans and most working-class people out of the developing suburban fringes. But the color line was no more permeable in the North than in the South. In 1897 the Woodlawn Improvement Association in Chicago threatened to "make war" on a hotel on the outskirts of the neighborhood that was renting rooms to black customers. Five years later a similar confrontation ensued with a hotel owner who sought to convert suites into apartments for African-

Americans. The association stopped him as well, and by 1910 it had effectively removed any black presence in the neighborhood.[20]

Around the time of World War I improvement associations in outer-city neighborhoods in the North began to shift their focus from neighborhood enhancement to neighborhood protection, from securing services to excluding lower classes and racial minorities, especially African-Americans. They now consciously resisted social change, advocated racial segregation, attacked "block busters," and even aligned themselves with right-wing organizations like the Ku Klux Klan. In 1919 in cities across the nation racial tension heightened as white ethnic neighborhood organizations, in alliance with city officials and realtors, sought to prevent African-Americans from moving into their neighborhoods.

Neighborhoods like Woodlawn in Chicago, once the preserves of the affluent, were now inhabited by first- and second-generation immigrants who had managed to climb a notch up the economic ladder. Segregationist hiring and residential practices continued to keep the black population poor and ghettoized. Until World War I they posed no "threat" to the homogeneity of the once upper-class, now middle-class, outer-city neighborhoods. From 1915 to 1920, however, in cities like Chicago, the African-American population more than doubled as black laborers came north to fill industrial jobs created by the war. As housing deteriorated in the black ghetto under the massive population pressure and as competition for housing grew increasingly keen, the small black middle class sought to move out. Before the war this would not have been a problem. It was common in northern cities for a few blacks to move into a neighborhood and slowly but steadily for the whites to "relinquish" it, just as the upper class had relinquished it before to the white, ethnic middle class. As long as available new housing and space existed, class and racial conflict was generally avoided. But by 1917 there was little available housing, and tensions began to mount.

Resistance to neighborhood change and integration took many forms. Racial zoning had been declared illegal in 1917 when the Supreme Court in *Buchanan v. Worley* deemed unconstitutional a Louisville racial zoning ordinance that restricted certain areas in the city to whites and other areas to blacks. In the absence of outright judicial support, however, improvement associations in many cities formed a "united front" to keep their neighborhoods "white." In Hyde Park–Kenwood in Chicago the association used newspaper publicity, blacklisted realtors, held mass rallies, boycotted merchants, and intimidated black residents. When that failed to stop black immigration, vigilante groups armed with pipes, bricks, bats, and bombs stormed the house of black "invaders." From 1917 to 1921 fifty eight homes recently purchased by black families were bombed in Chicago, about one every 25 days. In the spring of 1919 two bombs went off each month. Efforts like these at "neighborhood protection" led to race riots in Chicago, St. Louis, and New York.[21]

Bombings and tension continued in "disputed" neighborhoods of America's large, northern cities in the first years of the 1920s but began to die down with the housing boom that began in 1922. The process of segregated neighborhood succession continued steadily, if slowly, in most northern cities from 1922 to 1926 as white, ethnic, middle-class neighborhoods bordering black ghettoes became middle-class black communities. For the duration of the housing boom, improvement associations did little to stop the pattern of residential racial change. When the boom ended around 1926, however, white homeowners and realtors sought a new device to protect their investments. Unable to secure legislation to create and zone exclusive racial areas, neighborhood improvement associations, supported by realtor associations like the National Association of Real Estate Boards (NAREB), drafted "restrictive covenants" primarily to exclude racial minorities. In 1924 NAREB gave state commissions the right to revoke the license of any realtor who introduced African-Americans into white neighborhoods against the wishes of that community. This policy was implemented prior to 1924 by local realty boards.

In 1926 the U.S. Supreme Court lent its weight to the issue, upholding the validity and enforceability of restrictive covenants. Covenants proliferated throughout northern cities. By 1930 more than 175 property owners' associations in Chicago had enforceable racial covenants and three fourths of all residential property in the city was bound by such restrictions. None of this property could be sold or rented to African-Americans.[22]

The history of neighborhood improvement associations in Chicago was repeated throughout the nation. Associations focused on community enhancement projects, especially when the neighborhood was first developing. Community development improved property values and the quality of community life. People were willing to move on to "better" neighborhoods, however, as long as housing was available and affordable. Commitment to "the neighborhood" was as transient as the urban population of the early twentieth century. In times of housing shortage or recession, however, when people did not have the money to move, white neighborhood improvement associations bordering black or lower-class ghettos took on a decidedly segregationist and militant stance.

The Cold War had a profound impact on neighborhood improvement organizations. U.S. competition with the Soviet Union abroad demanded something be done at home about institutionalized racist practices. American political and business leaders found it difficult to present themselves as leaders of the "free world" in Asia, Africa, and South America while the nation perpetuated a humiliating and exploitative system of legalized racial segregation within its own borders. As President Truman put it in 1946:

Our position in the post-war world is so vital to the future that our smallest actions have far-reaching effects. . . . We cannot escape the fact that our civil rights record has been an issue in world politics. The world's press and radio are full of it. . . . Those with competing philosophies have stressed—and are shamelessly distorting—our shortcomings. . . . They have tried to prove our democracy an empty fraud, and our nation a consistent oppressor of underprivileged people. This may seem ludicrous to Americans, but it is sufficiently important to worry our friends. The United States is not so strong, the final triumph of the democratic ideal is not so inevitable that we can ignore what the world thinks of us or our record.[23]

The National Association for the Advancement of Colored People (NAACP) was quick to capitalize on this new "liberalism" in Washington. While its opposition to restrictive covenants had begun in 1925, in 20 years of nearly constant litigation the NAACP had made little headway in securing a clear-cut decision against them. The situation, however, seemed more promising in 1945. In addition to Cold War pressures, masses of black people had migrated from southern rural areas to northern industrial centers during the war, found jobs, tasted a better life, and were willing to go to the polls or even protest to defend it.

In the wake of these developments, property associations organized to resist social change. In Washington, D.C., the Federation of Citizens Associations, formed to prevent residential integration, had 69 neighborhood affiliates by 1944. Neighborhood improvement associations won lower-court cases supporting racial covenants in Los Angeles, Chicago, Columbus, New York City, Detroit, and

Washington, D.C. They lost only one local case, in St. Louis, in the Marcus Avenue Improvement Association area, but since it was lost on a minor technicality they appealed it and had the case reversed by the Missouri Supreme Court in *Shelley v. Kraemer.* The Marcus Avenue Improvement Association (MAIA), like most neighborhood associations, had a good deal of strength in local courts where they could marshal the force of local public opinion. They packed the courts with association members, got prominent businessmen and realtors to testify about the harmful effects of residential racial change, and were thus able to win their day at the state level.

But when the case got to the U.S. Supreme Court, the local neighborhood improvement association had no national organization, no allies powerful enough to counteract the liberalizing pressures of the Cold War. The Court declared racial restrictive covenants unenforceable. J. D. Shelley, the plaintiff in the case, and his family were allowed to remain at 4600 Labadie Avenue, on the fringe of the Marcus Avenue neighborhood. Within a short time the segregationist MAIA had folded, most white residents had fled from the neighborhood, and it became a black middle- and working-class community.[24]

Of course, the history of improvement associations prior to 1948 varied widely, depending on the unique historical situation and local conditions of each neighborhood. Improvement associations appeared in lower-class as well as upper-class, black as well as white, inner-city as well as suburban neighborhoods, in metropolitan environs as different as New York, St. Louis, Atlanta, and Los Angeles. Nevertheless, certain general patterns of development are discernible. Most started out the same, designed to coordinate and lobby for local services. To the extent that neighborhood racial and class homogeneity was threatened, however, to the extent that the neighborhood bordered lower-class and minority communities, improvement associations took on a decidedly protectionist and reactionary caste. Those improvement associations that were not threatened by social change—either because their class background and the spatial structure of the metropolis isolated them from poor and minority people or because the social control mechanisms of the city, especially in the South, prevented integration—focused fundamentally on neighborhood conservation and enhancement. Without social change pressures, neighborhood organizations in these communities emphasized securing such amenities as new schools, playgrounds, and swimming pools to enhance the quality of life in their neighborhoods as well as to increase property values. The nature of any given neighborhood organization was thus directly related not only to national developments, such as the "Shelley" decision, which transformed entire neighborhoods and local associations in less than a decade, but to the specific class, racial, and spatial relationships of each city and neighborhood. As we will see in the following discussion of neighborhood improvement associations in the 1950s, this was certainly as true after 1948 as it was before.

Neighborhood Improvement Associations after 1948: Houston Civic Clubs

We must all be on the lookout for [deed restriction] violations, report them, and stand ready to help the Restrictions Committee protest them.

—Southwest Civic Club (Houston)

While all neighborhood improvement associations concern themselves with the dual goals of enhancement and protection, the history of associations prior to 1948 indicates that some were far more protective and defensive than others. After 1948, however, the large majority of neighborhood improvement associations were organized in suburban areas geographically distanced from the neighborhoods of the central city, and thus these associations appear more akin in style and focus to the first generation of improvement associations, founded in affluent, elite neighborhoods on the urban periphery, which sought enhancement more than protection.

The massive suburban development boom of the postwar years, which spatially transformed the modern metropolis, was stimulated and engineered by the federal government. As military spending fueled the development of "critical defense areas" in the South and West, so federal expenditures opened rural areas on the urban periphery to suburbanization. Low interest, insured loans from the Federal Housing Authority (FHA) made it possible for the white middle class to leave their outer-city neighborhoods and move to newly developed suburban communities. Within a few years after the federal government in 1948, by court decision, had made it more difficult to restrict blacks from neighborhoods, it passed FHA legislation that encouraged white residents to "flee" outer-city neighborhoods and leave them to newer residents. The rub for minorities and the working class was this: the FHA program tacitly declared inner- and outer-city neighborhoods ineligible for low-interest loans, thereby condemning almost all interior neighborhoods in the metropolis to a slow but steady decline. Over the course of the following generation, the central city and its immediate neighborhoods were either abandoned or destroyed by neglect.

Similarly, the Federal Highway Act of 1956 constructed thousands of miles of inter- and intraurban roads, resulting in a transnational network of turnpikes and parkways. People now could move to the suburbs if they wanted to, if they had enough money, and if they owned a car. Corporations and factories also moved to the new urban periphery, following and leading workers out of the central city. Thousands of new autonomous suburban towns emerged and with them a new metropolitan form. Whereas the industrial metropolis represented a growth in city size from a radius of 2 to 10 miles, the new urban sprawl of the "multinucleic" metropolis encompassed a radius in each direction of 25 miles or more. Low-density, single-family housing, purely residential areas, automobiles, and freeways characterized the new metropolis. No longer were people dependent on the central business district, the downtown area, for employment or shopping. The new multicentered metropolis had employment and shopping opportunities scattered about in "industrial parks" and "shopping malls," all within driving distance from the new residential suburbs.

In most metropolitan areas the new suburban developments were autonomous entities, self-governing and independent of the central city. In many of the sunbelt cities, like Los Angeles and Houston, which first experienced large-scale urban growth after 1945, the newly formed suburban areas were annexed as part of the central city. But whether they were legally independent of the central city or not, the new suburban residents tended to join together to create a sense of community and order out of their subdivisions of houses, streets, sidewalks, and trees. One of the more prominent forms of organization was the neighborhood improvement association. These associations, like their counterparts in developing suburbs in the early twentieth century, focused primarily on securing and providing services. After all, the suburban boom of the 1950s had eased competition for space in the multinucleic metropolis. There was little need for neighborhood improvement associations in new suburban areas to adopt a protectionist cast.

Excellent examples of postwar community organizing are the neighborhood civic clubs—numbering more than 700 in 1990—which abound in the city of Houston. Such widespread neighborhood organizing in Houston comes as a surprise to most. Houston seems to be little more than a massive urban sprawl, connected solely by freeways and characterized by a boom-town atmosphere. Moreover, it has a well-deserved reputation as a highly conservative city, not the sort where one expects cooperative efforts like neighborhood organizing to abound. In 1947, for example, John Gunther in his *Inside America* said that "with the possible exception of Tulsa, Oklahoma," Houston was "the most reactionary community in the United States."[25] Curiously, while no single image suffices for the Bayou City, the blend of extraordinary growth since the early 1940s and a laissez-faire political environment has combined to forge a mass of conservative neighborhood associations throughout the city that are almost identical to associations in suburban areas throughout the nation.

In Houston, up until very recently, deed restrictions and civic clubs were said to take the place of zoning. Land use was determined by private interests and the profit motive ever since the Allen brothers, two New York City entrepreneurs, first began to market Houston in 1836. This is not to suggest, however, that the city had no form of land use management other than the speculations of land developers and businesspeople. In residential neighborhoods, once the land was developed, land use was determined, rather explicitly, by deed restrictions. Drawn up initially by the developer, such deeds included land-use controls, architectural restrictions, and, until recently, racial covenants. Under this type of land-use management, individual homeowners were and still are ultimately responsible for enforcing restrictions. They are the ones who have to take a "violator" to court to prevent a chicken farm or a Colonel Sanders from moving in next door.

To facilitate the enforcement of deed restrictions and remove the burden of enforcement from individual residents, many neighborhoods organized local civic clubs.[26] While Houston's neighborhood civic clubs, all situated in neighborhoods within the city limits, perform a rather unique land-use control function, their history, especially since World War II, is very similar to that of most neighborhood improvement associations in affluent suburbs that have zoning. These suburban communities, like most of their counterparts in Houston, are situated away from lower-class and minority neighborhoods and their associations therefore do not have to deal with pressures of class or racial transformation. Instead they tend to focus on neighborhood enhancement rather than protection.

Deed restrictions came into use in Houston in the 1890s with the development of residential subdivisions. Prior to the first subdivisions in Houston and other cities, land was purchased in small parcels, usually by individual homeowners. The initial six inner-city "wards" in Houston were settled in this manner without deed restrictions. After 1890 large parcels of land were developed on Houston's periphery, and these subdivisions were regulated by deed restrictions. In 1909, a brochure for Woodland Heights, one of the first outer-city neighborhoods in Houston, advertised its deed restrictions as one of the virtues of purchasing land there: "In order to keep Woodland Heights the strictly high grade residence section it is, and to guard against all undesirable features, we have placed certain restrictions on this property as to the character of the improvements and the nature of the use which are embodied in all our deeds, and are binding not only upon the purchasers, but upon their heirs and assigns."[27]

Civic clubs were quickly organized in these new "streetcar suburbs." Their raison d'etre was restriction enforcement, but they also functioned as traditional improvement associations, supplying necessary services and lobbying city hall for street repairs, park development, and schools, just like associations in the North. As development boomed on Houston's periphery, some three miles from downtown in the 1920s, so did neighborhood civic clubs, as each new subdivision came complete with a set of enforceable deed restrictions. But Houston civic clubs in the 1920s did not pursue restrictions with the reactionary zeal of their outer-city counterparts in Chicago or St. Louis. Deed restrictions were seen primarily as a means of protecting property values and preserving neighborhood homogeneity, not a means of excluding African-Americans; white homeowners in this bastion of racial segregation were less threatened by neighborhood racial transformation than were their northern counterparts.

Deed restrictions in Houston in the 1920s included racial clauses limiting ownership and tenancy to "Caucasians and whites only." But competition for housing between blacks and whites was slight and well controlled. With some 138,000 people, the city had a relatively small population. The number of African-Americans in the city was sizable, around 34,000, but the percentage, 24 percent, was not expanding. Most important, this was the South before the civil rights movement of the 1960s. Segregation was the law of the land. The entire system—institutions, power brokers, police, and day-to-day relationships—enforced Jim Crow laws. Two separate societies existed, one black, the other white. African-Americans were concentrated in three older areas of the city. Moving into a white area was suicidal, if not impossible. People "knew their place." Before 1948 residential racial transformation was not a "problem" for Houston's neighborhood civic clubs.

Civic clubs in Houston achieved their heyday in the decades after World War II. So did the city. From 1940 to 1960 Houston's population increased from about 400,000 to nearly 600,000. Suburban construction boomed as well. Federal highway development made the outlying areas more accessible, and federal housing loans put the purchase of a single-family home within the reach of the middle class. Developers rushed to meet the demand.

The Braeswood area, located in the southwest sector of the city, was one of the more popular new subdivisions for upper-middle-class whites. Less expensive middle-class housing could be found in other parts of town, but the Braeswood area offered ranch homes with central air conditioning and central heat, three bedrooms, modern kitchens, and two bathrooms for around $20,000. In many ways the subdivision was undistinguished: small plots of land, gridiron street pattern, few trees, only a few house models from which to choose. But it was pleasant enough, accessible to downtown, and on the "right" side—the west side—of the city. The Braeswood development opened in 1951 and by the end of the year there were 6,000 people living there.[28]

The Southwest Civic Club (SWCC) was organized in the Braeswood area on 13 February 1951 and held its first meeting one month later. Eighty-eight residents attended. The goals of the organization were clear: enhance and protect the neighborhood and enforce deed restrictions. Like earlier neighborhood improvement associations, initial activity focused on securing neighborhood physical necessities. Houston prided itself on limiting the role of government in the affairs of "private" citizens. This meant that taxes were low and public services few. Neighborhood residents were expected to furnish their own needs. Accordingly, civic clubs coordinated neighborhood support and financing for services the city would not supply, like mosquito fogging or street lighting.

But the SWCC did lobby city hall, often with success, for improved services. Residents paid sizable property taxes compared with other neighborhoods in the city, and they expected something in return. A meeting on flood control in November 1951 brought out some 200 neighborhood residents. They resolved not to support county officials who were seeking two new tax measures unless promised road and ditch repairs were completed. The county government responded slowly, but eventually met the neighborhood's wishes. Over the next few years the SWCC effectively lobbied for traffic signs and lights, improved water pressure, road paving and repairs, and a new library, park, elementary school, and fire station. To accomplish their objectives, the club might hold mass meetings or sponsor letter-writing campaigns to pressure city hall and county officers. But most often club successes resulted from personal contacts between club leaders and city officials and prominent businesspeople. SWCC leaders over the years included state representatives, realtors, lawyers, and urban planners, each with some contacts and varying degrees of influence in the city and county. In neighborhoods like Braeswood, the prestige and contacts of individual members, enhanced by the backing of a civic association, enabled the organization to be heard and win services.

From its inception deed restriction enforcement was a central activity of the SWCC. The process of private deed enforcement maintained neighborhood homogeneity effectively, but not without serious drawbacks. The first steps in restriction enforcement were informal: a resident would complain to the civic club, the club president would write a letter or pay an informal visit to the "violator." Most often people were simply unaware they had broken the deed. In one case a young boy was raising two lambs in his backyard for a Future Farmers of America project. The deed prohibited the keeping of livestock in the neighborhood. The resident reluctantly complied. Sometimes more formal action, like the threat of a civil lawsuit, was required, and it was here that a fundamental problem faced neighborhood civic clubs. Court cases were few and far between because defendants realized the potential expense and the court's support of deed restriction enforcement. On one occasion the SWCC secured a "permanent injunction" against a chiropractor from practicing in his home. On another, they took a motel operator to court, forcing his business out of the area. But court expenses were high for the club as well as the defendant. One violation pursued all the way through the courts could wipe out the club's entire restriction fund, and more. Only the wealthiest civic clubs, like the River Oaks Property Owners Association, could finance frequent court battles. Deed restriction enforcement was potentially an expensive means of protecting property values.

It was also divisive. Neighbors had to keep watch on, oppose, and threaten one another with court suits. It was easy to oppose a filling station trying to move in the neighborhood. But what about telling neighbors that they could not extend their carport to the lot line or convert their garage into an apartment for the family of their son or daughter? Given the problems of constant enforcement, potential expense, and intraneighborhood tension, neighborhoods with active civic clubs, surprisingly, also ardently supported zoning proposals in 1948 and 1962. Civic clubs preferred to make enforcement of deed restrictions a public rather than a private function, one supported by tax monies and administered by local officials.

While the SWCC, like all civic clubs in Houston, established a democratic structure for resident participation, the affairs of the club were handled by a half-dozen men, usually businessmen or professionals. Membership was not opened to women until 1956, and then only to women who were "resident owners of real property." The club had 4 elected administrative officers, 10 "area directors," and "block captains." Meetings were run democratically, in that all members could vote, but generally resident participation and interest was slight. The early years of the SWCC were the peak time of resident activism. The neighborhood was young, people were just getting to know one another, and basic amenities still needed to be secured. The residents wanted a community organization. In 1955 85 percent of the residents paid $6.75 per year to join the club: $1 for membership, $1.25 for the restriction enforcement fund, and $4.50 for mosquito fogging. Meetings that addressed an "emergency issue," like flood control, could bring out 200 residents. But even in the heyday of the SWCC most monthly meetings were poorly attended. "Everybody is willing to do everything they are asked to do, but [they] don't attend the meeting," lamented an officer in 1955. Often no more than 10 or 20 people came. Block captains and a regular newsletter kept neighbors informed of club activities, and this sufficed for most. Elections for club officers were rarely contested. Residents willingly accepted the suggestions of the ad hoc nominating committee, which was appointed by the board of directors. Members were grateful that someone with leadership skills and, quite often, political or business influence, was willing to assume the burden.

Over the years the organization became even less participatory and less democratic. In 1956 the number of annual general meetings was reduced from 12 to 5. The board of directors continued, however, to meet monthly and direct the affairs of the club. In 1958 membership hit a low point of only 43.5 percent of neighborhood residents. The reasons were obvious. The Braeswood area was becoming more stable, and most initial services and amenities had been provided. Many people, moreover, were not pleased with the club's mosquito-spraying service and chose to do without the fogging. Perhaps most important, neighbors did not feel threatened. The board of directors proclaimed the need to "Sell the Civic Club" in the neighborhood, but to little avail. In 1963 membership was up slightly to 48 percent, but remained a far cry from dues payments in the initial years. This pattern of elite leadership and declining resident interest seems nearly universal in Houston civic clubs. The SWCC, like other neighborhood civic clubs, was, after all, fundamentally a neighborhood-based interest group, and interest groups, especially those in affluent communities like Braeswood, do not require democratic or active citizen participation.

Despite their overt political function as neighborhood interest groups—as coordinators and lobbyists for neighborhood services and protectors of property values—civic clubs picture themselves as nonpolitical. While they do not directly support candidates for public office, the most effective civic clubs, like the Southwest Civic Club, serve a parapolitical function by influencing local officials and power brokers on behalf of the neighborhood and by serving as informal conduits of information about the needs and developments in the community.[29] The SWCC never shied away from addressing political issues. Over the years it invited speakers and sponsored programs that reflected the conservative politics of club leaders. Speakers warned club members of the hazards of federal deficit spending and taxing powers. The club coordinated civil defense programs at the neighborhood level. It showed films like *The Land of the Free* and *Communism on the Map,* the latter advertised in press releases throughout the city as "a fully documented film on how the communists are spreading their doctrine throughout the world." These activities were not seen as political because residents supported them. Issues that might cause dissent within the civic club, like partisan politics, were off limits. But political activity was acceptable when it preserved, or at least did not disrupt, neighborhood homogeneity.

The fundamental issue facing most outer-city neighborhood improvement associations in the 1950s was racial integration. In response to black activism and the pressures of the Cold War, segregationists organized in the North and the South in both neighborhood-based and broader organizations like the Citizen Councils to resist residential and school integration. In Houston, civic clubs located in neighborhoods contiguous to the black ghettos on the east side of town actively resisted integration. For example, Riverside—called by some "the Jewish River Oaks"—situated east of Braeswood along Braes Bayou, was a select white neighborhood in the 1940s. With the "Shelley" decision in 1948, white residents in Riverside grew alarmed about the expanding black ghetto to their north. In 1952 they formed the Greater Riverside Property Owners Association (GRPOA) to prevent integration. They told white residents to sit tight, not sell, remain in the neighborhood, and they tried to raise money to buy property for sale and to "buy out" blacks who had already moved into Riverside Terrace.[30] Signs declaring "This house is not for sale" were frequently seen posted on porches. Bombs exploded at the house of the first African-American family that moved to Riverside in 1953. But none of this was very effective. Once the pattern of residential change was apparent, white homeowners sold quickly, even at lower prices, and realtors were eager to help them do so. The white residents of Riverside moved to newly developed subdivisions in the southwest of the city, like Braeswood, which provided good housing and appreciable distance from the black ghetto.

Because Houston was growing at a breakneck pace after World War II, competition for living space was minimal, limited only to those areas, like Riverside, that bordered the black ghettos of the city. Residents in neighborhoods like Braeswood shared similar segregationist sentiments with their white counterparts in Riverside. As late as 1970 only 13 of the neighborhood's 8,654 residents were black. But residents of Braeswood, like most suburban residents in the 1950s living 5 to 10 miles from the central city and the black ghetto, were not as threatened or affected by integration pressures as residents of neighborhoods that bordered the black ghetto in both southern and northern cities. Nevertheless, organizations formed even in southwest Houston to address this issue and protect property values.

In the 1950s an umbrella organization of local civic clubs in southwest Houston, the Allied Civic Clubs (ACC), formed to deal with district-wide issues that went beyond subdivision boundaries. Among other activities, the ACC organized workshops on community leadership training and restriction violations, supported a drive toward district representation on the city council, and became a strong advocate of zoning. The ACC also helped coordinate opposition to residential desegregation in southwest Houston. ACC leaders recognized that the "Shelley" decision made it difficult to prevent a black family from moving into a white neighborhood. Indeed, "there is no reason now to believe that this is possible," they lamented. But ACC could stop wholesale neighborhood transformation and panic selling; ACC leaders called this objective "neighborhood stabilization."

Where integration threatened to destabilize a neighborhood, the ACC advised its constituents to remain calm. "Emotional panic of white neighbors solves nothing and is, indeed, self-defeating. The way of neighborhood stabilization is much better." Be alert to potential problem houses, such as a G.I.-financed home that did not sell quickly. If an African-American moves into the neighborhood, call a meeting quickly with residents of the immediate area. Urge them to sit tight. Beware of "unethical" realtors who "stir up race prejudices." If "wildcat realtors" are put out of business, then "every all-white area in Houston that wishes to remain all-white will have a much better chance." The ACC further requested residents to report wildcatters to the Houston Board of Realtors, the Better Business Bureau, and the ACC, so that such realtors could be singled out and ostracized. The advice was clear: "neighborhood stabilization" was the best way to protect property values.[31]

The SWCC, a member organization in the ACC, followed the recommendations. As late as 1970, when a black family moved into the neighborhood the civic club president quickly wrote a letter to residents in the immediate area, advising them that "a frantic rush to get out will devalue our properties and deteriorate our neighborhood." The letter identified the realtor who sold the property, and went on to praise the quality of the two African-American families who currently resided in the community: one a doctor, the other an attorney, both "educated and cultured." "Sit tight and face this situation with realism, courage, and goodwill. . . . The value of your property and the future of your neighborhood depend entirely on what you people do."[32]

In summary, the strategy of neighborhood stabilization sufficed to "protect" Houston's more affluent white neighborhoods. Most African-Americans could not afford to move there, and for those who could a few other areas of the city were opening up that were equally attractive and more hospitable. Neighborhood improvement associations in the North before and after World War II tried the "sit-tight, don't panic" strategy, but with little success in white communities contiguous to the expanding black ghetto. Similarly in Houston, where white neighborhoods bordered the black ghettos, as in the Riverside area, neighborhood stabilization was equally ineffective. Throughout the nation where pressures by African-Americans for more and better housing were great, violent conflict ensued, bombs exploded, whites resisted militantly, and then, ultimately, moved out.

This was not the case in the Braeswood area or in other affluent suburban neighborhoods—north and south—more removed from lower-class and minority inner-city areas by geographic distance and class barriers. In Houston the largest concentration of African-Americans remained on the east side of town, away from suburbs in the west like Braeswood. Protecting the neighborhood from racial change was less important to the SWCC than were the routine tasks of service acquisition and maintenance. Throughout its history the SWCC concerned itself with enforcing deed restrictions, keeping out commercial development, and doing mosquito fogging. The extraordinary distances separating races and classes in the new multinucleic cities in the South and the metropolitan areas in the North clearly enabled affluent residents to segregate themselves more successfully and easily than before. Prior to the 1950s such separation had been a "luxury" shared only by residents in the most affluent suburbs. But with the federal government subsidizing through highway and housing programs the mass suburbanization of metropolitan centers, upper-middle and middle-class suburban developments, whether within or outside the city limits, were removed and isolated from the central city as never before. In turn, improvement associations in these neighborhoods took on the role of maintenance and service lobbying efforts, rather than the combative and defensive style of racist associations in white neighborhoods that bordered the black ghetto.

Chapter Four

The Neighborhood Organizing "Revolution" of the 1960s

Poverty and Race in the "Affluent" Society

> *I, for one, believe that if you give people a thorough understanding of what it is that confronts them, and the basic causes that produce it, they'll create their own program; and when the people create a program, you get action. When their "leaders" create programs you get no action.*

> —Malcolm X

As preceding chapters have demonstrated, the stop-gap solutions and tenuous class and race relations of one decade often become the central problem and basis for change in the next. And each new situation seems to breed new forms of neighborhood organization activity. For example, in the postwar decade military Keynesianism did not resolve the fundamental inequity and instability of the economic system. Large numbers of people, especially nonwhites, did not share in the fruits of U.S. expansion abroad. Repression served as only a short-term political solution to the threat of dissent and rebellion, and as it let up in the late 1950s disaffected groups organized to protest their condition and to win power. If conservative neighborhood organizing was the dominant style of the 1950s, then radical organizing efforts responding to the contradictions of life in the "affluent society" characterized the succeeding decade. The shift in organizing styles and goals was similar to that which occurred from the 1920s to the 1930s.

The most innovative efforts in neighborhood organizing in the early part of the 1960s were the quasi-anarchist experiments initiated by the Student Non-violent Coordinating Committee (SNCC, pronounced "Snick") and Students for a Democratic Society (SDS).[1] Each emphasized the value of radical, community-based organizing and each focused its attention on developing new forms of grassroots political action based on the concept of participatory democracy. These groups were important innovators in a new style of community organizing, but only one of many types of grassroots efforts during the decade. These early projects of SNCC and SDS were followed by a most dramatic, violent, and unorganized community response to the inequities of the "affluent society," the inner-city ghetto rebellions of the years 1964 through 1968. As in the "progressive era" and the thirties, the federal government responded to this disorder with programs designed to undercut radical activity and palliate conditions. Its Community Action Program (CAP) launched the largest, most systematic neighborhood organizing project ever tried. The various "war on poverty" programs of the decade successfully defused social disorder and coopted a good deal of political militancy. But the events of the decade, especially the urban rebellions and the rise of revolutionary leaders like Malcolm X, pushed many radicals further left rather than into the "establishment." Calls for participatory democracy of the early 1960s were often replaced after mid-decade by avowedly socialist, anticapitalist critiques and programs for revolution. The decade's political and economic concerns, the early programs of SNCC and SDS, and the "Great Society" projects are the subjects of this chapter.

In the 1950s and 1960s, conservatives, liberals, and radicals shared a prevailing opinion that military expenditures and wars helped ensure prosperity in capitalist nations.[2] The signs of material wealth that adorned the "affluent society" reinforced the perception. By 1971 GNP exceeded a trillion dollars, whereas 20 years earlier it was one fourth that. Almost everyone owned a refrigerator, a television, and a vacuum cleaner. More than a third of the population had an air conditioner, a freezer, a color television, and more than one car. Large numbers of Americans, through increased real wages, installment buying, or both, were able to improve their economic standard of living. Thrilled by this success, apostles of the Cold War economy proclaimed the beginnings of a new economic era. Business leaders had made similar pronouncements in the 1920s, but this time, postwar boosters declared, it was true. America, they said, was in the process of building a "people's capitalism," characterized by ever-rising real incomes, the abolition of poverty, and the rapid spread of stock ownership among masses of Americans. Prosperity for all, spread more equally throughout the population, was the promise. It turned out not to be the reality.

Real income and wages (adjusted for inflation) did rise from the late 1940s until 1973. For some 25 years the fruits of America's international economic empire, federal deficit spending, and new technologies promoted the longest sustained period of economic growth in our history. Average unemployment in the 1950s was very low and the recessions that occurred were relatively minor. But a greater degree of economic democracy did not accompany this prosperity. The class-based prosperity of the "affluent society" did little to resolve income inequities, and stock ownership did not increase enough to warrant claims of a "people's capitalism." As conservative a source as *Business Week* noted in 1972 that the concentration of wealth had changed little in the United States from 1929 through the 1960s: "If anything, it increased slightly."[3]

Social theorists began to warn of impending class and race conflict if the glaring inequities of postwar prosperity were not addressed. In 1958, in his facetiously titled book, *The Affluent Society,* liberal economist John Kenneth Galbraith questioned the vacuous quality of life created by America's single-minded penchant to produce, purchase, and consume new products. He warned that amid America's material affluence there was a large population living in poverty that would one day revolt and cause costly social disorder. Michael Harrington's *The Other America: Poverty in the United States,* published in 1962, was an even stronger statement. According to prosperity's evangels, Harrington wrote, providing basic human needs, such as food, shelter, and clothing, was no longer a problem; the central concern now was how to live happily amid all this luxury. But this vision of a luxurious, affluent society was class-limited and distorted; poverty was widespread in America. Harrington estimated that some 40–50 million people were trapped in a "cycle of poverty." Poverty was a rural as well as inner-city, southern as well as northern problem. It hit the aged, female-headed households, and the young the hardest. Suburbanization had simply made it "invisible" to those who did not want to see it, Harrington added, by heightening class segregation in the postwar metropolis.[4]

While nearly 80 percent of those below the federal government poverty line of $3,000 in 1960 were white, the 22 percent who were African-American represented nearly half of the entire black population in America. But poverty in the 1960s came to be seen as a "black problem" not simply because of its extraordinary concentration among African-Americans. That had always been the case. What was different in the early 1960s was the intensity of opposition by blacks to this economic oppression.

The rising threat of black, urban disorder resulted in part from demographic shifts underway since the turn of the century. As late as 1910, 90 percent of African-Americans lived in the South and 75 percent lived in rural areas. After 1910, partially in response to the lure of industrial jobs created by World War I, black farmers began to leave the rural South. They headed first to southern and then northern urban areas. This trend accelerated during and after World War II as 1.5 million black agricultural workers left the South in the 1940s. In the next decade another 1.5 million departed, so that by the mid-1960s 75 percent of the black population in the United States lived in cities and more than 50 percent lived outside of the South. This extraordinary population shift equaled the massive migration during the late nineteenth and early twentieth centuries of Southern and Eastern Europeans to the United States and rural native whites to the cities.

The mass migration of African-Americans, especially after World War II, was more a result of "push" rather than "pull" factors. The modernization of southern agriculture after the war reversed a period of economic decline in agriculture begun after World War I. In no more than two decades, large-scale, highly mechanized, industrialized farming replaced small, labor-intensive operations in the South. Between 1940 and 1960 half the farms in the South disappeared, while the average farm size nearly doubled. Ten years later the average farm size had doubled again. Mechanization, new technologies, new crops, and federal policies dramatically reduced the need for tenant labor in the South. Between 1950 and 1965, as reported by a presidential Advisory Commission on Rural Poverty, new methods and machines increased farm output in the United States by 45 percent—and reduced farm employment by the same percentage. Agricultural workers were literally thrown off the land. Some white tenant farmers found jobs in the newly developing industrial mills in southern cities, but black agricultural workers continued to find themselves barred for the most part from such employment. In response, more than 3 million African-Americans left the rural South and headed north to cities such as New York, Chicago, Newark, St. Louis, Detroit, and Cleveland.[5]

In the course of a generation from 1940 to 1970 a black rural peasantry was transformed into an unskilled urban proletariat. The number of black residents in New York City tripled in 30 years, from 458,444 to 1,668,115, increasing from 6.1 to 21.2 percent of the city's population. In Chicago the jump was even more dramatic, from 277,731 and 8.2 percent in 1940 to 1,102,620 and 32.7 percent in 1970. In 1940 Newark was a city of primarily first- and second-generation Eastern European immigrants; African-Americans made up only 10 percent of the population. By 1970, reflecting both black in-migration and white out-migration, Newark was one of the growing number of northern cities with a majority of black residents.[6]

In many ways the economic position of the new black migrants was little better than it had been in the rural South before the war. Socially, culturally, and politically northern cities were more open. But ghetto and slum living, job ceilings, color lines in all areas of life, and powerlessness repeated in northern cities the same severe economic hardships and impoverished circumstances, in new and unfamiliar communities, that black workers had experienced in the South for generations. The median income of black workers was half that of their white counterparts. Unemployment figures for African-Americans were startling. In Watts, the Harlem of Los Angeles, just before the first riot in 1964 up to one third of all black residents were unemployed. Black teenage unemployment nationally was 22 percent, low in comparison to 1970 figures but more than double that of white youth. Four million blacks subsisted on welfare programs in 1966, and this was only a portion of those who needed or qualified for assistance. A 1967 Department of Labor study noted that more than 20 percent of black ghetto residents who were *work-*

ing full-time had earnings below the government poverty line of $3,000. In total, 37 percent of ghetto families reported incomes below that figure.[7]

To make matters worse, at the very moment that masses of unskilled, uneducated, poor black farmers were moving to cities up North, businesses and white property owners—the basis of the urban tax structure—were leaving the city for the suburban hinterland. At the very moment that more funds were needed for public services to train recent black migrants and at the very moment that masses of unskilled laborers arrived looking for work, much of which required higher skill levels than ever before, the sources of jobs and the tax base to support public services were leaving the city. Worsening poverty, declining urban educational programs, deteriorating housing, increasing crime and drug use, booming welfare rolls, and spiraling infant mortality and disease rates combined to create an urban crisis and fan the flames of discontent.

The decade of the 1960s was thus something very different for the inner-city, minority poor from the society of abundance and prosperity pictured by most recorded observers of the American scene at the end of the 1950s. The fruits of empire and Cold War politics aided many corporations, stockholders, and those segments of the middle class who were able to secure the skills and perform the tasks demanded by the private and public sectors. But for farmers and minority and ethnic workers outside the mainstream, the 1960s offered a challenge of a very different sort. In response to the gap between the theory and reality of the "affluent society," in response to the discrepancy between the idea of a society of abundance and the reality of systematic poverty and powerlessness experienced by millions of citizens, people did not sit idly or passively by. An important and influential minority of poor people and activists joined neighborhood and national organizations, participated in demonstrations, teach-ins, and civil disobedience actions, carried signs and threw molotov cocktails, and demanded "Freedom Now" and "Power to the People." Like the 1930s, the 1960s was a decade of important radical ferment and social change. It is certainly too soon for historians to evaluate the period effectively and probably too late to capture its boundless spirit, vitality, and hope. Such limits aside, the decade is a critical one in a history of neighborhood organizing because of the quantity, variety, and impact of its neighborhood organizing projects.

New Left Organizing Projects: SNCC and SDS, 1961–1965

[The civil rights movement] was an experience that totally changed the lives of people who participated in it. . . . I had grown up in a society where there were very clear lines. The older I got, the more I found what those lines were. The Civil Rights Movement gave me the power to challenge any line that limits me. . . . [It] said that if something puts you down, you have to fight against it.

—Bernice Reagon, SNCC organizer

[We need] a politics of responsible insurgence rooted in community after community, speaking in comprehensive terms to the felt needs of their locales, offering specific alternatives to specific problems of inequality, industrial stagnation, inadequate schools, civil defense, and so on. . . . We have no more difficult and more necessary task today than a race to create genuinely independent political constituencies who will not be satisfied with the New Frontier.

—Tom Hayden, SDS organizer

In the history of neighborhood organization, the 1960s will be remembered as a decade of mass insurgence, radical politics, and youthful experimentation, as a time when the notion of democracy was reinvigorated with participatory content. The most innovative efforts were the student-initiated projects of the Student Nonviolent Coordinating Committee and Students for a Democratic Society. In southern rural and urban areas and in northern urban ghettos these student activists, black and white, experimented with what it meant to develop democratic grassroots organizations. From 1962 to 1965 SNCC's community organizing work in the rural and urban South focused on registering voters and protesting segregation in public accommodations. From 1963 to 1965 SDS, through its Economic Research and Education Project (ERAP), focused on community organizing in poor neighborhoods of large, northern cities. Independently, SNCC and SDS forged two autonomous but interrelated groups of radical activists—a "new left"—the likes of which had not been seen since the Cold War began.

The radical ferment of the 1960s grew out of the civil rights movement. The mass struggle for black equality in the second half of the twentieth century began during and just after World War II as it became clear to increasingly militant black leaders that the battle for democracy must be fought at home as well as abroad. After 1945 the Cold War increased pressure for racial equality. As President Truman put the liberal viewpoint: the "top dog" in a "world which is over half colored ought to clean his own house."[8] And with good reason. State Department officials estimated that approximately 50 percent of Soviet propaganda against the United States focused on the race issue. With Truman's order to desegregate the armed forces in 1948 and with the Supreme Court's *Brown v. Board of Education of Topeka, Kansas,* decision in 1954 to desegregate public schools in the South, the federal government lent support to the cause of racial integration. Given the rising militancy and activism of black leaders, these actions helped spawn an insurgent, mass movement for racial equality throughout the South.

Beginning with the Montgomery bus boycott in 1957, led by Rosa Parks and Martin Luther King, Jr., middle-class black leaders, with support from affluent, liberal whites, initiated a mass movement of nonviolent, direct action protest against the most obvious forms of racial discrimination in the South. They operated in organizations like the Southern Christian Leadership Conference (SCLC), the Congress for Racial Equality (CORE), and the National Association for the Advancement of Colored People (NAACP). But they sought to build a *movement* of moral outrage and civil disobedience, not a powerful civil rights organization. As such the movement took its character and leadership not from a specific organization but rather from a shared vision of "beloved community" and a strategy of "passive resistance." Martin Luther King, Jr., best articulated the conception of a true democracy, but neither he nor the SCLC developed organizational forms that could sustain the concept in practice. Instead they followed a strategy of elite-led, nonviolent direct actions designed to expose the viciousness of racism and win the minds, if not the hearts, of those in power. The movement, however, became more participatory and turned to greater militancy in 1960 when black students engaged in ad hoc sit-in protests at segregated lunch counters and joined "freedom rides" that challenged segregation in public transportation.

SNCC began in October 1960, on the heels of the student sit-in activities. Initially it was seen as the organized but independent student arm of the civil rights movement in the South. One year later, it was a good deal more than that, a group of full-time organizers working to stimulate protest and launch social change efforts throughout the Deep South. More specifically, SNCC organized voter registration drives and protests in communities where black people had not voted or collectively challenged racism since the days of Reconstruction and populism. Here were the cream of black and white youth, most of them college educated, 180 strong at their peak in the winter of 1965, organizing challenges to segregation in the den of the lion.

Despite important and fundamental differences, the early programs of SDS in northern urban neighborhoods mirrored, as much as differing conditions would allow, the origins, objectives, and style of SNCC projects in the South. SDS began in the spring of 1960, in the midst of the first sit-in demonstrations. But in its first few years the new, campus-based, highly intellectual organization was unsure of its role and its constituency. In 1963 SDS turned for direction to what was then the only compelling activist model, SNCC's community organizing work. In that summer the newly created Economic Research and Action Project received from the United Auto Workers a grant of $5,000 to "emphasize economic issues on campuses and communities." Influential SDS leaders like Tom Hayden and Rennie Davis pointed to the slum neighborhood, not the workplace, as the best site for radical organizing. By the summer of 1964 SDS had raised $20,000 and began 10 ERAP community organizing projects with approximately 100 student volunteers. The ERAP projects occupied SDS's attention for two years, through 1965. At its height the project involved some 200 organizers in 10 cities. The organizers were often the brightest, most intellectual, upper- and upper-middle class students at the most prestigious and academically demanding universities. As in SNCC many of the white, northern-born members were "red-diaper babies," the children of Communists and Socialists, and the southern white students were often the children of liberal ministers. And as in SNCC, organizing for SDS was more than a difficult and exhilarating experience. For most it became a way of living, seeing, and behaving.[9]

Both organizations identified themselves as "nonideological." This was not surprising for SNCC, which was rooted in the moral crusade of the civil rights movement. It was, however, more significant for SDS, since SDS was founded as the student branch of the "old left," the democratic socialist League for Industrial Democracy (LID). The world view and tactics of new left organizations, however, jibed with little of LID's socialist critique. It was not that the student activists were more "radical." The Port Huron Statement, written in 1962 and perhaps the best expression of early SDS thinking, was not a revolutionary document. It included little explicit criticism of capitalism, class domination, or imperialism. But it was quite clear in its rejection of old left thinking. In 1964 Rennie Davis articulated the thoughts of many SDS organizers when he stated: "We know of no satisfactory blueprint for full employment, shared abundance, equality and democracy. We have only limited ideas about the sources of power or the strategy of change which will carry us into a new society. We have found little information on organizing in the 1930s that has proved relevant to our operations.[10] Bruce Payne, a SNCC activist, echoed the point:

SNCC people generally refer to themselves and their organizations as "non-ideological." By this they mean that they do not have any *total* view of political and social life that enables them to offer a blueprint for the kind of society they would like to see in the future. They also mean they are not committed to the views of any existing political organization—that they are not Marxists, Socialists, or Democrats. The absence of a full-scale program has as its concomitant an emphasis on immediate action.[11]

Nevertheless, both organizations shared definite ideas about the future of society and "the movement." They advocated in their words and behavior a moral revolt and nonconformity to "the system," which they said restricted self-expression and self-realization. They rejected the liberal faith in modest reforms and anticommunism. Accordingly, earlier left strategies of building coalitions with liberal and mainstream labor organizations were replaced with an emphasis on direct action and the formation of locally autonomous, insurgent, community organizations. Moreover, SDS and SNCC, the former more explicitly, rejected all centralized, bureaucratic, hierarchical forms as practiced in both democratic socialism and corporate capitalism.

This critique led SDS away from the old left's concern with organization and power, but the group did not replace it with an alternative formal theory of society, history, and radical change. Instead they substituted an all-embracing political credo that emphasized democratic action and relationships, processes, and values. "Participatory democracy," they called it. "Let the people decide." In SNCC and SDS participatory democracy became an ideology of both goals and methods, a vague vision of how to get people together, act together, and win power together.[12] This perspective was fundamentally anarchistic, not socialistic. New left activists in SNCC and SDS wanted to create a spontaneous, decentralized, antiauthoritarian movement that would

stand in marked contrast and as an alternative to the dominant system
of bureaucratic structures, representative government, and leadership
by professionals. The current system perpetuated elite control over
the poor and powerless, they said, and offered people little opportunity
to participate in public decisions. Because of this, most people felt ill-
equipped to do so and left politics in the hands of the elite.
The outlines of the new left vision were drawn by the conditions of
Cold War America. Psychologist Kenneth Keniston described this historical response well:

The fear of the abuse of power, or irrational authority, and of dominating
leadership is in many respects a legitimate reaction to a world in which
power, authority, and leadership are used cruelly rather than benignly. The
various positions, styles, and forms that cluster around the concept of participatory democracy are an important attempt, no matter how incomplete and
experimental, to devise new forms of organization and action that will human-
ize the organized and vitalize the actors.[13]

A unique organizing style resulted. Simply put, the new left
approach to community organizing included these common ingredi-
ents:
   1. *Be a catalyst, not a leader.* Given that uneducated, poor people
can represent their own interests effectively, the organizer ought to
be a catalyst for social change, not a community leader. The organizer should give community people skills and confidence and, as
Alinsky had suggested in Back of the Yards, work her or his way out
of a job.
   2. *Let the people decide.* Jimmy Garrett, a SNCC activist in
Mississippi, described the organizer SNCC sought. The organizer
"got the people together and said, 'You decide, you make decisions
about your life. You decide about voting. You decide about demonstrating. Just as you are. You don't have to be articulate or politically
developed. You know your conditions better than I, better than any
one.'" An ERAP staffer in Cleveland put it this way: "We just talked
with the women. They decided they wanted to do something. We said
we'd help them do whatever they wanted."[14]
   3. *Develop loose organizational structures.* This would encourage
maximum, meaningful participation by community people. They practiced consensus decision making. They rotated meeting leaders.
Tasks were assigned on a voluntary, ad hoc basis. SDS and SNCC

organizers believed a loose structure enabled people with no prior political experience to speak and act without being embarrassed about the opinions they expressed and without being dependent on "higher-ups." In the Newark ERAP project, for example, the program committee was composed of "representatives from all the blocks, the staff, and *anyone who could attend the meeting,* one man, one vote." The committee would meet weekly and make all policy decisions, decide its own organizational forms, and be chaired by an elected president rotated once a month.[15]

4. *Establish places in the community free of external restraints.* In ERAP the "community union" (the local office site) belonged to the neighborhood people. It was, one organizer said, probably the only "institution in the world where a destitute alcoholic can stand up and give a lecture, occasionally brilliant but usually incoherent, on political strategy and be listened to with complete respect."[16] You could find activity at community unions that ranged from leaflet preparation to sleeping and carousing. Keys to the centers were often distributed liberally to neighborhood people. Because SNCC generally was better grounded in the local culture, its community shelters ranged from churches to community centers and the SNCC office. They used any site where people could meet and talk comfortably and in safety.

5. *Develop indigenous leaders.* The organizer was to use his or her "dynamism to project other people—tell them they can lead—ask people questions rather than give them answers."[17] SNCC, for example, rejected the traditional organizing style of SCLC and CORE in which elected or appointed leaders from outside the local community directed activities. These same leaders, SNCC was quick to note, left as swiftly as they came, leaving community people leaderless and vulnerable. SNCC and SDS emphasized that leadership had to be developed among the people so that *they* could advance and protect themselves.

6. *Create supportive personal relationships.* Organizers had to be willing to remain in rural communities and urban neighborhoods and build strong personal relationships with local people. Trust and confidence between organizers and community people were the building blocks of grassroots organizing. From the standpoint of outsiders without a specific program that could attract people, the best way to get people interested was through developing personal as well as political ties. Supportive, nonmanipulative, noncompetitive relations between organizers and community people would prefigure future

ways of relating in the new, truly democratic society.

If those six tenets were the organizing theory of the new left, a position paper written by SNCC staffer Charles McLaurin, who grew up in Jackson, Mississippi, outlined the organizing process. First, become part of the community. Find a family to stay with, preferably a family well-known in the community. "It may just happen that you are not able to find a place for weeks; but do not give up." Make contacts. Talk with people about the community; they are the ones from whom you will get a real community education. Canvas the whole community one afternoon. Talk with them, laugh and joke with them. "Do most anything that gets some attention on you." Find out what bugs people. Take down names and addresses of people you talk with, especially those who seem like potential leaders. These will be key contacts later. Identify a core group of talkers and interested people. Set up a meeting, in a church or empty building, perhaps even in the home of the family where you live. Plan some action at the first meeting. "You put suggestions before the group. Let them talk over the suggestions, about paved streets, stop signs, street lights, or recreational facilities, and how the vote can get these and more." It might take 10 or more of these meetings. Let the group elect a chair and appoint committees. Stop by the homes of core group members, talk with them regularly. Visits show that you are interested in the community and people's family and personal life, not only in political meetings. Developing a feeling of being close together will help people overcome the fear of getting involved. "Suspicion comes from mistrust. So many have led us wrong, that it is hard to trust people we don't know. You must be friendly, reliable, and most of all trustworthy. With this, suspicion will disappear. When the people trust you and trust your judgment, suspicion will be a thing of the past."[18]

At its best the development of leadership was a two-way street in which the poor provided courageous models of insurgency for the students in SNCC and SDS. For example, McLaurin recalled one day in Indianola, Mississippi, when he took three elderly black women to register to vote at the court house.

As I opened the [car] door to got out I got a feeling in my stomach that made me feel weak. . . . At this point I was no longer in command, the three old ladies were leading me, I was following them. They got out of the car and went up the walk to the court-house as if this was the long walk that leads to the Golden Gate of Heaven, their heads held high. I watched from a short distance behind them; the pride with which they walked. The strong convictions that they held. I watched as they walked up the steps into the building. I stepped outside the door and waited, thinking how it was that these ladies who have been victimized by white faces all their lives would suddenly walk up to the man and say, *I want to vote.* This did something to me. It told me [that] . . . the people are the true leaders. We need only to move them; to show them. Then watch and learn.[19]

A vivid example of the actual process of community organizing in SDS was the ERAP project in Chicago. While conditions in Chicago differed from other ERAP communities, the organizing process there demonstrates nicely how SDSers sought to put their theory of participatory democracy into practice. SDS sent Joe Chabot, a student at the University of Michigan, to Chicago in September 1963 to organize primarily white unemployed workers. He attended dozens of meetings over the course of several months, observing the activities of established neighborhood organizations like settlements and churches and educating himself about local conditions and politics. Chabot made little headway initially. He attributed this to the lack of "readiness" of white unemployed youth to join political organizations. A break came when he was able to form an alliance with the Packinghouse Workers Union (UPW), the same left-oriented union that Alinsky linked up with in Back of the Yards. The UPW wanted someone with resources and energy to do organizing among the unemployed, and Chabot was eager to do so. SDS based its ERAP organizing on the theory, advanced by a number of economists in the early 1960s, that the postwar boom was about to end, and SDS thought a vast constituency of discontented, potentially radical unemployed would result from the impending economic crisis. Chabot, with the assistance of some UPW staff and an organizer from the American Friends Service Committee, assembled a core group to plan how to organize the unemployed.

This core group labeled their operation JOIN—the Committee for Jobs and Income Now. They established offices on both the South Side and North Side. Each morning Chabot and others would hand out leaflets at the unemployment office, talk with people at the JOIN offices, answer the phone, hold meetings, and serve coffee to folks who dropped by. By the sixth week of operation, 400 to 500 men had come to the North Side JOIN office and participated in discussion with ERAP staffers. Thursday evenings ERAP staffers held organizing meetings for those members of the unemployed who seemed most interested in getting further involved in JOIN's work. Anywhere from 5 to 30 people attended these organizing sessions. More than a dozen workers were attending meetings regularly in the first few months after the office opened. For the experienced and skillful activist, organizing can be difficult and exhausting work, and it was even more so for ERAP organizers. Often fresh from college, with little or no organizing experience, they went to live in what were for most of them foreign colonies of poverty. They received no salary and lived on a subsistence allowance that kept them fed primarily on powdered milk and peanut butter and jelly sandwiches. Unlike settlement workers, who sought to create upper-class islands, like Hull House, in the inner-city, ERAP organizers sought to become part of inner-city life.

Hours upon hours were spent leafletting unemployment offices, talking with people, attending meetings, addressing the most rudimentary concerns and political positions, and often with few results to show for it. Rennie Davis, active in the JOIN project in Chicago, describes the process well:

Probably all of the ERAP community workers have developed a deeper sense of the extreme slowness of building a permanent community organization on a program of fundamental change. . . . An organizer can spend two or more hours with a single individual. Through hundreds of conversations, slowly, clusters of unemployed contacts are made and identified on city maps. One person in a large unemployment area is approached about having a meeting; he agrees, but has not the time to contact neighbors. So the JOIN worker calls every unemployed by phone or sees them in person. Thirty people are contacted; eight turn out. One is a racist, but his arguments get put down by the group. One (maybe) is willing to work and has some sense of what needs to be done. The others go round and round on their personal troubles. The process is slow.[20]

The JOIN strategy was most successful in Chicago, where ERAP focused on organizing unemployed Appalachian whites, but it was seriously limited even there by the fact that the impending economic crisis and high rates of joblessness never materialized. In other project sites the JOIN strategy to organize around the issue of unemployment failed miserably. What worked better in projects in black neighborhoods in Newark, Cleveland, and elsewhere was a new strategy oriented to other community issues and sarcastically called GROIN (Garbage Removal or Income Now). ERAPers found it more effective and easier to organize black women around issues like welfare, day care, schools, recreation, and rat elimination than to organize black men around unemployment problems. Women staffers in ERAP, however, were the only ones who felt comfortable organizing around GROIN issues such as food stamps or welfare benefits. Women organizers in both SNCC and SDS had always done some of the best organizing, while men always remained center stage and dominated the organizations. With the GROIN strategy, however, women organizers rose to the forefront in a number of projects. In Cleveland, where women assumed leadership, ERAP organized welfare mothers around social service issues. In Chester, Pennsylvania, a black community two miles from Swarthmore College, the GROIN strategy resulted in a public school boycott. Subsequent demonstrations there led to the arrest of 200 community people and 50 Swarthmore students and the formation of an executive committee of 15 Chester adults. This committee proceeded to write a platform with 37 demands calling for fair and full employment, new schools and housing, adequate health care, and police reforms.[21]

Such short-term successes aside, by almost every measure the ERAP program was a failure. Few of the projects were able to sink effective roots. Few were able to get many people, other than ERAP staffers, to meetings. Political education was minimal. ERAP organizers learned quickly that the impoverished recent migrants to urban America with whom they were working were not easily moved to mass collective action by outsiders who were young, white, and affluent. ERAP's stated goal of building "an interracial movement of the poor" remained a distant dream. Only a few of the projects, most notably in Chicago and Newark, even lasted beyond 1965.[22]

In some respect, working in SNCC was even more difficult. Organizing blacks in the Deep South meant risking your life. Reactionary elements there were well organized and had a long history of violence against black people and white "agitators." If you were black, from the South, and in SNCC, a visit to your hometown could mean jeopardizing not only your life but that of your family as well. Nevertheless, SNCC staffers had organizing advantages over their counterparts in ERAP. Southern black communities were knit more tightly by generations of experience and struggle than were northern black slums, and SNCC grew out of a civil rights movement that was widely accepted and very popular in black communities in the South. Moreover, the issue of voter registration provided a focus and a measure of success for SNCC that the ERAP projects never achieved. At the least, SNCC's voter registration and desegregation actions hastened the pace of civil rights reform in what seemed in the early 1960s to be an almost impenetrable system of segregation. But as a recent biographer of SNCC put it, the organization's major achievement was its "unparalleled success in breaking through the socialized inhibitions of blacks in the rural South by undermining the legitimacy of existing white dominated institutions."[23]

As the federal government took up the mantle of desegregation during 1964–65, however, new left organizers, and especially those in SNCC, found themselves in a quandary. What strategy should a radical organization follow now that the federal government had become a champion of civil rights reform. While SDS gave up on community organizing, returned to college campuses, and began to organize students in 1965 around the antiwar issue, SNCC in that same year began to splinter, with those on one side supporting a loosely structured participatory democracy and those on the other a tightly organized socialist revolution. By 1966 SNCC was advocating revolutionary black nationalism, and its style of organizing, best exemplified in later groups like the Black Panther Party, changed accordingly. But neither SDS nor SNCC had the historical impact each had hoped for.

Three factors most undermined their work in the period up to 1965. First, and perhaps the most serious problem facing the ERAP and SNCC projects, was the decimated state of the left in the early 1960s. This situation placed enormous burdens on the student left and deprived young activists of a national organization that could lend support. It also deprived them of a national program that could provide a radical political direction and context to their local work. The anticommunist purges of the 1940s and 1950s had effectively destroyed communist, socialist, and anarchist efforts, and the new left rejected the organizational and ideological remnants of what remained. SDS and SNCC were student organizations, doing community organizing for the first time, and often working with constituents of a different class and race; and they did so without guidance, without a program, and with almost no historical ties to radical predecessors. Being students with generally little political experience, they were ill prepared to be *the* left. Almost everything they did was developed from scratch, as if they were the first activists ever to do community organizing. They had to develop strategy, programs, ideology, and structures at the same time that they were deeply involved in the all-consuming, day-today tasks of community organizing. It was impossible for them to be *both* the left and the student vanguard.

Except for a few specific SNCC projects like the Mississippi Freedom Democratic Party, new left activity at the local level lacked a national focus. SNCC and SDS saw problems inherent in localism. While staffers were committed to decentralization and community organization, they also understood that the problems poor people faced were not limited to a neighborhood or rural community and that a national movement was the ultimate objective of their work.[24] But SNCC and SDS were too busy fighting for immediate and local issues and demands to be able at the same time to integrate their work into a larger national framework that could break the political provincialism inherent in local work and effectively deal with national problems like class and race divisions. Given the immense burden of their task, however, most SNCC people simply assumed that such problems would be handled successfully once African-Americans won freedom and equality.

But without a means of linking everyday problems and struggles to an analysis of national power, without a national program and critique that put local activities in perspective as steps toward larger and more fundamental changes, successful reform efforts at the local level, such as registering voters or securing welfare benefits, created the incorrect impression that the system was responsive and democratic, and that only reform, not radical change, was necessary. Kim Moody, an ERAP staffer, was right when he complained that "nothing in such [reformist] issues breaks through the localism of the poor. . . . What is there in the block programs that leads to 'revolutionary social change?'"[25] By 1964 and 1965 experienced SNCC staffers were fearing that if the reforms supported by SNCC succeeded, all that would be won was that black middle-class people, too, would have the right to worry about crab grass on their front lawn.[26] The new left knew that without radical change, the needs of the poor, especially the black poor, would not be met. They knew that reforms would only palliate the problems, ameliorate the most pressing and gross instances of poverty, as the later Great Society programs would demonstrate, but not attack the causes of poverty or racism and not give poor people the power they needed to alter their situation. But the new left lacked the national organization and direction that could help transform local reform efforts into a nationwide radical program.

Second, and this is more an internal than external problem, there was a critical contradiction within the theory of participatory democracy about the role of the organizer. How do you create a "leaderless" movement of "organizers?" How could you create an organization that organized community people but was fundamentally antagonistic to leadership and structure? Lerone Bennett, Jr., a prominent black intellectual, found SNCC "an organization in revolt against organization, a formless form." SNCC staffers at an ERAP meeting in 1965 pictured the ideal organizer as one "who never organized, who by his simple presence was the mystical medium for the spontaneous expression of 'the people.'"[27] The most extreme example of this antileadership, antiorganizational ethic was the ERAP Hoboken "nonproject" in which the strategy was to simply find working-class jobs in this industrial New Jersey city and let the tides take the organizing project where it would.

It is critical in community organizing to provide leadership, to do organization building, and to teach leadership and rudimentary organizational skills, but most new lefters thought this ran counter to the idea of letting the people decide. Clearly, letting the people decide made sense. It was especially applicable in SNCC, where local people often *had* to decide because they were the ones who knew how to survive. If local people did not become involved and exert leadership, the SNCC project would not only fail but the organizer and anyone associated with him or her would be in serious physical danger. Nevertheless, a tendency in the new left to romanticize the power and impact of participatory democracy often led local projects to become absorbed with issues of democratic process and individual freedom rather than focus on skill development, political education, or collective goals. The results often ended up disappointing almost everyone. A JOIN organizer lamented that most people who came to the Chicago office "are revolted by the word 'socialism' and claim to be strong supporters of free enterprise; many conceive of their jobless state as due to their own shortcomings . . . their perception of the 'enemy' is fuzzy or worse."[28]

In creating a theory of community organizing in poor neighborhoods that denied the possibility of nonmanipulative leadership, organizers were led to pretend (sometimes even to themselves) that community people often "were deciding issues that only the organizers knew about, let alone understood."[29] Equally important, they developed an impractical theory that did not correspond with the needs and realities of their daily organizing. This problem was more endemic in ERAP organizing, where staffers tended to be more theoretically oriented and less a part of the communities where they worked. In SNCC longtime staffers with a good deal of field experience were often pragmatic (they had to be to survive) and tended by 1964–65 to openly argue for a SNCC that was better organized to win collective power and argue against the romantic and counterproductive notion of a "nondirected," structureless organization.

A third, and more obvious, factor was the sheer physical and emotional drain of organizing. This was more the case in SNCC, but was true in ERAP as well. Neither group had the staff or resources equal to the task. Of course, most organizing efforts never do. But most organizers are usually trained and experienced. SNCC and ERAP staffers were often neither, and they certainly did not have the confidence and knowledge to reject or modify the furious pace of organizing. Many left SNCC and to a lesser extent ERAP out of exhaustion as much as anything else, the exhaustion that comes not only from fear but from always pushing to one's physical and mental limits. SNCC especially was hurt by its inability as an organization to help its organizers repair. They had no place to go to relax, to get out of the frontline, to replenish themselves. This meant that temporary "burnouts" were never recovered. People just left and did not return.[30]

Recognition of the flaws and limits of SNCC and ERAP community organizing projects should not lead us to underestimate their importance in the history of community organizing. Coming on the heels of nearly two decades in which progressive and left-wing activities had been destroyed by repression, capitulation to the Cold War consensus, and internal errors, the community organizing efforts of students in the new left, in both SNCC and SDS, were important breakthroughs. They were often brave and always innovative experiments with what democracy meant and what a democratic society should be like. They were significant challenges to the racial and class barriers that since the 1950s separated most radicals from the poor and minorities. Moreover, participation in these activities created the nucleus of a new generation of radical activists who had learned important lessons about community organizing, political power, and what it was like to be poor in America. After 1965 they continued to do community organizing and radical political work—in the antiwar movement, black power organizations, communities, training institutes, college campuses, social welfare programs, unions, and factories. The widespread belief in participatory democracy that bloomed in the late 1960s, prospered in the 1970s, and continues today owes a good deal, directly and indirectly, to the community organizing efforts of student radicals in the years 1961–65. Equally notable for our purposes, the new left projects reflected a shift of focus by leftists to the local and communal level. Classical radical theory, from Marx onward, had always slighted or ignored community-based organizing, choosing to focus instead on large-scale factory organizing as the proper locus of class struggle. As noted earlier, even in radical community organizing efforts such as that of the Unemployed Councils in the 1930s, the Communist party's priority was organizing laborers at the industrial workplace. There are, of course, good reasons for this decision, most notably that the workplace united working-class people in a clearly focused and common struggle against the owners of capital. A number of factors coalesced by the early 1960s, however, to cause a rethinking of this basic radical premise. Perhaps primary, the civil rights movement, the basis of all 1960s organizing, focused on community organizing because its demands for racial equality and human brotherhood were not limited to the workplace and because much of its constituency in the South was not employed in industrial jobs. In addition, important changes had been occurring in the U.S. economy since World War II, among them the declining importance of industrial labor and the fact that white industrial workers and their union leaders no longer were the progressive force they had been during the 1930s and 1940s. It was not surprising then that new left activists, who came from middle- and upper-class backgrounds and the southern civil rights movement, looked to communities as the natural locus of their operations. The new left was not opposed to workplace organizing. It saw, as noted earlier, the inherent provincialism in community organizing. But for these activists community and "issue" organizing at the grassroots level seemed most appropriate to the conditions of the early 1960s. Partly as a result of the factors that turned the new left to community organizing and partly as a result of the new left's efforts, it is no accident that the major social change movements since that time—the antiwar, women's, environmental, and the antinuclear movements—all have had as their locus grassroots, community organizing, not factory or labor organizing.

The Great Society Organizing Projects: Community Action Agencies

[The Economic Opportunity Act] must be a total effort to bring about broad community change. And this cannot be done by the Federal Government. We can only help by stimulating local action. It must be done by local people and local agencies working closely together.

—Robert F. Kennedy, attorney general

Few undertakings in our time have generated as much hope, produced as many immediate and beneficial results, or excited as much controversy as the anti-poverty program.

—Lyndon Baines Johnson, president

Student radicals were not the first or only ones to notice the widespread poverty and social disorder in the "affluent society." On the heels of the recession of 1956–58, which hit black workers in the North and Midwest the hardest, social workers, philanthropic agencies, and the federal government implemented programs to curb youth crime and delinquency. Efforts began in 1958 with a grant by the National Institute of Mental Health (NIMH) to fund an experimental, comprehensive, and systematic juvenile delinquency program— Mobilization for Youth—on the Lower East Side of New York City. The Ford Foundation followed in 1961 with a similar endeavor in Oakland, California, the Richmond Youth Project. That same year President Kennedy initiated the President's Committee on Juvenile Delinquency and Youth Crime under the direction of attorney general Robert Kennedy. In 1962 the president's committee issued planning grants to communities addressing youth problems in nontraditional ways, and the Ford Foundation established four new "gray areas" projects. All of these projects shared much common ground. They were planned as "comprehensive" programs to be operated by new community organizations, controlled by the local community, and funded by a national source. They focused on inner-city black ghettos. The emphasis was on using recent social science innovations, disregarding traditional social welfare approaches, and encouraging citizen action and participation. "Experiments in working with the black community," one participant called them.[31]

They were not, of course, the first neighborhood-based projects to attract national or federal funding. Most notable in the post–1945 era, the President's Advisory Committee on Government and Housing Policies in 1953 supported the development of "a broadly representative private organization . . . with congressional and/or Presidential sponsorship to mobilize public opinion in support of vigorous and responsible action by communities in urban renewal activities."[32] Likewise the NIMH, Ford Foundation, and federal projects were certainly not the first to emphasize the value of local control and citizen participation in social welfare efforts. What ultimately made them unique, however, was that the foundations and the federal government began willingly to initiate social change experiments that rejected traditional methods and encouraged grassroots citizen action, even protests against local public agencies.

The NIMH, Ford Foundation, and initial Kennedy programs were too small, however, to have much impact on youth problems or the rising tide of social disorder in cities. As these problems intensified, as SDS, SNCC, and Alinsky organizers continued to give political expression to some of the disaffected poor, and as influential, militant minority leaders such as Malcolm X advised black people to resist white racism "by any means necessary," the federal government responded with a massive antipoverty program. By the fall of 1963, Kennedy's staff had begun working on a comprehensive program, modeled on the innovative NIMH and Ford Foundation projects, to deal with problems of poverty and discrimination. First Walter Heller and then Sargent Shriver, advisers to Kennedy, provided direction, but with Kennedy's death in late November, Lyndon Johnson quickly assumed leadership of the project. The following spring Johnson described the outlines of his "War on Poverty" to Congress. Five months later the Economic Opportunity Act sailed through both the House and Senate, and the president signed it into law.[33]

The most innovative and central feature of the legislation and the one that most emphasized the ideals of "maximum feasible participation" and local control was the Community Action Program (CAP). The program established Community Action Agencies (CAAs) to sponsor neighborhood self-help projects, promote social action, mobilize local resources, and coordinate local programs. These CAAs would address concerns heretofore left to city, state, and nationwide organizations and would be directly supported by public funds, 90 percent of which would come from the federal government. If the city or town refused to put up the 10 percent seed money or in-kind payment, then private groups could do so. Equally significant, the CAA was to be a broadly based program that superceded traditional channels by receiving direct funding and authority from the federal government. As Richard W. Boone, one of the program's activists, explained:

It was an attempt to move administrative authority closer to people directly affected by federal legislation. Not only did it allow a bypass of states, it endorsed new administrative instruments at the local level, thus offering the opportunity to bypass traditional instruments of local government. . . . Concern over neglect of the poor by public and private programs, their oppression by political design and the insensitivity of service systems were reasons for permitting, even encouraging, new conglomerate arrangements for policy and program.[34]

Why? Why would the federal government fund new programs designed to supercede local agencies? Why was the federal government so interested in community organizing and the "maximum feasible participation" of the poor in community-based programs? Urban renewal officials in the 1950s had viewed grassroots organizations with a good deal of trepidation. Why did the federal government establish new programs to address the issues of urban poverty rather than go through established mechanisms like public housing, the Social Security administration, and urban renewal? Why were John Kennedy, Robert Kennedy, Walter Heller, Sargent Shriver, and Lyndon Johnson, not to mention the host of "professional reformers" who designed the programs, so interested in involving the urban, black poor in planning and implementing programs, in "giving them a real voice in their institutions?"[35]

Most significantly, NIMH, the Ford Foundation, and the President's Committee on Juvenile Delinquency designed their early efforts at community organizing to promote social harmony and ameliorate urban social disorder. Persistent unemployment had undermined traditional forms of social control such as religious, family, educational, and community institutions, and had caused an alarming spread of gang delinquency, vandalism, drug addiction, and serious crimes against people and property. The civil rights movement and its black clergy leaders ignited this disorder, most often unintentionally, by politicizing the poor and especially the young in nonwhite urban ghettos. Fueled by exacerbating ghetto conditions and the leadership of radicals like Malcolm X, urban disorder was transformed by 1963–64 from individual acts of violence to massive urban rebellions. Urban ghetto residents looted stores, burned property to the ground, and killed police with sniper fire from the rooftops of ghetto tenements. Something had to be done. This collective disorder was creating havoc in the nation's key economic and political centers.[36]

The Great Society, however, was more than a traditional liberal reform program to palliate and coopt mass insurgency. It sought not only to defuse protest from below but to reincorporate African-Americans into the political process and thereby solidify their support for the Democratic party. It sought in essence to create new black political organizations in the inner cities and the rural South that would strengthen black political involvement and electoral participation.

Changing electoral patterns were a crucial concern of presidents Kennedy and Johnson. In the early days of the New Deal the Democratic party had been able to forge an enduring north-south coalition. By the late 1940s, as African-Americans pressed their demand for equality and as the Democratic and Republican parties, responding to the pressures of the Cold War, became more liberal on issues of race and civil rights, the white southern segment of the Democratic coalition became less dependable and increasingly unstable, moving toward third-party "Dixiecrat" candidates or Republicans whose position on domestic questions, especially race, were more in line with their segregationist sentiments. In the extraordinarily close election of 1960, John Kennedy received overwhelming support in the black ghettos of strategic northern cities. At the same time the States Rights party won in Mississippi and Alabama, while Florida, Tennessee, Kentucky, and Virginia all voted Republican. To counter the loss of southern strength, the new administration began to seek methods of strengthening its base of support among minority groups. It had especially high hopes for the black vote, but while African-Americans continued to vote heavily Democratic, local impediments to their active participation in party politics jeopardized the extent of their total voting power and thus the value of their support.[37]

Kennedy and Johnson initiated a wide array of social reform legislation in the years 1961 to 1968 with the intent of using the managerial powers of the president and the allocation of federal dollars to deal not only with social disorder but the more partisan political problem of party realignment. The War on Poverty was fundamentally designed for urban nonwhites, especially African-Americans, not for poor people. While many CAAs, especially those programs in nonsouthern rural areas, included few African-Americans, their predominance is most obvious when CAP is seen from a national perspective. Only 25 percent of the funds, for example, went to rural areas, and more than two thirds of that was spent in the "black belt" area of the South. In many areas, people of other minority groups and the white working class played active and important roles, but in essence CAP was seen as an extension of the civil rights movement, as a "black program."[38]

Of course not all of those who designed the program, from the officials in the White House to the professional reformers, shared a single motive. Few of the professional reformers shared the electoral concerns of the political officials. The more radical ones claimed that the CAP was not intended to forestall social protest but rather to give it direction and organization. Many others believed that the primary objective was to address urban problems with the latest innovations in social welfare theory. That the architects of the program shared differing methods and objectives is apparent in their still continuing debate over what the program was all about. Nevertheless, the objective of the White House from 1961 to 1968, especially after 1963, and the fundamental animus behind the program was the response to disorder and the realignment of political coalitions in the nation.

Like the Wagner Act of 1935, which sought not only to defuse protest but bring industrial workers firmly into the ranks of the Democratic party, CAP became a double-edged sword of social reform. As the Wagner Act was a piece of class-oriented legislation intended to galvanize the white working class, so CAP was racial legislation intended to develop new local organizations that could assist and empower primarily African-Americans and other minorities. And as labor activists used the Wagner Act as a mobilizing tool to carry the union movement far beyond what FDR intended, so too did black and other activists see CAP as a grassroots organizing device that could be used to organize and advance the poor, especially the black poor, far beyond what the federal government planned.

The program spread like a prairie fire. Within 18 months of the passage of the Office of Equal Opportunity (OEO) legislation there were more than 1,000 funded CAAs in the United States. While CAAs differed dramatically depending on the local political environment, the fights for citizen participation and for neighborhood organizing dominated the first years of most locals. In few instances did citizen participation come without struggle. Initially, the OEO did not spell out any specific guidelines regulating the selection and composition of the boards of directors that governed local CAAs. So in the first Community Action Agencies a coalition of public officials, welfare agency leaders, and representatives from groups involved in liberal social causes dominated the boards. For example, when asked why there were no representatives of the poor on the local board, the mayor of Nashville, Tennessee, who made the appointments, asserted "you can't have unqualified people running good programs." In Atlanta, the initial CAA board had no poor people and only one representative of the poor, Martin Luther King, Sr.[39] In San Francisco, Mayor John Shelley made all 39 initial appointments, as did the mayor in Oakland. No elections were held in "target area" neighborhoods, and no means created by which poor people could ensure their "maximum feasible participation." Predictably, local leaders had no intention of helping local citizens supercede or oppose local agencies and authorities.

Struggles with community people over citizen involvement ensued. In San Francisco, one year after Shelley's initial appointments, local activists raised enough protest and exerted sufficient pressure to get the board changed from the mayor's initial 39 appointments to a more representative board of 47 people. Of the 47, 23 were mayoral appointees and 24 were elected neighborhood representatives, 6 from each of the 4 target areas. This happened in CAAs throughout the nation, not just in progressive centers like the Northeast and West coasts. But in the highly politicized CAAs, most commonly found in cities with large black populations, every issue—whether model cities, welfare, CAA funding and personnel, public housing, or service delivery—became an area of contention between neighborhood people and the local "establishment." Local politicians could no longer work behind the scenes, for neighborhood people now demanded a voice in what happened in their city and their neighborhood. Local officials, of course, were not used to this. Shelley complained in 1967 that the struggle over maximum feasible participation in the local CAA "expanded the social revolution in San Francisco into a chain reaction of unrest and distrust that has left its mark on every major civic improvement project attempted here in recent years."[40]

The level of conflict varied from city to city. In cities like Oakland, Newark, New York, and Syracuse, where political conflict between established authorities and citizen action groups was not uncommon, where there was a heritage of civil rights insurgency, and where there was generally a well-organized, militant black community, CAAs were often confrontational, dynamic, and militant. In such places, demands for citizen participation were aggressive and the CAA focused on neighborhood advocacy and organizing, not service delivery. Where the political environment was more conservative, in cities such as Chattanooga and Phoenix, where African-Americans were fewer and radicals in the poor and minority community were less well-organized, or in cities where the political environment was more constrained, such as Chicago, where the political machine tightly controlled the urban bureaucracy, CAAs tended to be less participatory and less confrontational. In these places, CAAs performed essentially service delivery and "watchdog" functions. In all CAAs, however, poor people and activists used the agencies to advance the level of politics in their cities and neighborhoods and increase the flow of benefits to the poor.[41]

The expanded participation of the black poor and their representatives pushed the more politicized CAAs beyond an emphasis on child and social welfare programs to neighborhood advocacy, organizing, and development. A large number of relatively autonomous neighborhood service centers, commanding 15 percent of the total CAA budget, were formed in target areas in 1965–66 by local CAA boards of directors. In the early years local CAA officials fought with neighborhood people and their board representatives over the content of neighborhood center programs. Chartered to perform "outreach" and "referral" services, neighborhood centers in the more politicized CAAs were often led by experienced community organizers who sought to go beyond the designated service functions. They did advocacy work, primarily defending the rights and advocating the needs of welfare recipients. They did community development work by setting up well-baby clinics and developing school lunch and rodent extermination programs to foster a greater sense of community solidarity and power. They engaged in social action work, for example, pressuring the public housing and public welfare bureaucracies and promoting rent control legislation. The advocacy and social action projects proved most threatening to local officials and accordingly received the lion's share of the program's publicity.[42]

The furor between local officials and neighborhood representatives in the more politicized CAAs in the nation between 1964 and 1967 obscured a widespread inability of the CAP to organize poor neighborhoods effectively. CAP programs had so many built-in bureaucratic restraints, most notably a hierarchical and bureaucratic structure with seemingly endless responsibilities, paper work, and regulations, all outlined in OEO guidelines, that it was impossible for community people to use the agencies as effective vehicles for representing minority-group interests. Exhaustive comparative and case study research of CAAs throughout the nation has concluded that, except in a few cases, local community action agencies served more as traditional service delivery systems to the poor than as social change organizations, and that "no radical redistributions of influence, power, service rewards and other benefits" occurred as a result of the Community Action Program.[43] Because of the intensity of the struggles in the early years of the more radical CAAs, both sides often exaggerated the extent of actual power gained and institutions changed by neighborhood activists.

At the peak of protest activity in the years between 1966 and 1968, national and local officials allied to defuse CAP. From the outset, local officials and agency representatives had been wary of a social reform program that skirted their political control. Such CAA actions as welfare protests and court suits initiated by legal aid lawyers mobilized the poor but further fanned the flames of distrust and political reaction. The conservative backlash that occurred in 1967, however, was not unprecedented. Since 1964 local officials in New York had attacked the community action projects of Mobilization for Youth. While MFY was not very successful in addressing problems of poverty, it did engage in some well-publicized confrontations with powerful groups in New York City—the Board of Education, the police, and local landlords. When MFY's talk about the "powerlessness of the poor" and "tenants rights" made opponents even more uneasy, the "red-baiting" began. An August 1964 editorial in the widely read *New York Daily News,* for example, accused MFY of being "infested with Commies and Commie sympathizers." Soon MFY's director was forced to resign and all MFY business was ordered to go through city departments.[44]

CAP followed a similar path. From early in 1965, when the federal government made clear that participation of the poor was a condition for receipt of funds, local politicians worked to undercut the legislation. Hubert Humphrey pressured Sargent Shriver, then head of OEO, to ease up on the demand for citizen participation. In 1965 the League of Cities and the Conference of Mayors both sought to limit the involvement of the poor in the running of local CAAs. At the mayor's conference, Shelley of San Francisco and Sam Yorty of Los Angeles accused OEO of "fostering class struggle." The federal government, performing a difficult balancing act, moved to appease local officials while allowing the local CAAs to continue their activities. Shriver declared in 1966 that "We have no intention, of course, of letting any one group, even the poor themselves, 'run the jobs' or 'run the programs.' That's not *community* action . . . [which is] maximum feasible participation by *all* segments of the community."[45] The OEO followed the rhetoric with action. It agreed to make private arrangements with mayors in 15 cities to clear all CAP grants in their areas through city hall. It passed regulations prohibiting partisan political activity and the employment of those in "subversive organizations" and not "of good character." By late 1966 the trend was clear. CAP was tightening the reins on local CAA activities, checking local militancy, and shifting to what Saul Alinsky called a "zoo-keeper mentality."[46]

The so-called Green Amendment passed by Congress in 1967 tightened the screws on community action. Like all federal agencies, the OEO had to secure new appropriations each year. By 1967 it was in serious political trouble, especially among Republicans and southern Democrats. Representative Edith Green of Oregon, an advocate of the antipoverty program but a constant critic of the OEO, offered an amendment to undercut the power of poor people in local CAAs. First, the amendment required that all CAAs be designated by state or local governments. This rerouted all grants-in-aid through local officials, instead of directly allocating it to local community organizations. A direct channel could be maintained, however, if local officials chose not to intervene. Curiously, eight months after the passage of the Green Amendment 97 percent of local governments chose to continue existing relations with local CAAs and not move to widen their control. Why? Because many local officials had come to terms with the CAA projects and found it easier to live with existing relations than to stir up a hornet's nest, and because the second provision of the Green Amendment made it unnecessary to implement the first one. This provision limited the size of the board of directors to no more than 51 people, composed equally of one third democratically selected representatives of the target areas, one third public officials, and one third representatives of business, labor, civic, and charitable groups. While community people in places where CAAs had little citizen involvement benefited from the Green Amendment's institutionalization of at least one third community representation, CAAs with far greater levels of citizen participation were undermined, as the poor no longer had a majority on any of the local boards.[47]

Equally significant, the character of the more democratic and militant CAAs quickly reflected the composition of their new boards. They became increasingly "professional." The impulse to confrontation, to fight the local welfare or rent control office, to demand increased community control or expanded allocations for Manpower (job-training) programs, for example, became mired and then lost in bureaucratic discussions about budgets, accountability, efficiency, and personnel. Increasingly, concerns of community planning, coordination of resources, and management required greater and greater sophistication and skills from board members. The professionals on the staff and on the board often possessed these skills and felt most comfortable with the new emphasis on organizational maintenance. Community people did not, and were relatively powerless to do much more about it than harass the "pros" or learn how a public bureaucracy functioned, both of which some activists did exceedingly well.

If the Green Amendment cut the heart out of CAA militancy, budgetary changes sealed the coffin. In 1966 all CAP funds, except Head Start, were discretionary. The local agency could use them any way they wanted. By 1968, 60 percent of all CAA dollars were directed to national emphasis programs like Upward Bound (an educational program for disadvantaged youths), Legal Services, and Manpower. And a sizable percentage of the remaining 40 percent went to administrative salaries and fixed costs such as building upkeep. From the start CAAs had little funding to wage a war on poverty. By 1968 they had a lot less at their disposal.[48]

Nixon's election in 1968 heralded the end of CAP, for the Republican party knew its constituency did not reside in the poor inner cities and rural areas of America. From 1968 to 1972 CAAs became even more absorbed in operating programs, certainly not advancing social change or citizen action. They became, as one historian wrote, "part of the problem, another service agency rather than a mobilizer and coordinator of agencies."[49] In some communities agencies informally continued to support social change efforts by offering meeting space and use of resources, such as photocopying and mimeograph machines, to radical organizations. When Nixon's New Federalism passed through Congress in 1972, however, the War on

Poverty was laid to rest. The New Federalism got the federal government out of the grant-in-aid business and into distributing block grants to states and cities. Nixon called this "revenue sharing." This program gave local officials and bureaucrats much more control over social welfare funds. The new program continued the pretext of citizen participation, but the participatory component of revenue sharing or community development block grant funding was always token, ad hoc, and purely advisory.

By the early 1970s meaningful citizen action and citizen participation in federally funded social programs was a thing of the past, a memory of the civil rights movement and the tumultuous 1960s. CAAs continue today under the Community Service Administration, as advisory social service organizations, directing low-priority federal programs like energy conservation and fuel assistance and serving as local administrators for programs funded by the United Way. Their work is often valuable and progressive, often not, but always a mere shell of what was initially intended by some CAP architects and hoped for by community activists.

Was CAP a success or a failure? For whom? For the Democratic White House in the 1960s it was a limited success. As a strategy for rebuilding the Democratic party it did not duplicate the effect the Wagner Act had on the earlier Democratic coalition, for party realignment and the causes of Democratic party decomposition could not be addressed so simply. Nevertheless, in less than a decade many civil rights activists did become government employees, and in many cities poverty programs became new black political organizations. It is no accident that the number of African-American mayors in the United States rose from almost none in 1968 to 108 in 1974. In Newark, the poverty program provided the organizational structure upon which Kenneth Gibson built a power base for his successful bid for mayor. Moreover, the community action programs provided new opportunities and resources, in the form of better salaries, skills, and job experience, which especially assisted the black middle class in taking advantage of the political opportunities created by the Civil Rights Act of 1964 and the Voting Rights Act of 1965. Great Society projects did not secure political equality for African-Americans in the United States, but they were not intended to do so. Rather, in a relatively short period of time and with a limited amount of funds, the programs not only coopted many of the most militant activists and groups but also channeled much of their energy into traditional electoral and bureaucratic structures. To this extent, the Great Society served the purposes of its Democratic designers.

For the tens of thousands of poor and black people who became active in local politics for the first time, CAP was an important educational experience. They learned how the political system functioned, how established agencies sought to coopt dissent, how people who were willing to take risks and stand up for their rights—individually and collectively—had power and could successfully pressure the political system for services, benefits, and jobs. They learned that simply bringing issues to light, bringing the problems of poverty, racism, and inequality to public view, was not sufficient. As David Austin and others have demonstrated in studies of CAAs, and as many CAA people learned, mass resistance, direct action, and protest were critical to effect change.[50]

The CAA experience also demonstrated to many the limits of "participationism." The political and economic system was willing and able to let poor people participate in an advisory and token capacity in social welfare decision making at the local level. It was not willing to give these people power, as limited as that power might have been. The class and race cleavages in the economic and political system, especially at the local level, ran so deep that even the slightest power at the bottom threatened to crack the foundation.

To its credit, the federal government, whatever its motives and intentions, did support and fund a grassroots citizen action program. To their credit, community workers, if only minimally, shook up the system, pressured local bureaucracies, gave people a sense of their latent power, and used this as a formative experience for political work in the 1970s. A number of organizations, the National Welfare Rights Organization, for example, evolved directly out of the experiences of the activists and architects of CAP. Ultimately, however, CAP did not appreciably alter the problem of poverty in the United States. It assisted in the expansion of a professional black middle class, but it did not affect the factors that kept many whites and most minorities impoverished. A more substantial program would have developed a national policy of services and jobs to ensure decent housing, health care, education, and, most important, employment as everyone's right.

Furthermore, the programs of the CAAs and the Great Society in general were based solely in rural and urban ghettos, which guaranteed that more widespread changes need not result from them, that people living in affluent communities need not be affected by them, and that the chief contradictions in society—namely, class and race stratification—would remain. Without a program promoting fundamental political and economic change from the national level on down to the neighborhood, liberal programs such as the CAP and its predecessors in the Progressive era and the New Deal ultimately served to maintain the class status quo rather than improve the position of people they were intended, in theory, to assist.

Chapter Five

The New Populism of the 1970s

Recessions, Inflation, and the New Corporate Conservatism

> *We believe in democracy—and average people controlling their lives*
> *and the right of every person to fulfill his or her God-given potential as*
> *a human being. We are willing to take that dream of a truly democrat-*
> *ic America and transform it into flesh and blood organizations of aver-*
> *age people, who through their own efforts, can make it into a reality*
> *for themselves and their children.*

—Jean Mayer, president, Illinois Public Action Council

The conservative consensus of the 1950s and the welfare-state liberalism of the 1960s were grounded in the continuous and often substantial growth of the United States economy after World War II. The
nation was faced with serious problems abroad and at home during
these years, but in general the fruits of being the premier world power
kept the economy in impressively good health. As economist Robert
Heilbroner notes, in the United States as well as other "advanced" capitalist nations the two and a half decades from 1947 to 1972 "were the
longest period of growth that capitalism had ever experienced, almost
a quarter of a century of nearly uninterrupted expansion."[1] Much of
the international capitalist economy's strength in the post–1947 period

rested on the ability of the United States to fuse industrial capitalist nations and dependent Third-World countries into a single economic system under the mantle of U.S. capital and corporations.

By the early 1970s, however, the sound economic foundation began to crack as the worldwide imperial system of U.S. capital faltered in the face of successful Third-World insurgency and heightened competition from Japan and West Germany. The crisis, stimulated by a 400 percent increase in OPEC (Organization of Petroleum Exporting Countries) oil prices, came in 1973–74, just after U.S. withdrawal from Vietnam, and began the most serious economic downturn since the depression of the 1930s. Unemployment between 1973 and 1975 rose 75 percent, but even that figure masks the concentrated impact on minority communities and working-class neighborhoods in northern cities. The recession produced "pockets of unemployment" in some black ghetto areas, for example, that ran as high as 90 percent of all black youth. Layoffs, plant shutdowns, and "runaway shops" (industries that leave one area for another to lower costs; they "run away" to Latin America, Asia, the South, and so forth) became commonplace in industrial cities in Ohio, Pennsylvania, New York, Michigan, and Illinois. Moreover, this recession was unique, and especially difficult to resolve, because it was accompanied for most of the decade by double-digit inflation.

Walter Hoadley, vice president of the Bank of America, reported that business reacted to the collapse with "sheer fear." No longer was the chief concern of the corporate community developing a "people's capitalism" or redistributing wealth in an affluent society. No longer was the problem how to live well amid luxury. This was an economic crisis, not a boom period like that of the previous two decades. How were corporations to deal with the unprecedented twin problems of high inflation and high unemployment? How could they resolve the problems of declining profits and productivity? How could widespread domestic and international insurgence be prevented as economic uncertainty and crisis grew? These were the new concerns of corporate and national leaders.

The beginnings of the new corporate response to the economic crisis of the 1970s emerged, political commentator Harry Boyte suggests, in 1972 with Treasury Secretary John Connolly's call for a "new level of partnership" between business and government in which government would curtail its restrictions on corporate activities and, at the same time, develop new means of aiding big business. A more complete corporate program emerged after Watergate. Corporate leaders and New Right theoreticians launched a concerted ideological attack on the "welfare state" of Keynesian economics. More specifically, the new corporate agenda called for an "age of limits" characterized by balanced government budgets, fewer public social service programs, lower corporate income taxes, higher corporate tax credits and depreciation allowances, and, in general, an attack on the progressive gains of the last generation—from minority and women's rights to health, consumer, and environmental regulations. The object was to get big government off of the back and out of the lives of the American people. It is inefficient, it is unwieldy, it is expensive, and it is the source of our economic problems.

Corporate leaders were well aware that it was not going to be an easy job selling this neoconservative program to the public. Surely people were receptive to the antigovernment aspects of the corporate agenda. Watergate, Vietnam, government corruption and scandals, haunting disclosures about CIA and FBI activities, and dehumanizing experiences with public bureaucracies had alienated citizens from official representatives and government agencies. But it was one thing for people to think big government was the problem; it was another to see big business as the solution. The social movements of the 1960s had changed people's political consciousness. Even those who opposed these movements learned about the value of active participation in realizing and expanding what is possible. A sense of grassroots self-assertiveness was a central legacy of the decade. People were energized and empowered by its events and not about to forget their dreams or acquiesce responsibility to either government or big business. The neoconservatives had their hands full. As a *Business Week* editorial put the problem: "Some people will have to do with less— cities and states, the home mortgage market, small businesses and the consumer will all get less than they want. It will be a hard pill for many Americans to swallow—the idea of doing with less so that big business can have more. Nothing that this nation or any other nation has done in modern history compares in difficulty with the selling job that must be done to make people accept the new reality."[2]

The neoconservative strategy was implemented most easily in cities. Elected national politicians such as Presidents Carter and Reagan were unable, given among other things their support of increased defense allocations, to cut the national budget deficit. At the local level, however, the situation differed. Fiscal crises, rising unemployment, welfare cutbacks, attacks on public unions, and declining services became the lot of cities in the 1970s. Much of this urban crisis was the result of the general economic situation. Historically when the national economy falters, cities—the central nodes of the economic structure—suffer badly. But not all cities were affected equally in the early 1970s. Northern cities, from commercial centers like New York, Boston, Cleveland, and San Francisco to single-industry towns like Youngstown, Ohio, suffered severe crises. Cities in the sunbelt, though not without problems of poverty, insufficient services, racial and class segregation, and pollution, to name but a few, did not experience the economic recession to the extent of their northern counterparts. Houston, for example, a city with vast social problems, experienced massive growth throughout the 1970s, with an unemployment rate consistently around or below 3 percent.

As long as the boom of the 1950s and 1960s kept going, the fiscal situation, if not the political and social situation, in northern cities remained intact. These cities were highly vulnerable in the late 1950s to fiscal crises resulting from residential suburbanization and industrial decentralization, which drew the affluent and the tax base outside the city's taxing borders. But "progrowth" coalitions, composed of central-city politicians, liberal bureaucrats, corporate executives, and real estate and construction industry representatives united in city after city to push for federal welfare and urban renewal programs, highway projects to connect the central city to the suburbs, and locally initiated and financed downtown redevelopment. They united, often successfully, to revive these cities by bringing money back in and renewing growth.[3]

But the economic base on which the progrowth coalition of the 1950s and 1960s operated was largely the product of the unprecedented economic expansion of those decades. As the recession and international economic problems hit in the early 1970s and as growth funds receded, northern cities became burdened by their declining tax bases, increasing city indebtedness, and deteriorating social services. Many of these cities, New York being the most notable, teetered on the brink of bankruptcy. No longer were the bankers, financial analysts, and corporate investors praising and supporting progrowth projects. Whereas cities like New York were previously applauded for their efforts to reinvigorate the central city and maintain social peace, now financiers and federal officials saw them as mismanaged, overly generous, unwieldy bureaucratic messes that needed to be taught the lessons of fiscal responsibility. The neoconservative solution gradually took hold at the local level. No money would be forthcoming from banks or the federal government unless cities mended their extravagant and wasteful ways. What this meant was that the corporate sector, especially financial institutions, would play a much larger role in the control and guidance of northern cities.

Neoconservative strategies for urban change became commonplace. Using models of "planned shrinkage" or "triage," officials planned to bulldoze or ignore the poorest areas of the city. They hoped the residents of these neighborhoods would be coerced into moving outside of the city's realm of responsibility, preferably to the sunbelt where jobs were said to abound. Roger Starr, the New York City housing and development administrator, went so far as to suggest in 1976 that fire and police stations as well as public schools be closed in slum areas as a method of accelerating population decline. No longer were the poor to be helped. The new corporate strategy saw them as bad investments, economic roadblocks to cutting city costs.

The new urban strategy began during the Nixon administration. In the first two years of the revenue sharing program, which replaced the Johnson administration's Office of Economic Opportunity projects, more than half of the funds were used to lower city taxes and much of the rest went to buttress law enforcement, uses intended to aid and protect business development and make the city more attractive to the affluent. Only 3 percent was spent on social service programs for those in need. By mid-decade the conservative strategy had accelerated. Urban economist George Sternlieb, reflecting the drift to the right, argued that "you can't support the poor without the rich, and every time someone rich stays in Manhattan it's a triumph for the poor."[4] But as Sternlieb was quick to point out, such an analysis was not an easy one to sell to poor and working-class people. It was not even an easy one to sell to New York's political leaders who, despite joining the chorus of "fiscal conservatism," found themselves in a terrible economic mess without any assistance from either the federal government or the banking industry. New York Mayor Abe Beame incorrectly saw it in partisan terms, as "a Republican pincer movement responsible not to the people but to financial institutions." But he was on the mark in decrying that corporate leaders, especially in the financial institutions, were "using cash as a weapon in an attempt to direct the social and economic policies of our city."[5]

Of course the people affected by urban renewal in the 1960s or planned shrinkage in the 1970s did not sit passively by and let the private and public sectors implement their programs. Urban rebellions in most large cities challenged the architects of urban renewal in the 1960s. More quietly and often more effectively, ad hoc neighborhood organizations formed to block urban renewal or highway development plans, win services, jobs, and other benefits, and demand greater community control. In 1970 there were 400 on-going community struggles in the nation against highway construction plans alone. In a climate of growth and prosperity, such neighborhood organizations were not able to completely stop development or fundamentally change the general plans of urban renewal or highway development. But they did slow down the process, slightly alter the plans to protect their community, secure marginal participation, and, most effectively, win benefits from a city hall and federal government willing to coopt rather than repress grassroots resistance.

The neighborhood response to urban problems accelerated with the economic crises of the 1970s. Media hype to the contrary, activism did not end with the turn of the decade, and not all activists became stock brokers, like Jerry Rubin, or born-again Christians, like Eldridge Cleaver. Most activists held onto their initial vision of social, political, and economic democracy, and brought it with them into the neighborhoods where they lived and into the schools, factories, social welfare and health care agencies, and legal and political offices where they worked. As Gale Cincotta, the leader of National People's Action, a national neighborhood coalition, put it in 1977: "I keep hearing that everything's dead and there's no big cause since civil rights and the Vietnam War. But that's a myth. There's a neighborhood movement that started in the sixties. It's not as dramatic with everyone out in the streets, but it's steadily gaining strength in every city and state. The base was there and people reached the point where they just had to do something."[6] While the media continued to tout the conservative drift of the nation and wondered what happened to the 1960s generation, many thousands of neighborhood organizations, single-issue groups, and progressive political action efforts formed in response to the economic crisis and the new corporate strategy.

By the end of the 1970s the neoconservative program had secured repeated victories. A *Fortune* reporter glowed that "suddenly business seems to possess all the primary instruments of power—the leadership, the strategy, the supporting troops, the campaign money—and a new will to use them."[7] While his claim of unmitigated success for 1970s conservatism was overstated—as were the death knells for 1960s activism—neither viewpoint was without some basis. People may not have been convinced that corporations were their natural allies, but their powerlessness and the absence of an alternative, left program led them to accept the dominant conservative choices presented. Nevertheless, what did not make the pages of the print media was the fact that based on the lessons and experiences of the 1960s, a multifaceted, "new populist" citizen action movement had developed in the 1970s to counteract the alienation most Americans felt from both the public and private sectors.

The Roots of the New Populism

The radicalism of the 1960s has become the common sense of the 1970s.

—Tom Hayden, political activist

In response to events of the 1960s and the economic crisis that followed, a widespread interest in neighborhood organizing arose throughout the United States in the 1970s. The *Christian Science Monitor,* in a series of articles in 1977, reported a "groundswell movement of citizens calling for the return of political and economic power to the local level."[8] More than 20 million Americans were active in hundreds of thousands of neighborhood groups throughout the nation. Several thousand block clubs sprang up in New York City alone after 1975. The National Commission on Neighborhoods listed more than 8,000 larger community groups throughout the nation. Communities Organized for Public Service (COPS) in San Antonio, one of the largest single-community organizations in the nation, was able to turn out 6,000 delegates to its 1976 convention, only two years after it began. The Association of Community Organizations for Reform Now (ACORN) claimed in 1980, 10 years after it was founded, some 25,000 active dues-paying members in neighborhood organizations in 19 states. Perhaps even more impressive were the more than a dozen organizer-training centers founded in the 1970s to serve the needs of citizen's groups. As people increasingly turned away from public and corporate leadership, they turned inward to spaces and interests where they could have more control, and nowhere was this more visible than at the neighborhood level.[9]

Many commentators saw the groundswell as a new populist movement in the making. Traditional populism, ranging from the writings of Thomas Jefferson to the more radical farmer and labor movements of the late nineteenth century, championed America's democratic mission and supported the struggles of "the people" against the "plutocrats." The new populism is very much within this tradition. As Mike Miller of the Organize Training Center in San Francisco describes it, the basic values of the new populism are the values of democracy. Its fundamental analysis is that "unchecked power has become concentrated in the hands of a very small number of people who are at the helm of the major corporations of the nation." Because government remains unaccountable to most people, it, too, along with business, is part of the problem. The solution is for people to organize in democratically controlled and administered community organizations built on "the democratic values and self-interests of the people."[10] Since the nineteenth century, populism has assumed a middle ground between the elitism of traditional liberalism and the class conflict analysis of socialism. While it is critical of elements of the economic system, it sees bigness and unaccountable power, rather than capitalism, as the fundamental problem.

It is not surprising then that much of the new populism began as a reaction against the revolutionary socialist organizing of the late 1960s. Harry Boyte, a prominent new populist commentator and theoretician, pretty much sums up the rationale behind the new populism when he says that "contemporary citizen organizing is more down to earth, more practical, above all more enduring and rooted in the social fabric [than sixties organizing]. It seeks to build ongoing organizations through which people can wield power. It is accompanied by a sense of the rightness, creativity, and vitality in people's traditions, folkways, and culture that sixties radicals were prone to scorn or dismiss."[11] Accordingly, new populist neighborhood organizing in the 1970s rejected the emphasis on anticapitalist political ideology, the focus on "consciousness raising," the sectarianism, the single-minded attention to a particular constituency—whether African-Americans or students—all of which, new populists contended, isolated late 1960s organizers from working people and prevented the development of effective grassroots neighborhood organizations. Instead, the new populism offered a "majoritarian strategy" rooted primarily in the communities and traditions of white and black, low and moderate income people. It offered an organizing approach that toned down the late 1960s emphasis on ideology and focused on winning power and building organizations owned and directed by working-class people. To accomplish such goals, these organizations often allied with traditional community institutions like churches, unions, and ethnic associations.

Notwithstanding their rejection of 1960s revolutionary politics, the new populism emanates directly from the experiences of young men and women, black and white, in organizations and movements of that decade. The new populism, above all, reflects a continuous effort since the early 1960s to find a successful radical program that presents, as an alternative to corporate capitalism, a vision of a more cooperative, democratic, and decentralized society. For example, Wade Rathke, the founder of ACORN, got his start doing welfare organizing and working with George Wiley and the National Welfare Rights Organization. Harry Boyte was active in the southern civil rights movement and a cofounder of the New American Movement (NAM), a new left socialist organization. Heather Booth, the founder of the Midwest Academy, a training and resource center for new populist organizers, was a leading figure in the antiwar, student, and women's movements, a veteran of both SNCC and SDS. Steve Max and Tom Hayden were both active in the initial ERAP projects of SDS and continue to be important theoreticians and leaders of new populist campaigns for economic and political democracy. Mike Miller was also prominent in ERAP; worked with SNCC, Cesar Chavez, and the United Farm Workers (UFW); organized with Saul Alinsky in Kansas City in the mid-1960s; became the lead organizer in an Alinsky-style project, the Mission Community Organization (MCO), in San Francisco; and is now director of the Organize Training Center in that city. By 1980 there were new populist organizers and political activists, living and working in neighborhoods and communities throughout the country, with nearly two decades of political and organizing experience under their belt. And while the 1970s altered their political perspective and tactics, the animating core of their experience rests with the anti-imperialist, participatory democracy struggles of the sixties.

It is no accident that the new populist critique of 1960s organizing was reminiscent of the salvos launched during that decade against the new left by Saul Alinsky. At his best, Alinsky criticized 1960s organizing for not being grounded in working-class politics and traditions. At his worst, his criticism smacked of the traditional populist error of throwing the baby out with the bath water, that is, a tendency to deny an entire radical left heritage rather than simply criticize its errors. The connection between Alinsky and the new populism is fundamental. Heather Booth called him the Sigmund Freud of modern community organizing. And as Freud and his disciples codified the field of psychoanalysis, so Alinsky and his successors have done with the tactics of populist-style community organizing.

Alinsky organizing experienced hard times from the late 1940s until the early 1960s. The Cold War repression kept Alinsky and fellow organizers defensive and ineffective. Their one success during this period was the Community Service Organization (CSO), an effort initiated by Alinsky-organizer Fred Ross in Chicano communities in California in the late 1940s. Throughout the 1950s Alinsky was pretty much forgotten, both in social welfare and what remained of activist circles, but he and his method were revived, along with many others, with the civil rights and antipoverty movements of the early 1960s. It was not until mid-decade, however, that Alinsky's work in lower-class black and white neighborhoods in Chicago came to popular attention. As other left groups became increasingly militant and revolutionary after 1965, as African-Americans rebelled and black ghettos burned, and as liberal leaders sought more "reasonable" alternatives, Alinsky, once ostracized as a "Bolshevik organizer," seemed more moderate and therefore more attractive.

Alinsky came to national attention as early as 1964 when *Fortune* editor Charles Silberman, in an influential liberal critique of race relations, *Crisis in Black and White,* touted Alinsky and his IAF (Industrial Areas Foundation) organizer-training center as the answer to America's race problems. For Silberman, the IAF organizing project in the Woodlawn neighborhood of Chicago, a neighborhood just south of the University of Chicago, of some 65,000 people, 86 percent of whom were black, was "the most important and most impressive experiment affecting Negroes anywhere in the United States." In a call for more Alinsky-style efforts, he lamented in the book's afterword that there was only one Alinsky and so many black slum areas. The praise and notoriety received by Alinsky and The Woodlawn Organization (TWO) were not accidental. Amid rebellions in comparable poor black areas throughout the nation, Woodlawn did not have a riot. Alinsky saw this as the result of effective, grassroots political organization; the residents in Woodlawn did not have to resort to spontaneous, undirected rebellion. People in power, however, saw Alinsky's populist organizing as a less threatening alternative, a less dangerous political program than the revolutionary black nationalism developing in organizations like SNCC. It was not surprising to find *Time* magazine shortly thereafter heralding Alinsky as the "The Prophet of Power to the People."[12]

Each of the numerous Alinsky projects of the 1960s was decidedly different. TWO was the first Alinsky effort to focus on an African-American community. The Organization for a Better Austin (OBA) in Chicago organized among local block clubs, while the Northwest Community Organization (NCO), based in a primarily Polish area of Chicago, organized Catholic church groups. In the mid-1960s, especially 1964 to 1967, Alinsky and the IAF ventured beyond Chicago, organizing three projects in black neighborhoods: CUA (Council for United Action) in Kansas City, Missouri; FIGHT (Freedom, Integration, God, Honor, Trust) in Rochester, New York; and BUILD (Build Unity, Independence, Liberty, and Dignity) in Buffalo, New York. But in each project from TWO to BUILD, irrespective of the differing local conditions, Alinsky organizers addressed immediate community concerns and worked to build "people's organizations" based on what they saw as the most prominent community traditions and sources of cohesion.

And despite important differences, Alinsky organizations in the 1960s generally followed a similar development, one most evident in TWO's history. Until mid-decade Alinsky-initiated organizing projects, most notably in Chicago, espoused and practiced the ideology of equality and the tactics of non-violent confrontation of the civil rights movement. From the mid-1960s through the early 1970s, Alinsky organizations shifted from a civil rights orientation to an emphasis on negotiation and community development. NCO continued the pressure group, conflict approach of the early 1960s, but TWO, FIGHT, and most others moved from "confrontation to coexistence." This development has wide applicability to new populist organizing today and underlines again some of the weaknesses of the Alinsky model.

For example, TWO, formed in 1961, was initially quite militant and confrontational. It held rent strikes and demonstrated against merchants accused of short weights—charging customers for more than they were really getting. It formed a procession of buses filled with more than 2,000 Woodlawn residents, and in a style similar to that of the civil rights movement went down to city hall to register to vote. Alinsky described one of the confrontational methods of the early TWO this way:

When TWO has a bunch of housing complaints they don't forward them to the building inspector. They drive forty or fifty of their members—the blackest ones they can find—to the nice suburb where the slumlord lives and they picket his home. Now we know that a picket line isn't going to convert the slumlord. But we also know what happens when his white neighbors get after him and say, "We don't care what you do for a living—all we're telling you is to get those niggers out of here or you get out." That's the kind of jujitsu operation that forces the slumlord to surrender and gets repairs made in the slum.[13]

By the late 1960s and early 1970s, however, TWO was no longer a confrontational pressure group advocating the needs of low-income people in the Woodlawn area. Increasingly it had become a community development corporation, run by the more middle-class segments of the neighborhood which tended to promote projects that primarily aided upwardly mobile blacks. TWO was able to survive in its new guise, no small feat for Alinsky-style neighborhood organizations, which usually had a life span of six years at most. But it survived in a different form than originally intended. It became the cosponsor and coadministrator of development programs funded and largely designed by private foundations and public agencies. It became part of the externally initiated antipoverty programs of the late 1960s. For example, TWO cosponsored a 762-unit, middle-income housing project in Woodlawn (which required the demolition of 2,000 units of low-income housing). It administered an early childhood development center, an OEO-funded Head Start program in the neighborhood, with a $100,000 annual budget. It received funds from the Zenith Corporation and later from the federal government to do job training, which ultimately resulted in TWO developing a career vocational institute supported by state and federal funds. It received other grants to develop experimental schools, training centers for mental health workers, and rehabilitated housing. TWO even became the owner of a neighborhood supermarket, a project begun to raise funds for the organization.

As a community development agency TWO was a success, the shining gem of all Alinsky organizations in the 1960s and early 1970s. The shift from "confrontation to coexistence" was remarkable in its level of measurable accomplishments. But TWO was now a neighborhood development corporation, not a "people's organization." It was run by a paid, professional staff whose attention was fixed on development and growth, organizational stability, and professional competence, not on social change or even on serving the needs of *all* the neighborhood people. Predictably, neighborhood resident participation declined as technical expertise grew to paramount importance. TWO became just another business in the community, a nonprofit business almost as removed from many of Woodlawn's problems and needs as the profit-oriented enterprises.

Moreover, in the face of powerful economic pressure, TWO was defenseless. In 1971, for example, Chicago newspapers ran articles about how East Woodlawn was being burned to the ground. In 1970 alone there were 1,600 fires in a mile square area. While the city did nothing and TWO was unable to mount effective opposition to these obvious acts of arson, developers waited for the complete destruction of this valuable chunk of land bordered by two parks, a golf course, museums, beaches, and the University of Chicago. There was no longer an opposition organization in the neighborhood, as TWO had been in 1961, to challenge the transformation of this area into a gentrified upper-middle class section of the city. Ultimately, TWO was unable to stop not only the gentrification of East Woodlawn but the continuing deterioration and impoverishment of residents in other parts of the community. The story of TWO and the Woodlawn neighborhood is more complex than related here. But the evolution of TWO into a neighborhood development agency that was unable to defend neighborhood interests results in large part from problems inherent in the Alinsky method, specifically its localism and its lack of a clear, long-term program for changing power relations at the city level and beyond.[14]

In essence the trend in Alinsky organizations was to ignore issues of social change or concerns beyond the neighborhood and simply bargain for benefits that could develop and improve the local community and assist its long-term residents, usually those who were "better-off." The cooptive pressures of federal and local programs assisted in this development. So did the disorganized state of the left. The late 1960s and early 1970s offered nonsocialist, predominantly white-led groups, such as Alinsky's, two weak alternatives. "Balkanization," a tendency to divide into small, isolated political units, was adopted by most neighborhood organizing efforts. "Single-issue coalition," on the other hand, such as the antiwar movement, was the preference for more nationally oriented projects but had no permanent structure and no staying power beyond the issue. TWO, MCO, OBA, and most other Alinsky organizations chose Balkanization, with its interest-group style, parochialism, and antipoverty program support.

In the early 1970s, the limits of Alinsky organizing were not well known or understood. People active in movements of the 1960s felt a deep need, especially after U.S. withdrawal from Vietnam, to continue moving the nation toward greater democracy, equality, and justice. They were attracted to Alinsky-style strategies based on their perception of what was wrong with the student-based and student-led movements of the previous decade. What they knew of the Alinsky method sounded good, especially the fact that it rejected the revolutionary rhetoric and openly socialist ideology of the late 1960s that isolated students from poor and working people. While many activists of the 1960s thought of themselves as socialists, the 1970s seemed to call for a rethinking of traditional leftist views of how to bring about radical change in the United States. The populist, democratic ideology of Alinskyism seemed to many to be a good, if imperfect, place to begin that rethinking.

Neo-Alinskyism

Some people say what does ACORN want? The answer is simple: We want sufficient power in our cities and states to speak—and be heard—and heeded—for the interests of the majority of citizens. We want to participate in community and civil affairs, not as second class citizens because we don't drive Rolls Royces, but as men and women committed to a better future where our concerns are met with justice and dignity; where wealth, race and religion are insufficient excuses to prevent equal participation and impact in government; where any person can protect his or her family and join with others in community strength; and where, as ACORN's slogan goes, "The People Shall Rule." That is what America is. That is what ACORN wants. Nothing more and nothing less.

—Steve McDonald, ACORN president

Many new populist organizations were directly initiated by Alinsky-trained organizers and their students. Tom Gaudette, for example, once a vice president for the Admiral Corporation, received his organizer training at the Industrial Areas Foundation and helped organize, among other efforts, the Organization for a Better Austin (OBA) in Chicago and the MidAmerican Institute in the early 1970s. The MidAmerican Institute, in turn, initiated community organizing efforts in Oakland, Baltimore, Seattle, New Orleans, and elsewhere. Most new populist efforts, however, had no formal or direct ties with Alinsky-trained organizers. Whether directly or indirectly related to IAF organizing methods, the more progressive new populist groups reflected a modification of Alinsky methods in the 1970s, the development of a "neo-Alinskyite" organizing strategy.

The essence of neo-Alinskyism in the 1970s was to develop mass political organizations rooted in neighborhoods, grounded in local concerns, and focused on winning concrete gains. The goal was to advance social and economic democracy, empower people, and challenge power relations within and beyond the neighborhood. Many organizations in this populist trend—which continues today—acknowledge that fundamental social change in this country demands a multi-issue, multiclass, multiracial, national effort that rests on grassroots organizing but goes beyond the neighborhood or community unit. They advocate a "majoritarian strategy" geared primarily to the needs of low- and moderate-income people, which they estimated in the early 1980s to be 85 percent of the population. In the 1970s they worked hard to hurdle the weaknesses of Alinsky-style neighborhood organizing in the 1960s, which defined and limited itself to a neighborhood, race, or ethnic group—often pitting one oppressed group against another—and which suffered a good degree of isolation in relation to other groups and the political system as a whole.[15] All neo-Alinskyite projects in the 1970s employed the ideology of the new populism—decentralization, participatory democracy, self-reliance, mistrust of government and corporate institutions, empowering low- and moderate-income people—and at their best saw themselves as grassroots organizations working to connect up with the national political process.[16]

Neo-Alinskyism differs in other respects from the practices of its founding father. In the 1970s it broke away from the highly professional orientation and reliance on large-scale institution and foundation support characteristic of the Industrial Areas Foundation model. It criticized Alinsky's overemphasis on the "super organizer," an emphasis that made it difficult for working people, who are not used to public roles, to assume leadership tasks and responsibilities. Moreover, neo-Alinskyite efforts did not require, as do IAF programs, a sizable capital outlay from community groups before organizers agree to enter the neighborhood. TWO, for example, was not begun until the IAF received a $69,000 grant from the Schwartzhaupt Foundation, a $50,000 contribution from the Catholic Archdiocese, and the promise of support from Presbyterian churches. Unlike most new populist organizers, IAF "professional organizers" were and are well paid, and their organizations well financed in comparison to most others.

Traditional Alinskyism remains most effective in Mexican-American communities in large southwestern cities where the Catholic church is a primary bond of unity and is often willing to play a social action role. Because of centuries of oppression, language barriers, and cultural factors, the Chicano community in cities like San Antonio had been kept politically isolated and inexperienced, ready for the low-keyed, self-empowerment skills offered by the IAF. Where IAF trained organizers, such as Ernie Cortes, have taken the time to work slowly through existing organizations, especially the churches, to involve what Cortes calls the "central core leadership" into citywide organizations drawn from Mexican-American neighborhoods, Alinskyite organizations like COPS in San Antonio, United Neighborhood Organizations (UNO) in Los Angeles, and The Metropolitan Organization (TMO) in Houston have had a considerable impact.[17] But even in these cases (discussed further in chapter 7) the traditional IAF model has been altered. Like all neo-Alinskyite organizations, these community efforts, while often localist and based among a single cultural nationality, are citywide in perspective and seek, at their best, to build "majoritarian" organizations that are allied with other low- and moderate-income groups..

One of the earliest and most successful examples of neo-Alinskyite organizing is the Association of Community Organizations for Reform Now. Begun in 1970 in Little Rock as Arkansas Community Organizations for Reform Now, ACORN has direct roots in the organizing strategies of Fred Ross, who studied under Alinsky, and the National Welfare Rights Organization (NWRO), perhaps the most effective, single-issue community organization of the late 1960s. Wade Rathke, ACORN's founder and director, received his community organizing training and experience, as well as support for the Arkansas project, from George Wiley and the National Welfare Rights Organization. Officially formed in 1967, the NWRO modeled much of its practice on the work of Fred Ross, not Alinsky. The Alinsky model emphasized organizing the leaders of existing neighborhood institutions, especially churches, to serve as the natural foundation for grassroots projects. In his work with the Community Services Organization (CSO) in the barrios of California, Ross saw the value of such institutional-based support, but found greater success organizing house to house on specific issues of concern to community members. And whereas Ross saw the need for a statewide organization that could more effectively advance the interests of neighborhood people, Alinsky feared the "fascist" potential of large organizations. The NWRO, and later ACORN, employed the door-to-door, issue-organizing approach of Ross.

ACORN, however, modified the NWRO strategy to include the development of a mass organization of low- and moderate-income people, the majority of people in the United States, which could pressure the political system from the neighborhood up to the national level. For ACORN the neighborhood was a "training ground" or "staging area" from which to mount larger campaigns for democracy, equity, and justice. The single-issue and single-constituency (primarily poor blacks) approach of organizations like NWRO came to be seen by George Wiley, Wade Rathke, and others as too limiting. Rathke, commenting on his organizing problems while working with NWRO in Massachusetts, put it this way: "The next-door neighbor to the welfare recipient was just as antagonistic to the recipient as anyone else. . . . With the welfare issue you're always dealing with a minority. We all knew that we had to break out of the single-issue campaign. I wanted to build on a majority constituency rather than on a minority, where the next-door neighbors are in it together, not fighting each other."[18] ACORN, then, was designed to be a novel effort at employing the new, "majoritarian" strategy in a mass-based, multi-issue, Rossian-style of community organizing.

In the 1970s ACORN attracted hundreds of primarily white, college students into community organizing. ACORN job advertisements in 1982 promised "A job you can believe in. ACORN needs organizers to work with low and moderate income families in 26 states for political and economic justice. . . . Tangible results. Long hours and low pay. Training provided." Most of the trainees, taught at the Institute in New Orleans, were novices, never having done much political work or community organizing. The Rossian method, as it is still taught by ACORN, is similar in many respects to the early efforts of SNCC and ERAP. The following general model of door-to-door organizing has been taught by ACORN, depending on local conditions, since its beginning.

1. *You, the organizer, are sent to a community.* You do not enter a neighborhood with an issue, but neither do you go in just for the sake of getting people organized, as Alinsky-trained organizers often seem to do. Your goal is to help bring about economic and social justice for low- and moderate-income people. Be guided by ACORN's slogan, "The People Shall Rule." The selected area, of some 300–1,000 households, should have the constituency you seek and natural geographic boundaries. See if there are any "external contacts" who can put you in touch with community people or give you a better sense of the neighborhood and its concerns.

2. *Develop internal contacts.* Get people's names and talk with them in their homes. Begin to sell people on the idea that they, too, can be organizers and that all people should be organized. You could say, "Doctors are organized, so why shouldn't we be?" Find someone willing to hold the first house meeting. All this time, you should be developing lists of people you talk with and those you need to see, and lists of community concerns. The more lists, the more information you have, the greater your knowledge of and interest in the community. All of the above should take between six and nine weeks.

3. *Organize the first house meeting.* At the first house meeting you organize make sure that you get a good representation of the community, but keep it under a dozen people. Take time here to get adequate representation. This initial organizing committee is a critical building block of the neighborhood organization. At this first meeting begin to identify issues. Perhaps you can even draft a letter at this meeting, declaring the group's concern about a winnable neighborhood issue. Direct the letter to the community and use it later as an organizing tool when you go door to door. This first meeting will often digress into people's personal and sometimes parochial concerns. It is important to let this happen; people do not often have the opportunity to air their concerns in such a forum. Listen well. You learn from listening, not from talking. If you have organized effectively before the meeting, you will have a good sense of what issues will come up. Nevertheless, meetings are critical for developing group solidarity and leadership skills, instilling confidence, and heightening people's spirit and willingness to struggle.

4. *Promote the organization.* During the next month go around town, door to door, with members of the organizing committee, talking to as many people as you can. This "door knocking" is perhaps the most important activity you will engage in. By talking directly with people in the informal, intimate atmosphere of their homes you can reach them in a personal way. Remember, people will get involved not only based on the issue but also because they like you, or trust you, or are looking for something meaningful to do. They are often frustrated and angry over local problems that they feel powerless to correct. The door-to-door approach enables you, as no other method does, to engage people and draw them out, to learn about them as they learn about you, and to give them a better sense of their collective power.

5. *Honor the organizing process.* During the organizing process, people will surprise you. Do not make assumptions for them or about them. Remain open. Develop a useful index file on each person you meet—you will never remember important things about their interests and their skills otherwise. The door-to-door process is especially valuable in discovering potential leaders. Invite them to join the organizing committee group. One of the chief strengths of door-to-door organizing, as difficult as it is sometimes, is that it finds people who never were or never thought of themselves before as leaders, people who were never before even asked their opinion. Hold more house meetings. Some people will quit; only a few will do work. Remain flexible and open.

6. *Identify an issue.* After talking with nearly everyone in the community the organizer has an incredible knowledge of community people and problems. It is likely that issues that concerned you and the organizing committee initially are no longer dominant. Identify the issue that your work thus far indicates is the best one, the one that will galvanize community people and show them they can win if they organize and work together. Remember, however, not to push people into an issue. It is not important what the first issue is. What is most important is to get people involved. The organizers should be presenting options, tactics, alternative ways of looking at things, information gathered from their full-time efforts. But let the people make the decisions.

7. *Hold a neighborhoodwide meeting.* Hold a major second organizing committee meeting. Follow this with telephone calls, flyers, and press releases about an upcoming neighborhoodwide meeting to dis-

cuss the identified issue. Make this as important an event in the neighborhood as you can. This is the meeting at which the organization will be born. Perhaps the night before, get together again with the organizing committee and agree on who will lead tomorrow's meeting. Get people to nominate one another for the election of temporary officers. You need only one nominee for each office. Make sure that everyone who attends the founding meeting gets a chance to speak. People came to have their say. Make a list of their comments. Hold an election at this meeting for temporary officers, which will provide an ongoing structure for the organization. Get people at the meeting to become dues-paying members ($1 a month, $10 a year in the early 1970s). The dues are significant not only because they provide some funding but, more important, because people relate differently to an organization that they own. This founding meeting should result in a community-wide action, which was planned roughly by the organizing committee beforehand.[19]

When ACORN first began in Arkansas in 1970, it focused on six neighborhoods of low-income residents in Little Rock. Using their NWRO experience, Rathke and others found a sentence in the welfare manuals that said poor people had a right to get furniture. Before long ACORN had negotiated with then-Governor Winthrop Rockefeller for a "furniture warehouse." ACORN caught on quickly after that victory. The Centennial Neighborhood Association, the Woodrow to Pine Neighborhood Association, and the Nine-Seventeen Community Organization, as well as others, seemed to spring up overnight. They focused on securing school lunch programs, demanding welfare rights, and improving public housing conditions.

Two years later ACORN expanded beyond its neighborhood bases, launching a grassroots "Save the City" campaign. The citywide effort respected neighborhood interests and at the same time cut across class and racial lines. It opposed blockbusting in white neighborhoods, demanded more parks in predominantly black neighborhoods, and worked on traditional community concerns like traffic, sewerage, and stray dogs. ACORN organizers stayed away from issues like racism that might jeopardize a victory. Opposition to blockbusting, for example, was carefully directed by organizers as being *for* neighborhood, *for* working people, not *against* African-Americans. The thinking, very much like that of Alinsky's, was to avoid issues that undermined unity and clouded the focus on the "real enemy." It was the job of ACORN organizers to isolate and expose any individual or group trying to turn the block-busting issue into one of white versus black neighborhoods.[20]

In his assessment of ACORN's first efforts commentator Andrew Kopkind noted that "winning is what is important in organizing, and it's almost an obsession with ACORN." Winning builds an organization, and build ACORN it did. In 1975 ACORN branched out into Texas and other states. By 1980 they had more than 25,000 dues-paying members in 19 states. Two years later their federated organization claimed 50,000 members with roots in neighborhoods in 26 states. When ACORN came to Houston in 1980, for example, it entered with a reputation. One of the city's two daily newspapers carried front-page stories on consecutive days, warning about this organization that wanted power for low- and moderate-income people, that believed "The People Shall Rule." The two white ACORN organizers sent to Houston, recent graduates of the University of Texas at Austin, had little firsthand knowledge of the city and found the organizing difficult. People in the black community, where ACORN often focuses its efforts, were little interested in the new organization. Nevertheless, ACORN's reputation for militant direct action, its successes in Arkansas, Dallas, and elsewhere, and its growing power worried Houston's conservative establishment.

As ACORN grew into a nationwide organization it became increasingly involved in electoral politics. This shift from pressure politics to pressure *and* electoral politics was increasingly apparent in the 1970s in many new populist organizations frustrated with the steady but minimal gains of grassroots, pressure-group tactics. In areas where ACORN was new and a less significant force, such as in Boston, where Mass Fair Share was the dominant new populist group, or as in Philadelphia, where the Consumer party and others were better established, ACORN emphasized militant direct action tactics, like house squatting, particularly in poor black neighborhoods, which are often ignored by "majoritarian" organizations. In areas where ACORN was more entrenched or where repressive conditions made direct action less productive, electoral political activity was emphasized. The move to electoral politics was consistent with the neo-Alinskyite objective of having low- and moderate-income people win power, rather than simply pressure those in power, and it is consistent with the goal of connecting grassroots organizing with the national political process.

More traditional Alinsky groups, like National People's Action, still adhered in the 1970s to the pressure group model, convinced that electoral participation would undermine the effectiveness and grassroots nature of community organization. ACORN, however, disagreed, emphasizing that real power could not be won solely by pressuring or exposing those with power. Real power is when low- and moderate-income people, or their true representatives, can make the actual decisions. The strategy used by ACORN in the 1980 presidential elections, for example, was to ask the two major national parties to incorporate into their party platform the issues in ACORN's people's platform. Similar statewide organizations, like Mass Fair Share and the community, senior citizen, and labor-based Ohio Public Interest Group (OPIG) also rethought their distrust of electoral politics, and plunged head first into the political arena, throwing their weight for and against issues and candidates much like populist political action committees. The assumption was that by organizing people and supporting candidates around programs that emphasize economic democracy and justice, a genuine—not doctrinal or isolated—democratic people's movement would arise and ultimately win power.[21]

A central problem with neo-Alinskyism in the 1970s was that any movement that rests on a reform-oriented populist ideology tends to be dominated by its organizers and highly vulnerable to cooptation by business-backed or conservative union-backed reform movements. Neo-Alinskyite groups sought to build a majoritarian left out of the traditions, hopes, and dreams of working- and middle-class people. With such a diverse constituency, they deemphasized political education, especially the anticapitalist vision of many of their organizers, for fear that "red-baiting" would divide support at a time when divisiveness might not be survived. This led to a strong tendency in ACORN and related efforts to remain staff intensive, to see the organizer as an "expert" who practices a method, almost a "science," of organizing. In some projects grassroots participation tended to appear only at selected and critical times—at mass meetings, direct actions, and elections; ACORN staff, for example, handled the day-to-day business and direction of the organization. Thus, the depth of political participation and real organizational democracy often remained shallow.

In communities where ACORN had developed a strong presence, they did "a damn good job" of identifying and training local people to be organizers. In many other neo-Alinskyite programs neighborhood people who never before were involved in political activity developed sophisticated organizing and leadership skills. For most neo-Alinskyite organizers, developing indigenous, working-class leaders is what organizing is all about. Ernie Cortes reflected this commitment when he noted that "No organizer should be so arrogant as to pretend he's going to organize an organization. I didn't organize COPS. The leadership organized them. I challenged them and I worked with them on a one-to-one basis. But they did the organizing."[22]

But even in the numerous instances where indigenous leaders were developed in the 1970s, the extent of political education was limited and the training tended to focus on organization-building skills—how an organizer can get people to join and build a neighborhood program. The political education of staff, indigenous leaders, and organization members—critical to any long-term, fundamental political change—was deemphasized. Part of the reason was new populist pragmatism, which encouraged winning victories and avoiding potentially divisive positions. Moving from one victory to another in rapid succession was easier than going slowly, giving people political education, and having to deal with some very sticky problems. Victories guaranteed that the organization would survive, and a strong argument could be made that people learn best from firsthand experience. But given the deemphasis on political education and ideology, it was not always clear whose traditions, whose hopes and dreams, whose community the new populism supported. Whose traditions were supported, for example, when some new populist organizations refused to take a stand on busing for school integration or on abortion?

To elaborate the point further, block and neighborhood associations organized around racial exclusion were as apparent in the 1970s as were those organized against redlining. ROAR (Restore Our Alienated Rights) in Boston demonstrated the right-wing possibilities of neighborhood organizations using the rhetoric of the new populism. In ROAR the ideology of participatory democracy was shrewdly manipulated by middle-class business leaders and politicians into an aggressive, militant, reactionary "a, b, c" program—antiabortion, antibusing, and anticommunism. "Let the people decide" and "community control" became the basis for actions against women and nonwhite minorities. In ROAR and in other reactionary, neighborhood-based organizations the multiclass call for "neighborhood power" loosely masked racist alliances between the white working-class and middle-class business-people and politicians. These alliances were often initiated by middle-class leaders who stood to profit financially and politically by preserving the segregated status quo. In the white, working-class area of South Boston, ROAR supporters saw the organization as a last-ditch effort in a period of economic hard times to defend their meager but relative advantage over blacks and to prevent the expansion of low-income housing and additional social problems into "Southie." These supporters, however, were mobilized and encouraged by "ward" political leaders who owned substantial property and had ties to local real estate and banking interests.[23]

ROAR was exceptional in its size and strength. It was well organized, with a staff in 1976 of 150 volunteers, 400 active members, and 200 paramilitary "marshalls" who did the organization's more "aggressive" work. But it was not unique. Linda Gordon and Allen Hunter, in an article on the New Right, made clear that democratic grassroots organizing, based on the folkways of church, family, and male authority, often led to conservative and right-wing advocates of the new populism. What political path a neighborhood organization takes depends to no small degree on its organizers, founding principles, and the way its victories and defeats are interpreted. In poor and working-class neighborhoods, people get involved to defend their neighborhood, and participation usually produces increased frustration and anger. But what becomes the object of the group's anger depends on its politics, ideology, and the extent of political education around issues of class, race, and gender.[24]

Most neo-Alinskyites saw organizations like ROAR as aberrations or as completely unrelated to the new populism. Accordingly, they avoided politically divisive issues related to class, racism, sexism, and nativism, and saw a program of conscious political education around an anticapitalist vision as more of a hindrance than a help. This may have been shortsighted. A political critique of the nation's economic, political, and social system that advanced specific programs and positions might have unified and strengthened such organizations, not to mention prevented conservative ideologies and groups from dominating in the 1980s.

The New Community Development

In the Bronx and on Manhattan's Lower East Side, in the barrios of East Los Angeles and ethnic neighborhoods of Chicago, across the

*country in communities once considered "garbage dumps" by city
administrators—redlined by banks for years and starved of traditional
social services—stirrings of a new spirit have become visible.*

—Harry Boyte, political commentator

While there was a tendency to see almost any inner-city neighborhood
organization in the 1970s as part of the new populist movement, it was
rather unclear exactly how much unity and common ground was
shared among the organizations. There appear to be significant differences in origins, goals, strategies, and structure among the multitude
of groups who spoke seriously on behalf of neighborhood organizing.
While the neo-Alinskyism of groups like ACORN represented the
most politically active and consciously left-oriented wing of the new
populism, there was another important trend in the new populism,
best exemplified by a community development orientation, which was
more localist and conservative than the neo-Alinskyite organizations.

Development-oriented organizations shared with neo-Alinskyite
groups a "let the people decide" ideology, a willingness to use conflict
tactics, and a deep frustration with the policies of elected representatives, corporate executives, and bureaucrats. They shared an opposition to social forces and public and corporate policies hostile to their
neighborhood's survival. Like most of the neo-Alinskyite neighborhood movement of the 1970s, they were generally found in blue-collar,
white "ethnic" neighborhoods where little left-oriented or civil rights
political activity took place in the 1960s, but they appeared as well in
African-American, Hispanic, and white working-class neighborhoods
with long histories of struggle. These were the neighborhoods in large
cities that experienced serious deterioration and displacement by the
mid-1970s because of redlining, absentee homeownership, blockbusting, urban renewal, gentrification, insufficient social services, and
nonexistent municipal capital improvements.

While neo-Alinskyite and community development groups overlapped in many other ways, they differed substantially in what they
saw as the problems, solutions, and future for neighborhood organizing. Simply stated, neo-Alinskyism in the 1970s sought to solve the
problems of inequality, injustice, and autocracy facing working people
by building a locally based, national movement to pressure and
change the system, perhaps even to develop a populist political party

that could wrest power from the current, corporate-dominated ones. The other trend, as one author describes it, included the host of localist neighborhood organizations that limited their focus to community development in a single, low- and moderate-income neighborhood and looked skeptically on projects "to build new institutions or amass power for 'external' uses." For them the emphasis was on maintaining and strengthening neighborhood networks and organizations, not creating social change or a new political movement.[25] They saw neighborhood decline, especially physical deterioration, fostered by working-class powerlessness, as the problem. And they sought to gain maximum benefits for the physical and economic restoration of the neighborhood by working in, maximizing benefits from, and even accepting the restraints of the existing political and economic system. Leaders in development-oriented, new populist organizations were most often the petit-bourgeoisie of the neighborhood, the owners of small homes and businesses, concerned that economic pressures were going to wipe out the value of their one major investment. Where such organizations lacked a class analysis, where they identified themselves solely as members of a racial, religious, or ethnic group, where they rejected alliances with other low- and moderate-income people outside their neighborhood and cultural group, then they, like ROAR, could take on a reactionary cast. More often, however, they adopted a conservative politics, as did the Back of the Yards Neighborhood Council and TWO, where the goals of neighborhood development and protection became paramount.

The Southeast Baltimore Community Organization (SECO) is a good example of the more localist, neighborhood development trend in the new populism. SECO began in 1966 with city council plans to put a six-lane highway through—and demolish hundreds of homes in—certain southeast neighborhoods of Baltimore.[26] A few people got upset enough to try and stop the road's destruction of the neighborhood. Southeast Baltimore is a white, working-class area of the city. Its approximately 95,000 residents in 1980 were mostly second and third generation, Eastern European immigrants—Poles, Ukrainians, Greeks, Italians, Germans, and Czechs. Southeast Baltimore was not a slum. People who lived there liked it, and have liked it for generations, which is why the residents who got together to stop neighborhood deterioration ultimately found so much community support. What got it all started was the formation of a "coalition," called SCAR (Southeast Council against the Road), to oppose the building of the highway through the neighborhood. SCAR was able to stop the development of Interstate 83 by shrewdly getting the Fell's Point neighborhood named to the national Register of Historic Places, making it off-limits to bulldozers. Community people noted with pride how this six-lane expressway "stops in downtown Baltimore as abruptly as the end of a diving board."[27] But as in hundreds of other neighborhood organizations that formed to fight "renewal" and highway projects in the late 1960s and early 1970s, the struggle in southeast Baltimore against Interstate 83 revealed that the highway was only one aspect of a much larger plan to alter the neighborhood. SCAR activists unearthed "development" plans that many people had suspected or had heard about, but about which most people felt little could be done. City planners wanted to rezone one area of the community for industry. Another section was slated for demolition and "renewal." Social services were declining throughout the area and some were in jeopardy of being eliminated entirely. For example, no new school had been built in southeast Baltimore for over a generation. As the city government had boycotted the neighborhood for decades, contributing to the neighborhood's deterioration, so banks had "redlined" it. Redlining is the practice whereby banks withhold mortgage or home improvement loans to "high risk" areas. Through this practice banks encourage a so-called "neighborhood cycle" of slow deterioration, demolition, and renewal. As the causes of southeast Baltimore's problems were brought to light, groups working independently to keep a library open, to stop a rezoning plan, and to set up a recycling center joined with SCAR to establish a community "umbrella" organization to oversee and unite all grassroots efforts.

On a rainy evening in April 1971 more than 1,000 people, representing more than 90 organizations, came to what was to be the founding meeting of SECO. From the outset SECO was a coalition of neighborhood groups—block clubs, church groups, union locals, ethnic fraternal organizations—begun, in the Alinsky mold, by uniting leaders from local organizations and institutions and thereby grounding the community organization in the traditional structures of the people who live there. And, like Alinsky organizations, SECO initially used direct action, confrontation tactics to achieve its goals. Mothers with baby carriages blocked and diverted truck traffic to keep trucks off of residential streets. A wheelchair protest march helped keep open the community's only public nursing home. An ongoing battle with city officials secured lower density zoning and thereby discouraged further subdivision of homes into rental units. SECO stopped the library from being shut down; it demanded and secured improved services from the city, including two new schools. It organized housing inspection teams, a neighborhood-based health cooperative, a public school reform program, and a youth diversion project, which is said to have successfully reduced neighborhood juvenile delinquency recidivism rates.

SECO members, working closely with city officials, also got the local Department of Housing and Community Development to formally investigate the practice of redlining by local savings and loan associations. The commissioner's report confirmed SECO's claims, concluding that most of the city's lending businesses were practicing redlining. Neighborhood residents, especially homeowners, united to fight against the banks, whom they now knew to be major contributors to the neighborhood's decline. In a compromise with SECO, the banks agreed to stop redlining Baltimore's poorer neighborhoods if southeast neighborhood people supported lifting the 8 percent usury ceiling imposed by the state legislature. This compromise seems to have marked the end of SECO's "confrontational" phase and the beginning of its neighborhood development approach. The change is one quite similar to that which occurred in other Alinsky organizations, the BYNC and TWO most notably.

Organizers and activists in SECO never completely agreed on what the organization stood for or on what goals it ultimately sought to accomplish, other than defending the neighborhood and advancing neighborhood interests. Even in its confrontational phase it was always willing to work with, even depend on, city officials, like the commissioner of housing and community development. Barbara Mikulski, the "godmother of SECO" who was later elected to the city council, the U.S. House of Representatives, and the U.S. Senate, put it this way: "We knew we had to be tough and militant. But the 'issue' was always the enemy. And we knew the very institutions that we challenged were the ones that we would have to work with when peace broke out. So it was never 'the Mayor is our enemy' or 'the City Council is the enemy.' We never attacked people. We attacked issues."[28]

Nevertheless, SECO never spoke on behalf of the need for fundamental political, economic, and social change in Baltimore and the United States in general. Some of the more leftist members, however, believed so privately and argued their position within the organization. What ultimately happened, as was the case in so many other new populist groups in the 1970s, was that SECO split over the direction of the organization. Those more to the left saw SECO becoming just another part of the establishment, another "successful" neighborhood development agency able to improve the quality of some aspects of the neighborhood but unwilling to tackle the broader problem of powerlessness faced by low- and moderate-income people. They argued that only through struggle and confrontation at the neighborhood, city, state, and national level could the political power and economic security of working people be raised sufficiently to give them effective participation in determining the future of their communities, not to mention their own lives.

SECO's first president, Jack Gleason, saw the problem differently. "We knew we could stop the city from doing things through the usual confrontation tactics. But if we were going to achieve the revitalization of southeast Baltimore, there were things *we* had to do, from the positive standpoint—housing, school reform, and so on. That's when we went into the neighborhood economic development stage."[29] Many others, inside and outside the neighborhood, supported the shift in priorities. Robert Cassidy, discussing the SECO experience in his *Livable Cities,* suggests that the litmus test of a neighborhood organization's maturity is when it effectively uses, as did SECO, both organizing/confrontation tactics *and* development/partnership strategies.

In SECO's case the immediate results seemed to reinforce the revitalization strategy. Because it was outside the channels of power, SECO's tactics were initially confrontational. But it learned that effecting modest reforms in an urban environment is not that difficult, at least for predominantly white, multiclass neighborhoods, if conditions are right and neighborhoods are willing, if need be, to collectively and openly challenge the economic and political powers in the city. SECO established Neighborhood Housing Services as a community corporation with bankers and neighborhood residents on the board of directors. In its first three years the service helped 245 families become homeowners and assisted another 100 with house renovations. SECO formed a partnership with government, business, and other institutions to create Southeast Development, Inc., which created jobs and business opportunities for neighborhood residents. It also established a community-controlled company—Southeast Arts and Crafts—that produced and marketed the crafts of elderly and handicapped residents; a primary health-care facility that served 3,000 patients a month; and the Highlandtown Revitalization Corporation, which gave technical assistance to merchants. SECO also received a grant from the Ford Foundation to buy attractive properties before real estate speculators did so.

In a six-year period SECO grew from an organization with a single underpaid community organizer working out of a church basement to one with a staff of 41, a budget of $650,000, and responsibility for another $16 million in neighborhood programs. In a nutshell, southeast Baltimore was no longer the unattractive slum area banks and city officials used to see it as. "SECO has restored entire blocks of new houses. It has restored community pride," one commentator applauded. "In short, southeast Baltimore has become a classic model for reviving the inner city."[30]

Lest we too get carried away with these results, the history of localist, self-help neighborhood organizations in working-class neighborhoods questions SECO's long-term potential and underlines the difficulty of replicating even such a short-term, new populist success. At certain unique times and places, the interests of specific neighborhoods, brought to light and advanced by insurgent and aggressive neighborhood organizations, are not incompatible with the interests of the business community and politicians. The primary concern of the economic and power elite in declining cities in the post–World War II era has been the revitalization of the central business district. In Pittsburgh the revitalization project was called "The Golden Triangle." In Detroit, it was "Renaissance Center." In other cities, like San Antonio, Boston, and Portland, Maine, it is the River, Waterfront, or Old Port District. While the focus is on revitalizing the downtown commercial area to attract business investment and the more affluent back to once declining urban centers, demands from certain neighborhoods whose upgrading could support the city's revitalization, and perhaps even house a new urban "gentry," are not ignored as they normally might be.[31]

Nevertheless, improvement activities that benefit working-class residents are few and far between. As Phillip Clay writes in *Neighborhood Renewal,* "The bootstrap efforts [of the 1970s] are credited with reversing the imminent decay and cynicism that have plagued low- and moderate-income neighborhoods." But such efforts at "incumbent upgrading," Clay suggests, are "manifestly small." Self-help efforts at rehabilitating a rundown neighborhood make for good news copy and neoconservative boosterism, so the media and business groups exaggerate and romanticize these developments. But the extent and impact of such neighborhood renewal efforts are quickly diminished when compared with the number of families who continue to move to the suburbs, who are pushed out of declining neighborhoods by disinvestment, or who are ultimately forced from upgraded or gentrified neighborhoods by rising rents and tax assessments and by new, white-collar, professional residents.[32] Another commentator suggests that the next step for successful upgrading efforts, like that of SECO, might well be "to mobilize to prevent the improvements it sought from backfiring." It would be ironic, though not unusual, Robert Rosenbloom adds, if the people who fought successfully to restore and preserve their communities found themselves powerless to resist the process of neighborhood gentrification.[33]

The strategy of SECO was not to stop "upgrading." Rather the goal was to get as much out of it for the neighborhood's middle- and working-class residents by working with and within the existing system. At the neighborhood level, it is interest-group politics pure and simple. For those with power already, interest-group politics can succeed. For working-class people, like those in southeast Baltimore, the community development strategy succeeds for a time under highly auspicious conditions, but ultimately it works only in proportion to the size, power, activism, and threat of militancy of the neighborhood organization. A single-neighborhood organization is ultimately too small to effect the necessary changes in, and counter the existing pressures against, a low- and moderate-income community. In comparison, while the neo-Alinskyite emphasis on developing statewide and mass-based organizations has its limits, it clearly recognizes the need for a national "people's organization" that could begin to address the underlying causes of community transformation that rest outside and beyond any one neighborhood.

Building Confidence and Developing Working-Class Women Organizers

[Organizing] is building confidence. It is saying, "Hell, if I can do it, you can do it. If I can stand up and have something to say, so can you." It is telling them you are a person, an individual; you've been

kicked around long enough, the hell with this noise—they can't do that to you. I like you; let's have at them.

—Phyllis Hanson, neighborhood organizer

Serious limitations notwithstanding, there was a power and potential to the new populism of the 1970s, especially neo-Alinskyism, that seemed to reflect the beginnings of a political realignment in the United States. The great hope of the movement, as Roger Friedland wrote in 1975, was that "by transforming urban daily life into national partisan issues, the large number of poor and working class people who have no meaningful connection or place in the national electoral system could be given choices that make a difference."[34] To their credit, community organizers, leaders, and members were able to develop a nascent national grassroots movement in a decade—the 1970s—when there was no single catalytic issue. New populist victories in Burlington, Vermont, and Santa Monica, California reflected not only individual successes or unique circumstances but the budding of organizing efforts nurtured throughout the nation during the decade.

One thing is for certain, however: new populist organizing in the 1970s raised the personal self-respect and political consciousness of tens of thousands of Americans. If it is true, as Lawrence Goodwyn suggested in his study of agrarian populism in the nineteenth century, *The Populist Moment,* that democratic movements are initiated only by people who have attained a high degree of personal self-respect, then the new populism, as well as its new left predecessor, made a significant contribution to any future progressive movement that develops in this country. A truly democratic society cannot develop without a confident and skilled citizenry capable of self-government. To the extent that people are given dignity, self-respect, political knowledge, and confidence they tend not to be intimidated by highly educated government officials, professionals, and corporate leaders, and they are certainly less willing to accept continued injustices. As organizer Si Kahn expressed it: "The dignity that comes from self-esteem is one of the most important tools the organizer can give to poor people. Belief in one's dignity as a man or a woman is one of the strongest motivating factors; from it comes the refusal to be used or abused, the assertion that 'I been pushed around too long, and I ain't gonna be pushed around no more.'"[35]

People learned a good deal about democracy from their experience in neighborhood organizations in the 1970s. They learned that authority can be challenged, that people generate power in numbers, that there is a long and important history of insurgent people's movements in the United States. They learned to work together politically and to see how "being political" meant more than voting or participating in electoral politics; it meant taking responsibility for and doing something about the decisions that affect your life. In the process people learned about themselves, their neighbors, their community, and, to a lesser extent, the larger political and economic system. Activism opened their eyes and made them conscious historical actors. "[Public officials] think we're all very stupid and we don't know what's going on. . . . They just automatically assume we're ignorant. . . . Awareness. That's the thing that [the organization] has given us, awareness," was how one working-class woman activist in Chicago put it.[36]

Organizers learned, too. Alinskyism assumes that people get and stay involved in community organizations out of self-interest. They get involved to put up a traffic light, expand a park, stop a highway, or oppose a slumlord. But neo-Alinskyite organizers came to learn that successful organizations are not built on self-interest alone. Rather, a central element is the vision the organization advances and how it raises people's expectations about themselves, their families, and their communities. If an organization is effective, people come to see themselves and their participation differently after only a few "self-interest" victories. If people stay involved, organizers learned, they do so to develop themselves personally and to accomplish the larger sense of purpose that being involved in the organization has opened to them. As Heather Booth noted, people "*stay* involved not simply for self-interest but for broader reasons—the sense of power and of community, of living out their idealism and their vision."[37]

Nowhere has the impact of the new populism on personal and political development been more pronounced than its work with working-class women. As a result of the women's movement of the 1970s, college-educated women began to play increasingly larger roles as both organizers, leaders, and active members in social change efforts. Of course, upper- and middle-class women have always played important roles in neighborhood organizations. From the settlements to SNCC and SDS, women did much of the day-to-day organizing while men got most of the credit for it. Women from affluent backgrounds have typically had the time and opportunity necessary to devote to political and social work, if they were so inclined. Settlement houses and most of the social welfare organizing projects of the Progressive era were staffed largely by women, and while men assumed leadership roles in far greater frequency than their total number, women too, like Jane Addams, Mary Simkhovitch, and Lillian Wald, were nationally prominent advocates of the movement. More commonly, women have played fundamental but less visible roles in neighborhood organizing efforts. In the 1930s, for example, women played active roles in the CPUSA and the Unemployed Councils, but again men assumed the public leadership positions.

As noted earlier, the upper-and middle-class women who joined the SDS community organizing projects in the early 1960s faced similar circumstances. Women played key organizing roles in ERAP, but their history was one of male domination. Men and women did the organizing, the going from door to door, the endless hours of going to meetings and talking with people. But the men in the organization, up until the late 1960s when the women's movement began to emerge, assumed and held the key leadership and decision-making roles.[38]

Working-class and minority women have also played important roles in neighborhood organizing efforts, though rarely in prominent, leadership positions. From the earliest days of the tenant movement in New York City around the turn of the nineteenth century, for example, working-class women pioneered as protest organizers in their buildings.[39] Many of the organizers in SNCC were black women from working-class and sharecropping backgrounds. These are not isolated examples. Nevertheless, the white working-class housewife has historically been the least likely person to get involved as an organizer or leader in community political activity. In the new populism, however, these women began to follow the paths of traditionally more activist black and college-educated women. As Kathleen McCourt describes in a study of women active in neighborhood organizations in the 1970s on Chicago's Southwest Side, "In many of these new assertive community organizations, still struggling for strength and direction, women offer important leadership. Often, too, women are the most active and most numerous rank-and-file members. All along women have been supplying the bodies for demonstrations; they are now beginning to make decisions, speak publicly, and assume more responsible positions in the organizations."[40]

Getting actively involved in a neighborhood organization, struggling on a daily basis with important political and social questions, is an

exciting and empowering experience for most people, and it was especially so for those working-class housewives who tended to shy away
from public, political, and leadership roles. Involvement often brought
with it dramatic personal and political changes. Participation gave
activists a better sense of their power as individuals, as workers, and
as women. It was not uncommon for working-class women to begin to
see themselves relatively quickly as natural community organizers. "I
think it's the women on these [community] issues who have to take
the stand. We need men, but they can only give so much of their
time," was how one participant put it. "We have the contact in the community . . . my husband doesn't know the number of people in the
community that I know just by virtue of involvement in the school."
Another said, "For my husband to be involved in the community, it's
jeopardizing a little bit of that security he has. . . . I don't think they
can take the chance that a woman can take."[41]

Activism in new populist neighborhood organizations led many
working-class women to become more cynical about and angry with
public officials and corporate leaders, but this did not lead them to
political defeatism or despair. On the contrary, their organizing experience generally empowered them. It gave them a better sense of self-
esteem, a confidence in their ability to convince others to fight back
and join the organization, a confidence in their abilities vis-à-vis traditional power brokers. This was often a dramatic political break-
through. As one woman described: "I always thought [politicians and
corporate officials] were probably very shrewd, very wise, had minds
like computers—and they don't. And that came to me as a kind of a
shock and it helped my ego and I wasn't afraid to fight them. They're
just ordinary human beings. They're not very bright at all. . . . You
don't have to fear them at all as far as your mind being able to cope
with their mind, not at all. And that helps you."[42]

Participation also affected women's home life and attitudes toward
the community, the former being stretched, oftentimes both being
strengthened. In many working-class households the participation of
women in public roles and in organizations where cross-sex friend-
ships were developed often caused strains with their husbands. What
usually happened, as one woman put it, was "now he had to adjust to a
new reality." Sometimes the new reality threatened marriages; more
often it created new roles and forged new bonds. In both cases, however, the role of the women was strengthened. Regarding the community, activist women tended to develop greater emotional attachments

to the community than nonactivists. Their lives became filled with an excitement and challenge rarely experienced before. Community organizing is a challenge and growth experience for anyone. It is not uncommon to hear organizers in ACORN or other neo-Alinskyite efforts say that their skills were tested more strenuously and that they learned more from a year of community work than from their entire four years at college. For working-class women, their new role was equally demanding and energizing.

Without doubt the new populism of the 1970s and especially the neo-Alinskyite trend, was quite skillful in introducing working-class women to neighborhood organizing. The legacy of the decade may be in its development of working-class leaders—both men and women— who continue to be politically involved and who know how to build organizations, pressure city hall, write leaflets, build coalitions, and organize demonstrations. In the 1970s, a vast number of people got experience doing neighborhood organizing and learned the necessary skills to build insurgent community organizations. What they tended to lack was a knowledge of political and economic systems and an alternative vision. Without such knowledge and vision there was the possibility that the nature and direction of the organizations people learned to build would perpetuate rather than solve their needs. The task of the 1980s was therefore to consolidate the people who received training and experience in the 1970s around a clearer left political vision and agenda than had been offered by the new populism of the 1970s.

Chapter Six

Community Organizing in the Conservative 1980s

The Economic Crisis Continues and Worsens

The dirty little secret about the 1980s is: In economic terms, it was America's worst decade since World War II.

—Walter Russell Mead, author

We live in a society that is like a house on fire, and it's arson.

—Heather Booth, organizer

It really is not much of a secret. The United States has been in an economic crisis since the early 1970s. This is the third consecutive decade of economic decline. True, as defenders of supply-side economics would argue in rebuttal, the economy expanded from 1983 through 1990 and price inflation fell from the double-digit highs of the late 1970s. The approximately 30 million people who earned between $50,000 and $200,000 per year did well. And those at the top flourished, so much so that being a millionaire, the epitome of wealth 20 years before, was dubbed "meaningless" by one conservative commentator. By the end of the decade there were some 100,000 "decamillionaires," those whose worth is above $10 million.[1] These were the symbols of the decade's economic success. The goal of "supply-side" economic policy, as promoted by economists Milton Friedman and Arthur Laffer, was to unleash the creativity and daring of American entrepreneurs, whose success, wealth, and reinvestment would "trickle down" to all segments.

In fact, as the authors of *After the Wasteland,* a critique of U.S. political economy, argue, "the much vaunted economic recovery of the 1980s did little or nothing to pull the country out of the economic crisis that began in the late 1960s and deepened during the 1970s and early 1980s."[2] Throughout the decade the average weekly wage fell, so that by 1990 it was back to $258, which wiped out about half the gains U.S. workers had made since World War II. The percentage of employees working full-time and earning a low wage—currently defined as less than $12,195—increased from 12 percent in 1979 to 18 percent in 1990. Low-wage work even increased among college graduates, from 6.2 percent to 10.5 percent.[3] More banks failed between 1989 and 1991 than in all the years from the end of the depression until 1980.[4] This was notwithstanding the savings and loan scandals and bailout, which will cost the American people some $500 billion. Key economic indicators such as output and productivity growth and investment and profit rates, in addition to real wage growth, were well below levels of the 1950s and 1960s. Homeownership declined precipitously. Overwhelming trade deficits turned us from the largest creditor to the greatest debtor nation.

"Military Keynesianism" continued fueling the economy and the federal deficit soared as massive allocations to the military were accompanied by tax cuts for the rich. Under Ronald Reagan's presidency the top personal tax bracket dropped from 70 percent to 28 percent in only seven years. The 1986 tax reform law, sponsored by Republicans and Democrats, reduced the tax on the top income bracket from 38.5 percent to 28 percent, while the next lower income bracket actually paid a higher rate of 33 percent. Corporate and capital gains taxes followed suit. The fundamental policy was to collect less from those who could afford it most.[5] Corporate mergers, buyouts, and leverages were so common that they became the subjects of daily conversation, TV programs, and movies. This "paper entrepreneurialism," in which assets simply change hands, turned millionaires into billionaires. It also intensified the decline in economic productivity, adding nothing in terms of investment in new plants, equipment, products, processes, or research.[6]

The economic crisis results from factors discussed in chapter 5. In response to the worldwide economic competition that began in the late 1960s and early 1970s and that replaced the glory and growth years of unchallenged U.S. economic hegemony, political and corporate leaders in the United States developed a neoconservative strategy to assist American business and the wealthy. But this strategy of sacrifice for most and benefits for few did not work. It benefited only some multinational corporations that were able to concentrate their power, a handful of people who were not affluent before and happened to be in the right place at the right time with the right skills, and, most of all, those who were already wealthy. In the 1980s the rich got much richer while the society around them deteriorated.

Numerous studies, by authors on both the right and the left, document the extraordinary redistribution of income upward in the United States during the 1980s.[7] The top 1 percent of income after taxes in 1990 almost equalled that of the bottom 40 percent; in 1980 the top 1 percent had only half the total income of the bottom 40 percent.[8] Of the total income gain from 1977 to 1989, 70 percent went to the richest 1 percent of Americans.[9] The incidence of poverty, declining in the late 1960s and early 1970s, jumped again to 1964 levels, hitting women, children, and people of color the hardest.[10] The figures are staggering. Twenty percent of all children in the United States are poor and 40 percent of the poor are children. Moreover, about 40 percent of poor families have incomes equivalent to half the poverty line or less. It is impossible, for example, to raise two teenagers in a major U.S. city on less than $5,000 a year. The United States has the terrible distinction of being the only major industrial nation where children are the largest impoverished group, and disproportionately these are African-American and Latino children. In most of our major cities 50 percent of the children of color are growing up in poverty, often in households way below the poverty line. In Texas, where at least one in four children live in poverty, 42 percent of African-American children, 43 percent of Hispanic children, and 9.7 percent Anglo children are poor.[11]

Arson may be a strong word, but these conditions did not come about by accident. Neoconservative politicians such as Ronald Reagan, George Bush, and their corporate supporters implemented a politics of deregulation, new tax laws, capital gains benefits, and a host of other policies to aid the affluent. At the same time they sought to eliminate policies such as affirmative action; cut expenditures for food stamps, Aid to Families with Dependent Children, Medicaid, and 57 other social programs; and loosen public regulation of and responsibility for worker safety, environmental standards, and even public education, that helped not only the poor but the middle class. The 'architects of neoconservative policy, such as David Stockman and Edwin Meese, threw the responsibility for social and public services back on the states, which did not have the economic resources or capability to handle it. As things grew worse many neoconservative analysts, most prominently George Gilder and Charles Murray, blamed government and the victims. The conditions of the poor, people of color, women, children, and people with AIDS were said to be due to the pathological behavior of the "underclass," or to drug use, unwed single mothers, promiscuity, broken families, and homosexuality. As Gilder argued in *Wealth and Poverty,* "in order to move up, the poor must not only work, they must work harder than the classes above them. Every previous generation of the lower class has made such efforts. But the current poor, white even more than black, are refusing to work hard."[12]

Worst hit were cities, from which most middle- and upper-class people fled. As the federal government removed support and as city tax bases eroded, affordable housing became increasingly scarce and jobs, especially manufacturing jobs, left town. Inner-city poverty rose from 30 percent of all poor people in 1968 to 43 percent in 1988. Federal spending on cities fell more than 60 percent from 1981 to 1992; the federal share of city budgets plummeted from 18 percent in 1980 to 6.4 percent in 1990.[13] Crime rates, drug use, racial and ethnic conflict, gang violence, infant mortality, teen pregnancy, homelessness, inadequate health care, and AIDS, to name but the most publicized problems, all increased in staggering and alarming proportions. Urban infrastructures collapsed after years of neglect.

The impact varied from city to city and year to year. Capital had never before moved so easily or rapidly. Information technology moves money around the world in seconds. Booms and busts now strike cities with astonishing rapidity. Houston and the sunbelt boomed in the early 1980s as the frostbelt suffered the flight of capital to better "investment sites." Then capital investment, primarily in real estate and manufacturing, left the sunbelt, forging prosperous cities on both coasts. Boston, Baltimore, Seattle, Portland (Maine and

Oregon) all did well while middle America, the supposed source of supporters for Republican politics, suffered most. By the early 1990s coastal cities like Los Angeles and Boston were in the grip of serious recessions while capital began to return slowly to areas with depressed real estate markets and lower wage rates, such as sunbelt cities like Houston and some Great Lakes factory towns.

Primary cities, like New York, Chicago, and Philadelphia, boom in good times and buckle under critical fiscal crises when they are no longer "hot." Small and medium-sized cities with fewer resources and less diverse economies, like the once thriving industrial towns of Flint, Michigan, and Bridgeport, Connecticut, barely survive or go bankrupt, while cities like Portland, Maine, bob up and down on the wave of the next boom or bust. Few cities have enough resources to address their problems. To survive they must channel scarce resources to uses that position them better in the global economy, where the principal activities include corporate and government management, investment, entertainment, and tourism. But in all cities social problems worsen. Many wondered, along with a feature article in *Newsweek* in 1991, "Are Cities Obsolete?"[14]

The disastrous conditions of our cities pose serious obstacles to progressive neighborhood organizers. Some are new: crack cocaine drug use and escalated violence have residents clamoring for tighter controls, more authoritarian tactics, less democracy. Others are old, but vastly expanded in scope and magnitude, such as poverty or racial and ethnic tension. The solutions to these problems far exceed the grasp of any single neighborhood or city. Complicating these conditions is the politics of privatization. "Free-market" thinking, policies, and programs—the hallmarks of the global economy and politics in the United States in the 1980s and early 1990s—pose serious new structural challenges to organizers.

Those who hatched the neoconservative strategy in the early 1970s, ,as discussed in chapter 5, knew that the nation could not continue to provide both "guns and butter" if corporate profits were to continue to increase in a highly competitive global economy. For the strategy to succeed, proponents of liberal social change and supporters of government social programs and services had to be muzzled.[15] Social programs raise social costs. They boost wage rates and either increase the deficit or increase taxes. Meanwhile, various New Right movements, such as religious fundamentalism and antifeminism, gained legitimacy and support in the atmosphere of social conservatism that permeated the White House during the Reagan-Bush years. Right-wing views on everything from education to abortion began to dominate public debate, pushing political discourse in the nation farther right and the proponents of progressive social change on the defensive.[16]

But the central component of neoconservative strategy to keep social costs down and free up capital was the ideology of privatization, of free-market economics. In this view unrestrained capitalism is blessed and government evil. Capitalism means economic growth and profits; the government stifles them. Neoconservatives such as Jack Kemp, echoing earlier free marketers such as Edward Banfield, said liberal government social programs caused poverty, destroyed inner-city families, created dependency, undermined values and traditional social controls, and generally wreaked havoc on American cities.[17]

This ideology quickly captured the attention of American politicians and the media. The laissez-faire capitalist vision of the National Association of Manufacturers and Chamber of Commerce was now back in favor. For them, *laissez-faire* meant government "assistance" on the side of business when business wanted it, not government "intervention." No longer, the credo went, was government responsible for the social welfare of its citizenry. Government could conduct armed interventions in Grenada, Panama, and Iraq, and, of course, build more prisons. ("When there's no social program, always there's a violence program," opined journalist Alexander Cockburn.[18]) Now the private sector, with the assistance of local government, would be responsible for solving social problems. George Bush counted on the enlightened self-interest of business and private citizens—those renowned "thousand points of light"—to pick up, at least in token fashion, the social concerns dropped by the public sector. Actually, most federal programs were too embedded in American political and social life to be dismantled. The essence of privatization on the federal level meant deregulation and delegitimization for social programs. The federal government was no longer interested in spending money to address social problems.

In *The Private City* Sam Bass Warner, Jr., puts this strategy in proper historical perspective.

Under the American tradition, the first purpose of the citizen is the private search for wealth; the goal of a city is to be a community of private money makers. . . . The private market's demand for workers, its capacities for dividing land, building houses, stores and factories, and its needs for public services have determined the shape and quality of America's big cities. What the private market could do well American cities have done well; what the private market did badly, or neglected, our cities have been unable to overcome. . . . The twentieth-century failure of urban America to create a humane environment is thus the story of an enduring tradition of privatism in a changing world."[19]

Privatization strategies here refers less to the turning over of government functions to for-profit business and more to the wholesale privatization of economic, social, and cultural life, that is, turning over cities, states, and the nation to corporate values, needs, directives, and leaders. Neoconservatives such as Stuart Butler argue that the marketplace solves social problems better than government programs *and* empowers people at the neighborhood level.[20] In the hands of self-described "communitarian conservative" William Schambra, a director in the Department of Health and Human Services in the Bush administration, this argument sounds reasonable and appropriate:

More and more, it is understood within the highest reaches of the federal government that our most urgent social problems—drug abuse, the spread of AIDS, infant mortality, teen pregnancy, homicide and violence—result precisely from a collapse of genuine local communities, and the structures that generate, collect, refine, and reflect local values and political beliefs. All too often in the past, we now see, the federal government contributed to this process by absorbing functions and authority from—thereby undermining—local communities. . . . I draw great encouragement from this sort of shift in policy focus—away from cumbersome, centralized bureaucratic programs, toward policy that is rooted deeply in the wisdom, values, and democratically determined wishes of the local community.[21]

Privatization is touted as the democratic alternative to a costly, unresponsive social democratic state. The free market lets the people decide. They are empowered by being assimilated into the business milieu in their communities. Through self-help strategies they empower themselves, determine their needs, and decide how to meet them.

In reality privatization has meant the opposite for our cities. The attempt to dismantle and delegitimize the public sector has burdened communities with few resources while simultaneously encouraging the development of insufficient self-help efforts. As Gale Cincotta of National People's Action puts it: "The message, ringing out clear across the land, from federal government and its bureaucrats, from

Congress and Big Business, is that low-income people should pull themselves up by the bootstraps on the boots they don't have."[22] Not only do social needs not get met, privatization tends to result in a "load shedding" of public responsibility. It makes citizen action, actually almost all public activity, more difficult. Paul Starr, in a critique of privatization, offers that "the removal of decisions from the public arena diminishes the individual incentive for community participation."[23] Certainly the "use of the political process to control 'private' activity," argue Susan and Norman Fainstein, "is vastly more difficult than employing it to affect government itself."[24] And Jeffrey Henig notes that privatization shifts "key decisions to an arena in which market power is the dominant currency, and the poor are well aware that this is an arena in which their victories come very hard indeed."[25]

More than that, privatization withdraws the public targets to undermine those groups whose needs, if addressed, would increase society's social costs. Privatization delegitimizes social action, dissolving public issues into private matters.[26] Seen from this perspective, current privatization strategies seek to remove government responsibility and accountability for the welfare of citizens and society so that social claims on the government—whether for more AIDS research, tighter restrictions on toxic waste dumping, or increased welfare benefits— are seen as illegitimate and anachronistic. As R. Emmett Tyrell, Jr., put the right-wing argument, rather flamboyantly:

The chloroform of egalitarianism was spread everywhere in the 1970s. Prior American values of self-reliance, personal liberty, and competence were heaved overboard. . . . Along with this abandonment of older American values came a new class of busybodies to elucidate the new hokum and to harass the productive elements of the Republic. The welfare state had turned many therefore toiling Americans into parasites, and this new class of busybodies lived as superparasites, deriving nourishment from the dependence of the welfare clients.[27]

As argued in the conclusion of this book, new social movement theory suggests that a primary target for contemporary grassroots efforts must be a responsible public sector. Organizing at the site of production (the factory) in a postindustrial society is not enough. Effective community organizing requires a legitimate and accountable public sector and a zeitgeist, a spirit of the time, that encourages its citizens to be active in public life. Privatization represents a serious threat to both.[28]

In sum, neoconservative politics called forth a harsh paradox. The drive to privatize that intensified urban problems and thus made community mobilization more important also made community social action more difficult.

The Reemergence of Voluntarism

Our belief is that the resources to solve community problems are at our fingertips. They lie in loaned talent and expertise, in cooperation and dedication, in thorough planning, and in careful implementation. They lie within the goodness and concern of all Houstonians for the well being of our community.

—Houston Committee for Private Sector Initiatives

Today you have to find ways to resemble the real for-profit world. Otherwise you won't be around.

—Joe Giron, Brothers Redevelopment, Inc.

Yesterday's neighborhood organizer is today's not-for-profit enterpriser. . . . Corrective capitalism is in.

—M. W. Newman and Lillian Williams, Chicago *Sun-Times* reporters

Neoconservative policies and global restructuring put community organization in ambiguous circumstances. On the one hand, grassroots voluntarism grew considerably in the 1980s. There are now millions of community-based, self-help groups working on a wide range of issues. In every large city, small town, and rural area, voluntary community organizations help address local problems. The United States has long been renowned for its voluntary organizations, though the penchant for voluntarism that Alexis de Tocqueville wrote about in the 1830s increasingly took a back seat in the twentieth century as centralized state responsibility for citizen welfare expanded in the Progressive, New Deal, and Great Society eras. In the 1980s and 1990s, however, voluntary citizen action organizations reemerged as a dominant strategy to address social problems.

This reemergence results partly from the proliferation of new social movement groups developing their own self-help efforts, such as women organizing domestic violence shelters or gay men building AIDS community centers. But the voluntary sector expanded primarily because of the decline in public social services that accompanied privatization policies. More than ever before, community organizations, such as neighborhood centers, housing and community development projects, social service agencies, cultural and arts societies, and nonprofit health care institutions, assumed functions previously shouldered by the government. "Policies designed to shift responsibilities to voluntary groups," geographer Jennifer Wolch notes, "led to an explosion in the aggregate size of the voluntary sector."[29] There was not a shift of power to the grassroots but rather a disavowal by—and in some cases the inability of—those with power to exercise it on behalf of those without it.

The explosion in volunteerism is the plus side for neighborhood organizers. Gary Delgado of the Applied Research Center, in a study of community organizing in communities of color, noted the following organizational configurations: single-issue mobilizations, like the Committee against Police Violence in Los Angeles; professional advocacy organizations, such as the NAACP or LULAC (League of United Latin American Citizens); economic development efforts, such as community development corporations (CDCs); immigrant rights organizations, like La Mujer Obera in El Paso; community-based workplace initiatives, such as Fightback in New York; multiracial community organizations, like DARE in Providence, Rhode Island; and single race, multi-issue organizations, such as Native Action in Montana.[30] The proliferation can be seen in every city in the nation.

The negative side is that the explosion results more from push than pull factors. Although those involved in social justice work are drawn to citizen activism by their politics, ideology, and heritage and some have been involved since the 1960s and before, most are pushed into it. Mounting social problems and cutbacks in public funding for social and public programs during the 1980s drove people into community organizing. In the absence of social programs and policies, people got involved. Power in the United States, however, became more, not less, concentrated in the 1980s. Consequently, these citizen initiatives had to address massive problems with scanty resources and the knowledge that most problems originate far beyond community borders.

The mismatch is evident: organizations proliferate, but social conditions worsen.

Some of the mismatch results from neoconservative forays into neighborhood organizing; such activism is no longer the sole province of the liberal, left populist, or radical organizers of the 1960s and 1970s. Because its decentralized organizational form mirrors corporate restructuring efforts, serves as an alternative to public and federal programs and costs much less, community organizing has been embraced by neoconservatives. The neoconservative movement, in fact, sees itself, not the New Left and new social movements, as the true proponent of "the community revolution" of the 1960s and 1970s.[31] Community-based efforts, New Right advocates proclaim, give "power back to the people" by "allowing local people and organizations to take the lead in tackling their own problems and opportunities—with the minimum of outside interference."[32] And by outside interference they mean the federal government and radical organizers.

Of course, such proponents of community organizing are not new to the 1980s. There is a long history of community organizing designed to protect property and strong conservative traditions to oppose social change, as discussed in chapter 3. But in the past even the reactionary and conservative forms of organizing tended to be indigenous efforts, grounded in the reasonable, if sometimes unjust and parochial, claims of workers, and peasants before them, who sought to protect what little they had.[33] Current neoconservative community programs differ. Their business-like efforts tend to be initiated from above by corporate leaders and groups or heavily influenced by "partnerships" with banks and other businesses. They seek to demonstrate in small projects such as community development corporations or "enterprise zone" ventures the advantage of private sector over public sector initiatives and decentralized over centralized social interventions. They try to demonstrate a shared, mutual interest between the poor and oppressed on the one hand and the economically privileged and politically connected on the other.

Most grassroots efforts do not see voluntarism this way. To put it mildly, "the reasons for the new emphasis on voluntarism are not everywhere the same."[34] The Neo-Alinskyite Industrial Areas Foundation (IAF) organizes public schools, registers voters, supports and opposes bond proposals, holds "accountability" sessions with politicians, and builds low-income housing. Jobs with Justice organizes public sector workers and builds solidarity between union and new social movement groups. Gay activists offer AIDS prevention work-shops or hospices. Social ministry workers cultivate community garden projects. All seek to address community problems, empower citizens at the community level through self-help projects, and demonstrate the chronic need for more public funding. Their aim is to meet community needs and to attract more people to a politics and vision of social, economic, and political democracy, one that will challenge the prerogatives and processes of corporate and political elites. The goals of new populist grassroots voluntarism—be they to stop toxic dumping or open a multiservice center in a poor, racially and ethnically segregated community—reflect its left-wing populist heritage and roots in the oppositional social movements of the past generation.

The neopopulist and neoconservative movements are at opposite ends of the class struggle. They do agree, at least in theory, that decentralized, grassroots structures offer numerous advantages over centralized public and private service programs. These include a decreased bureaucracy, greater efficiency, cheaper costs, increased innovation, heightened sensitivity to local conditions, extended services to heretofore ignored groups, enhanced potential for individual and collective empowerment, commitment to the theory and practice of grassroots democracy, restored civic life at the community level, and greater diversity in terms of who gets to participate in the decision-making process.[35]

Curiously, another stretch of common ground has emerged, one forced on all community activists by the conservatism of the 1980s and early 1990s. Most activists agree that dissent and confrontation are less salient than in the past. Mass protests, direct action, and citizen resistance are labeled icons of the 1960s. Organizers must now be more "proactive," more development minded. Neo-Alinsky organizer Shel Trapp sees that change as a natural progression. Defend the neighborhood, then take an "offensive" stance. "That's when you start to link development with organizing."[36] Robert Rivera, an IAF organizer, argues similarly: "There are two types of organizing. One that is *for,* the other is *against.* Now you have to be *for* something. It's a different style of organizing."[37] But at play in the 1980s was more than a shift in the "life cycle" of organizing. Community economic development and the building of community partnerships with local economic and political powers became the dominant form of neighborhood organizing because of the demands and constraints of organizing in a neoconservative political economy. Organizers were willing to rewrite history (good organizing has always been *for* things) in an effort to distance themselves from the radicalism of the past, maintain current support, and/or tap new private revenue sources.

Community Economic Development

"Local governments have become openly preoccupied with economic development almost everywhere," write John Logan and Todd Swanstrom in *Beyond the City Limits*, "and most will say it is their first priority."[38] As public economic support for communities, social services, and social problems declined because of lack of interest or opposition at the federal level and shrinking tax bases at the local, and as political discourse in the nation revolved around free-market solutions to all problems, community efforts moved into the business of economic development, partnerships with local businesses, and more consensual strategies. This is nowhere more evident than in the rapid growth of community development corporations (CDCs).

The focus on economic development is not a new phenomenon. John Davis, housing director for Burlington, Vermont, argues that indigenous property interests are the foundation of all neighborhood organizing and that people in neighborhood organizations act collectively on interests endemic to the locality itself.[39] "These common interests of property and place provide a basis for collective action even in the most communally and productively denuded locality." People organize over "rights of tenure," the right to stay put.[40] Davis's definition is too narrow to accommodate all the neighborhood organizing types discussed in this book, but it does place current CDC efforts in a neighborhood maintenance tradition tied to the individualist, capitalist foundation of private real estate in the United States and the desire of residents—homeowners, those who want to be homeowners, and tenants to a lesser extent—to protect their turf or improve their economic situation.

Others see the emphasis on community economic development as more recent. According to Renee Berger, community development organizations, like CDCs, are nonprofit organizations that serve a low-income community, are governed by a community-based board, and develop commercial/industrial, business enterprise, or housing development projects, with housing far and away the most prevalent undertaking.[41] They first sprang up, Neil Pierce and Carol Steinbach propose, in the 1960s, tied to the civil rights and antipoverty movements and funded by a few foundations and Great Society programs. This first wave numbered only about 100 organizations, but included well-funded, significant efforts such as The Woodlawn Organization (see chapter 5) and the Bedford-Stuyvesant Restoration Corporation. For its multitude of important projects, the Bed-Stuy CDC received about $4 million in federal support annually. The second wave of community development organizations in the 1970s saw a tenfold increase in the number of projects. These were smaller efforts that began as opponents of urban renewal, redlining, factory closings, or irresponsible landlords who abused tenant rights.[42] Most funds came from foundations, primarily the Ford Foundation, and federal sources, such as the Community Services Administration—which replaced OEO in 1974—and the Office of Neighborhood Development, begun in 1978. The idea of community economic development caught on in the Carter administration; by 1980 "there were over a dozen federal programs providing important sources of support for local staff and projects."[43] In the late 1970s CDCs, with all their virtues and drawbacks, were central components of the limited, but significant, federally assisted neighborhood development movement.

Beginning around 1980 CDCs found government support drastically cut. The new, third wave of CDCs that developed in the privatization campaigns of the Reagan years were forced into becoming much more businesslike than their predecessors. They had to exhibit "business talent and development skills once thought to be the exclusive province of the for-profit sector."[44] The Community Services Administration and the Office of Neighborhood Development were dismantled. Other sources of federal funds were dramatically cut back. The bottom line for CDCs, as with seemingly everything else in the decade, was economic success. The primary goal was to "correct the market's failure to provide jobs and services to the community" and, for the CDCs in minority neighborhoods, to help build a non-white middle class by developing highly specific and measurable development projects in which community people could work for their own economic betterment.[45] But the new CDCs became less like community organizations and more like small businesses and investment projects, evaluated on their ability to be economically successful.

Reflective of these changes is the Southeast Baltimore Community Organization (SECO), discussed in chapter 5. SECO is a second-wave community development organization, one that has not lost its ideology of opposition but whose practice has become more mainstream.

A recent pamphlet celebrating its 20-year history assailed "drastic cuts in public resources beginning in 1980 with Ronald Reagan" and criticized city hall's creation of "Two Baltimores"—a flourishing downtown amidst low-income residential neighborhood decay. SECO's roots were militant and confrontational. Participants saw themselves in the early 1970s as an "alternative governance structure for southeast Baltimore."[46] But SECO now focuses on social service programming, around such issues as lead paint and adult literacy, and on its CDC, the Ford Foundation–funded Southeast Development, Inc., which offers assistance to low-income home buyers and builds and manages housing.[47]

Proponents see community development as a third way to address community needs, superior to both social welfare liberal policies of centralized government programs and laissez-faire conservative strategies of private charity and voluntary self-help. They point to the substantial contributions CDCs make to their communities. They bring new services or goods into the neighborhood, employ local workers, displace higher-cost providers, engage in job training, and make other needed neighborhood improvements. The process of neighbors getting together, making decisions, seeing a project through to the finish, and then using *their* finished product builds a sense of community and enhances individual and collective empowerment. CDCs also serve as vital alternatives to for-profit businesses in the community, whose revenues almost always leave the neighborhood.[48]

Community development efforts represent a progression for some organizers. "It's been a remarkable transformation," says Norm Krumholz, former city planning director in Cleveland. "What began in the early '70s as a group of grass-roots activist organizations, very strident in style and confrontational in expression, has been transformed into a set of enormously competent community development corporations that are now doing economic development, housing, and commercial development."[49] New skills have been acquired, more coproduction with government and other providers rather than confrontation strategies adopted, more tangible neighborhood improvements made. The first edition of this book suggested that the greatest impact of neighborhood organizing occurs intangibly in the activation and empowerment of people. Over time, CDCs have done less and less of that. Unlike most social action organizing, however, they do offer tangible results. Berger's survey in late 1988 of 834 groups, estimated at less than half of those now operating, reveals that CDC projects produced some 125,000 units of owner-occupied and rental housing and repaired 275,000 additional units; developed 16.4 million square feet of offices, retail space, and industrial parks in poor communities; loaned money to some 2,000 enterprises, mostly for amounts under $25,000; and created or retained nearly 90,000 jobs in the five years prior to the study.[50] For organizers who found past efforts too idealistic or vague, for middle-class professionals alienated by the class-based antiprofessionalism of early efforts, CDC projects make it possible to contribute to solving urban problems in alternative, reform-oriented, community-based organizations.

But there are serious inherent constraints in the CDC approach that tend to limit it dramatically as a strategy for social change. First, resources are too few and the projects too small to counteract massive urban problems. Dramatically expanded federal support is essential if the conditions that oppress so many people in American cities—widespread poverty, crime, substandard housing, ineffective public schools, inadequate health care, and the lack of jobs at a decent wage—are to become the exception rather than the rule. Most of the CDC projects developed in a neoconservative environment interested in curtailing public expenditures on urban problems, but the community movement quickly outstripped the ability of private supporters to finance it. The first two waves depended heavily on federal funding. The first wave was built on large Great Society grants. Even the second wave was heavily subsidized; in 1980, during the last year of the Carter administration, the federal government allocated approximately $2.6 billion for CDC projects. By 1987 this figure was down to $1.1 billion.

States and cities have not had the money to take up the slack in funding, though they still contribute more than private foundations or corporations combined.[51] Some cities have created innovative "linkage" policies that raise money for community development by taxing other items (real estate transfers in Dade County or luxury apartment and large commercial projects in Boston, for example). Foundation support is growing and plays an increasingly important role in project startups; the Ford Foundation has contributed more than $170 million since it started funding the Gray Areas Projects in late 1961, which preceded the Great Society programs. It continues to fund programs that propose innovative strategies at the grassroots level, including both technical assistance and community empowerment, to help build a middle class of people of color. But this amount is nowhere near that of foundation support for other causes and a mere pittance compared with the amount tax payers contributed through federal programs during the same period. Even with the deep cuts in federal spending for community development, federal funding remained in 1989 the single largest source of financial support for CDCs, providing about one third of their income, according to a New School for Social Research study.[52] Even in the neoconservative heyday of the 1980s, corporations contributed only 15 percent of funding.[53]

Most current grants are little more than "seed" money to revitalize neighborhoods. They are designed to stimulate development projects and attract additional funds. In 1987, from a total of 1,402 grants from 196 foundations, amounting to just over $68 million, the median grant was about $20,000.[54] The private sector will not and certainly cannot be expected to voluntarily allocate the funds necessary to address urban and social problems in a comprehensive way. In Houston in 1990, New Foundations: A Partnership for Neighborhood Revitalization—consisting of a major bank, the national and local United Way, the City of Houston, Private Sector Initiatives, and the Ford Foundation–funded Local Initiatives Support Corporation (LISC)—developed a three-year budget to foster CDC development and neighborhood revitalization. The cash and in-kind support amounted to $879,000, over three years. This is the proverbial drop in the bucket. Such efforts may be useful as a pilot project or good for public relations, but they are not sufficient to "revitalize neighborhoods."

Most proponents now agree that because of the absence of a strong federal presence, CDC efforts continue "to suffer from inadequate coordination and undernourished capacity."[55] Franklin A. Thomas, president of the Ford Foundation, after years of funding CDC efforts, says that "there is just no substitute for the federal presence."[56] This does not mean that the federal government should develop, fund, administer, lead, and own community projects. Universal programs in health care and income maintenance, for example, that provide people with basic income and services, make sense. Sociologist Dick Flacks suggests, however, that we also need to reconceptualize the public sector as a source of capital for communities. This may be the best function left for government in a context "that is both globalizing and decentering."[57] The federal government needs to be brought back in *and* democratized. It is not clear as yet whether this is the direction of the Clinton administration, which in one of its first acts expanded support for CDC projects and community development banks. The democratization of government usually results from mass movements and social turmoil, which force those with power to address the needs of those largely without it. It would be surprising if any substantial support for community organizing efforts working for social change came from any administration without insurgency and demands from the grassroots.

Second, because CDCs are heavily influenced by business and development concerns, there is a tendency for participants to lose sight of their roles and goals as community organizers. Dennis Keating suggests that most CDCs tend to be apolitical, fail to empower the poor, and emphasize development over organizing concerns. Political scientist Benjamin Marquez and others argue that market demands make CDCs so profit oriented "that the traditional goals of community control and empowerment have been abandoned."[58] Bill Traynor of the Community Training and Assistance Center in Boston puts the problem this way:

> If the primary success story of the last 25 years has been the development of a legitimate, skilled nonprofit development sector with the proven capacity to create and preserve housing, jobs and businesses, the major failure has been the proliferation and dominance of a narrowly focused technical-production related model of community development which is estranged from strong neighborhood control or direction and which does not impact the range of issues which affect poor neighborhoods.[59]

These critics are correct. Most CDCs avoid political controversy, are dominated by professionals with a technical orientation, have narrow membership bases, and avoid social activism—though not always by choice.[60] The absence of public support, IRS restrictions on the political activity of nonprofit groups, and the necessity of seeking funds from and joining in partnerships with private sector leaders all push CDCs away from politics and an analysis of power. "This lack of fiscal and political support has forced CDCs to accommodate themselves to rather than redirect the course of the free market."[61]

There are, of course, exceptions, often from the first and second waves, which see community development corporations broadly, as one aspect of a much larger program of community work that also includes organizing, empowerment, advocacy, and social action.[62] They come out of the political activist, not neighborhood maintenance, tradition of neighborhood organizing, and, equally important, they are sustained by a strong belief in social justice and the limits of free-market capitalism. City Life in the Jamaica Plain neighborhood of Boston focuses on getting citizen ownership of housing and throwing out drug pushers. Its community development efforts focus on developing both cooperative housing and an eviction-free zone. They seek to make cooperative home ownership possible for more people, but at the same time try to protect people from slumlords and speculators. National People's Action lobbies around the Community Reinvestment Act of 1977 and around linkage of community economic development to the savings and loan bailout.[63] ACORN has also found itself deeply involved in community development, but as a part of "the fight for democratic control over finance and capital."[64] "Communities live or die based on investment decisions made by elites," argues ACORN organizer and fund-raiser Steve Kest, "and over the past five years ACORN has been in the forefront of an emerging community-based movement to democratize those decisions."[65]

ACORN's CDC work casts a wide net. ACORN activists organize against the bank bailout; act as a watchdog over the enforcement of the Community Reinvestment Act, which requires savings and loans to make loans to poor neighborhoods; and organize "squats" at vacant houses. More recently, ACORN has worked less militantly with banks and city officials, turning abandoned dwellings over to "homesteaders"; local homesteading programs have so far been set up in five cities. ACORN helps do rehab work on these and other sites, setting up "coops" for the new occupants or getting deeds of abandoned houses and doing "sweat equity" projects to put them back into shape for the new homeowners.[66] ACORN also joins partnerships with mainstream politicians and corporate funders. In its joint home-acquiring and rehab efforts in Chicago, ACORN works with Citibank, Mayor Richard M. Daley, and the Federal Home Loan Bank's Affordable Housing Program.[67]

In some respects ACORN looks like more traditional CDC efforts and even like groups such as Habitat for Humanity. The difference is that ACORN sees the CDC work as part of a larger political movement to challenge and change the systematic features of capitalism and traditional politics. Unlike those working for most community development efforts, which have shifted from protest to consensual strategies, ACORN members have over the past five years lobbied, marched, rallied, squatted, sat-in, and gone to jail. They even stormed the Chicago headquarters of the U.S. League of Savings Institutions for concealing problems in the banking industry and demanded that the league support ACORN's proposal to tax only the rich to pay for the bailout.[68]

Nevertheless, groups like City Life and ACORN are the exceptions to the nonconfrontational rule.

Most CDCs would probably defend their consensual approach as the most appropriate for the Reagan-Bush years and even for the current political and economic climate. If community development is to have a chance, organizers must be in tune with capitalist economic development and have a working relationship with the powers that be in the public and private sectors. CDC activists often have to be—and want to be—grassroots entrepreneurs. As community businesses, they must focus heavily on quantifiable projects, technical solutions, and a consensual strategy tied to the style and politics of the private sector.[69] Because the agenda of business dominates the economic structure of all cities in America, the most feasible strategy, some suggest, is "to devise ways to insert local concerns into the equations by which businesses make decisions."[70]

Consensual Community Organizing

Out of CDC work has come a novel form of community organizing, a blending of political activist and neighborhood maintenance approaches. Like political activism, it seeks to empower the poor and working class and mobilize community participation. Like neighborhood maintenance, it promotes a consensual approach, eschewing conflict and confrontational strategies, while working with the more conservative elements in the community.

Mike Eichler's work is representative. A social worker by training, his organizing experience includes both Alinsky and CDC efforts with LISC, the Ford Foundation–funded community development effort designed to provide communities with technical assistance and to help strengthen community organizations. He made a name for himself as a community development organizer by helping to put together CDC projects in the depressed steel manufacturing area of the Monongahela Valley near Pittsburgh. Since then, as a LISC program manager, he has established projects in Houston, New Orleans, Little Rock, and Palm Beach. Now with nine full-time organizers, Eichler has helped organize a total of 19 CDCs, most of which produce real estate projects.[71] When he was hired by the Houston Committee of Private Sector Initiatives— again assisted by a grant from LISC—to organize CDCs in low-income neighborhoods in Houston, he put into practice the strategy that worked in the Monongahela Valley. If the private sector could do more, as neoconservatives suggested, then organizers should go to the private sector for support. Committed to empowering the poor, he had to "sell it as a real conservative program."[72]

This meant altering the traditional political activist approach: making it more consensual and less confrontational, making sure to include business interests and to work with established power brokers. The consensual strategy of his "development team" approach unites the community to gather resources rather than identifying the causes of problems and pressuring the sources of power. Unlike the Alinsky "conflict" style, Eichler's is fashioned around building consensus and unity among all segments of the community: neighborhood residents, bankers, businesspeople, religious leaders, politicians, and government officials. No one is to be embarrassed, no resentments rubbed raw. Older forms of organizing are conflictual, confrontational, and strident, concurs Robert Zdenek, president of the National Congress for Community Economic Development. "If you're doing development, it's more collaborative."[73] More similar to the locality development and social planning models of community organization found in social work education, consensual CDC organizing strategy tends to see the fundamental goal as rebuilding community, forging a sense of unity among fragmented elements, and gathering resources to perform specific community tasks.[74]

Eichler's approach and that of other CDC organizers is congruent with the demands placed on local communities not only by neoconservative politics but also by the pressures of global economic competition, which spurred the development of neoconservatism. As economic conditions become more uncertain and competitive, leaders promote cooperative relations between business, government, and citizens. This is as true for communities as it is for nations, states, and cities, perhaps even more so. Faced with tremendous competition and scarce resources, nations and cities, let alone communities, can't tolerate costly political divisions or oppositional redistribution demands. Instead of mounting opposition in a climate that can't—or won't—sustain it, Mike Eichler and others like him offer consensus in return for support and long-term relationships with business and government leaders with power and resources[75] They work, as organizers have always done, to get what the given environment will yield. Eichler argues that by participating in the CDC consensual approach corporate types become more active and aware of social problems, city officials see community organizing as valuable instead of threatening, and neighborhood residents feel empowered and get more control over some community resources.[76]

The contradiction in this approach lies in the relation between democracy and corporate capital in the global economy. Jane Mansbridge suggests that the ideology of most community-based efforts rests on a dual conception of democracy. In the community activists practice a "unitary democracy," which assumes a predominant concern with promoting the common interest. To change national, state, or urban politics they practice an "adversarial democracy," which presupposes conflicting interests.[77] "Adversary democracy" embodies the consensus/conflict strategy inherent in most Alinsky organizing. In most CDCs, however, the elimination of conflict translates as no opposition. No conflict inside the community and no conflict with the local or even national powers outside the community. Causes of problems are set aside, differences deemphasized, and working relationships established with all segments of the community except those who insist on being confrontational. This leaves out a critical understanding of power and the role conflict plays in helping people to demand it and get it.

The new partnerships between the community, voluntary, public, and business sectors will remain problematic as long as the latter are the chief causes of the problems communities face. Business may help communities when it makes good business sense. Corporate leaders and neoconservatives might even think that community-based approaches are the strategy of the future. But the profit motive and investment demands destroy low-income communities much more often than they help them. Businesses often overcharge for products, especially in poor areas; they oppose higher corporate or wealth taxes, which could fund social programs; they flee communities when wages rise or other communities offer better "sweetheart" deals that lower taxes and startup costs; they depress wages rather than limit profits; they lay off workers because of "restructuring"; and they support urban policies that channel money away from neighborhoods and into downtown development or economic growth councils set up to attract new businesses with tax-subsidized deals.[78]

Of course, all community-based efforts in capitalist cities are in a bind. This is especially so in an era of heightened global competition and neoconservative policies. Poor communities do not have the resources to rebuild themselves. No number of minority-owned businesses or parents taking more interest in their children's education is going to make a significant difference. More resources, as well as effective programs, are needed. It is logical that communities would turn in the 1980s and 1990s to the private sector for assistance. That was part of the politically dominant strategy of privatization. Because the private sector is where people were forced to turn does not mean that the answer rests there. It is shortsighted to assume a consensus of interest where oppression and deep class divisions remain. Dissent is a critical element in democratic politics. Conflict is a powerful educational tool. Sacrificing democratic discourse to accomplish local tasks and failing to acknowledge the real political/economic roots of problems in poor neighborhoods have always been, throughout the history of neighborhood organizing, a self-defeating strategy for low-income people. Neighborhood maintenance strategies work best in middle- and upper-class neighborhoods, where residents use them primarily to defend their communities and enhance property values. Some organizers fear that CDC efforts deflate and divert social movements, that they are a trend away from social change. This analysis argues that for poor and working people CDC activity has a place, but only if it is part of a larger political activist strategy.

Neopopulism

The Alinsky legacy lives on today. In spite of the general political help-lessness and hopelessness felt by most Americans, in communities across the country people are joining together to act powerfully on issues of deep concern to them, their families, and their neighbors.

—Mike Miller, Organize Training Center

Nobody has enough good organizers to rub together to make a fire.

—Wade Rathke, ACORN 8

Not all community organizing meshed so well with the conservative politics of the 1980s as the CDC approach. But all efforts were deeply affected by the demands of privatization and consensual politics. Neo-Alinskyite groups begun in the 1970s continued working for economic and political democracy. Organizing efforts proliferated.[79] The expansion of new populist ventures included neighborhood-based, door-to-door efforts such as ACORN; coalitions grounded in canvasing and lobbying strategies such as Citizen Action; institution-based, religious-affiliated groups such as the Industrial Areas Foundation; and a myriad of political, service-oriented efforts organized around meeting the need of constituencies such as African-Americans, Hispanics, gay men, lesbians, women in general, battered women, and other aggrieved populations and victims of oppression.[80]

Social change organizations did not disappear. As noted earlier, the more substantial ones celebrated tenth and twentieth anniversaries in the late 1980s and early 1990s. But the groundswell movement forecast in the late 1970s, the "backyard revolution," was forced to veer right in the 1980s. Increasingly the pressures of the global economy and the conservative political climate altered goals, moderated strategies, and diminished the resources available to political activist efforts.

Most neopopulist organizers in the 1980s and early 1990s moderated their strategies and their politics. Battle lines shifted. "To a surprising extent, the grass roots no longer 'fight the power.' They fight for a share of the power. Sometimes they win a sizable share. . . . [Sometimes they] team up with the established elite that they once derided and that once spurned them."[81] Even the National People's Action (NPA), criticized by some organizers as too confrontational, opposed being "out in the streets making symbolic statements, when you can be in the boardroom negotiating specific agreements that win for neighborhoods."[82]

Relatedly, neopopulist efforts in the 1980s and early 1990s suffered from an absence of resources. This included not only diminished actual dollars for social action, but, perhaps even more important, a decline of active members, new leaders, and real community support. In the conservative environment money was channelled away from oppositional causes. That is one reason why some community organizations adopted more moderate strategies. But the conservative atmosphere also heavily influenced the number and type of people interested in community-based social action. "It is much easier now to convince people that times are bad, but much harder than in the 1970s to convince people that something can be done about it," concludes Bill Cavellini, an activist based in Cambridge, Massachusetts.[83]

A Strategy of Moderation: IAF Organizing

Perhaps the most touted organizing is done by the Industrial Areas Foundation network, the direct descendant of Alinsky organizing. IAF has 28 organizing projects in New York, New Jersey, Maryland, Tennessee, Arizona, California, and Texas, but it is in Texas, where the IAF has 10 organizing efforts, that it is the strongest. Throughout the state, in San Antonio, Houston, El Paso, Austin, Fort Worth, and the Rio Grande Valley, IAF organizers and active members struggle for utility reform, improved public education, government accountability, health care for the indigent, and basic public services, including water and sewers for the "colonias" populated by poor Mexican-Americans. Most visibly, they organize "get out the vote" efforts to promote bond packages to IAF neighborhoods, hold "accountability sessions" to keep politicians publicly in line with IAF objectives, encourage voter registration, and work to improve schools by halting the dropout rate, stopping drug use and violence, and getting parents more involved. More quietly, in the day-in, day-out practice of community organizing, they serve as "schools of public life," empowering community residents by giving them "an opportunity to do something about things that have . . . frustrated [them] all their lives."[84]

They do all of this remarkably well, as commentators have been quick to realize. Peter Applebome in the *New York Times* proposes that the IAF is "in ways large and small . . . changing politics in Texas."[85] Mary Beth Rogers, former chief of staff for Texas governor Ann Richards, concludes in her study of Texas IAF organizations that they "are virtually the *only* organizations in America that are enticing working poor people to participate in politics."[86]

While still pursuing Alinsky-style organizing, IAF has made some significant changes in its organizing method to meet the needs of new constituents and adapt to the demands of a new conservative context. IAF has continued its institutional approach to community organizing. It organizes only existing community institutions, usually churches. Unlike ACORN, which goes door to door to build a neighborhood organization, and unlike Citizen Action, which builds large coalitions through direct-mail campaigns, canvassing, and lobbying, IAF groups get invited into a community by local institutions willing to pay for their organizing expertise.

Since the late 1970s, and especially in the 1980s, however, the institutional approach of IAF has focused increasingly on churches as the community base. Alinsky also depended on religious congregations for economic support. IAF "has made a radical shift in direction since Alinsky times," John Moyer asserts, "namely to view the Church as the one institution in society with the potential to work positively for the empowerment of people."[87] Religious institutions no longer serve only as the funding base. Now they also provide a pool of activists and leaders and, perhaps even more important, the ideological core around which to organize constituents. Current IAF leaders now understand, as Alinsky did not in his "nonideological" later years, that for the long haul people must organize around more than self-interest or material needs.[88]

In 1978, six years after Alinsky's death, IAF's "Organizing for Family and Congregation" campaign reflected this new approach. It focused on a "war of values" against a materialistic, corrupt, greedy, media-dominated world. It argued that IAF should organize in community institutions, primarily religious congregations.[89] The Bible became the organizing text, the Judeo-Christian source of social justice values. A training session with Texas IAF organizers Ernie Cortes, Robert Rivera, or Christine Stephens, a former nun, is now filled with biblical stories, metaphors, and lessons. By incorporating progressive religious values into the process of grassroots democracy, IAF provides the "inherent" ideology—grounded in people's lives and traditions—so critical to initiating and sustaining social change.[90]

Of course, IAF does not call its theological glue an ideology. According to the organizers—and to what has become a standard IAF text, *In Defense of Politics,* by Bernard Crick—ideology is dogma foisted by organizers on the people.[91] IAF organizers like to say, citing Crick, that IAF practices the art of politics, the craft of compromise and conciliation, in which there is no room for fixed analyses or critiques. The Bible and Judeo-Christian values provide a diverse crop of ideas, not all of which would be considered "progressive." The key point, however, is that IAF organizing now explicitly emphasizes the importance of ideas and values in the organizing process.

The second major change in IAF organizing in the past decade is a shift from an oppositional politics to a strategy of moderation. The IAF's counterpart to the consensual strategy of Mike Eichler and others active with CDCs is the politics of "standing for the whole."[92] To be sure some of those in power still see IAF as a radical protest group, and even during Alinsky's lifetime some IAF projects, such as TWO, shifted from "conflict to coexistence." Now, however, this has developed into an organizing credo. IAF seeks to organize "community sustainers" and "core moderates," especially women in mainline religious congregations and civic organizations. It wants the civic volunteers who already work tirelessly for the PTO or church group, the folks, IAF says, who already protect the community, who stand for the whole. Like most moderates, IAF organizers distance themselves from radicals and social movements. Whereas Alinsky took pride in being a radical, in the current IAF radicals are seen as alienated outsiders. "IAF now almost makes a fetish of its commitment to '"moderates,'" notes organizer trainer Mike Miller.[93]

While they distance themselves from the left, IAF asserts that the true extremists are those who through personal greed, a lack of values, materialism, and a corrupt political system seek to destroy traditional communities.[94] This is more than a clever tactical jujitsu that makes the activists conservative and the conservatives extremists. "Standing for the whole" means legitimizing grassroots organizing in the eyes of both the powerless and the powerful, both of whom IAF assumes, as do CDC proponents, to be fundamentally moderate. It means creating a working relationship between those with and without power to promote the interests of its members. Uniting selectively with the powerful can help the powerless. To stand for the whole is to try to restore public life by redefining politics: getting citizens to become activists and politicians to become public servants.[95]

Citizen education is critical. In church-based organizing it demands challenging established relations between pulpit and congregation. "In effect, religious institutions which continue to rely on a pedagogy of passivity cannot hope to move individuals in ways that can fulfill the church's responsibilities to humankind or to God. What is needed is a rededication to learning through doing, so that basic ethical values can become operationally meaningful."[96]

Reeducating politicians to become public servants is equally essential. They must learn to deal with citizens in a "respectful" and "collaborative" fashion. In the 1980s and early 1990s confronting government officials became, according to IAF, less and less productive. Local government officials argued that they, too, were sympathetic to the issues but did not have the resources to address them. So standing for the whole now includes developing working relationships with business and government leaders to further the goals of both IAF constituents and the larger community. In Baltimore organizers have developed a wide-ranging partnership, the Baltimore Commonwealth, with IAF

BUILD (Build Unity, Independence, Liberty, and Dignity) at its core, to address public school issues. Increasingly, standing for the whole means IAF taking responsibility for what it calls "governance."[97] Running a job-training program in San Antonio. Doing policy initiation and implementation as well as organizing. IAF takes great pride in the changes it has been able to effect by becoming a key player in the politics of some major cities, like San Antonio, New York, and Baltimore. As one IAF organizer boasts, Communities Organized for Public Service is "now part of the power structure in San Antonio"[98]

Standing for the whole reconceptualizes the very concept of power. Power is no longer seen as simply something others have or as something gathered for personal aggrandizement. Power "is what you teach others to get for themselves."[99] Like the Spanish word *poder,* Texas organizers like to say, power means to be able, to have capacity. Like a true Alinsky organization, IAF knows power is good, that the powerless should thirst for it. To empower constituents, organizers must "never do for others what they can do for themselves."[100] But this is now a disciplined power limited by values. It is a sensitive power, more relational and reciprocal than coercive. For Ernie Cortes, "organizing is a fancy word for relationship building." Power, like organizing, forges a political relationship that grows out of association with those "with whom you share action."[101] When you stand for the whole, organizing communities and affecting policy, building relationships with the people and with politicians, IAF asserts, you share action with a wide variety of people and come to see power as the craft of arguing, listening, revising views, and compromising "in exchange for respect and a willingness to compromise from those who now hold power. What matters to us is not consensus, but a stake in the ongoing dynamic of controversy, resolution, and change."[102] Win what you can this time. Continue to develop working relationships of trust with the people and respect with the politicians. Abide by Hannah Arendt's philosophy that public life is an arena of equals. Convince both sides of it.

Most commentators sing glowing praises of IAF's work, as Charles Silberman did of Alinsky's work with TWO many years ago. The daily work, long-term objectives, and organizing creativity represent a clear democratic alternative to the neoconservative politics of the late 1970s and the 1980s. But not all organizers and progressives join the chorus. At issue is IAF's politics of moderation.

The strategy of moderation, the commitment to moderates, the grounding of IAF efforts in mainstream religious institutions, and a definition of power that emphasizes relationship building leads to a politics that limits the parameters of IAF work and excludes alliances with other movement activists and organizations.[103] It encourages IAF to work alone with its constituency and mainstream allies and avoid confronting the causes of the imbalance of power that oppresses its constituents. In a highly stratified society like the United States in the 1980s and early 1990s, power may be redefined (and defused) as a process of relationship building, but the exercise of power remains primarily in the hands of a privileged few who are interested in protecting that privilege. It is therefore not enough to work on the Baltimore Commonwealth and to take great pride when one kid from the inner city gets accepted by Johns Hopkins University.[104] Increasingly, with its emphasis on moderation and negotiation, standing for the whole brings IAF closer to interest-group politics, which changes the role of the organizer.

Standing for the whole moves IAF away from the Alinsky idea of the organizer being in the background, working his or her way out of a job, focusing on getting community residents to lead the organization. The more IAF gets involved in negotiating with government officials and corporate executives, the more its organizers come center stage to be the brokers and spokespersons for the organization. Increasingly the division of labor in IAF gives much of the public role and visible power to the organizers, which makes sense in interest-group bargaining but not in community organizing if the goal is to empower community residents and, as Alinsky suggested, to work your way out of a job.[105]

The natural progression of the broker/advocacy model is that neighborhood residents may increasingly become clients to work for, rather than allies and activists to work with. IAF sees its work more broadly. Brokering an issue or project is a means to an end. They see their work as "a search for an approach to public life which is more about understanding life and meaning than just dealing with a particular issue."[106] There is, as Steve Max of the Midwest Academy reminds us, "no one right kind of organizing."[107] But doubts remain about where IAF's strategy of moderation and brokered politics will lead it.

Radical Organizing

Not all neopopulist efforts follow the IAF model, although most are direct or indirect descendants of Alinsky organizing. Radical approaches continue. ACORN continues to follow a social justice movement model, committed to radical ideology and confrontational tactics. It has a clear political program. Its "people's platform" emanates from but goes beyond neighborhood politics to integrate both a constituency and class-based mode of organizing and a critique of American political economy. Other approaches, like the many efforts influenced by the Center for Third World Organizing, pursue multiracial organizing, with an inherent critique of the systemic, institutional basis of racism and ethnocentrism. Community-labor alliances unite constituency and class-based organizing.[108] ACT-UP blends a radical critique of American power with organizing around gay and lesbian issues.[109]

Reflecting the widespread growth of grassroots responses to the dramatic decline of American cities, hundreds of other groups not directly connected to a national coordinating project continue to practice a social action type of organizing begun in the late 1960s and early 1970s. It is not uncommon for contemporary urban neighborhoods to have an array of grassroots organizations, including community development, service delivery, and social action. In Cambridgeport, Massachusetts, for example, the struggle over the Simplex property (discussed in the introduction) between the Massachusetts Institute of Technology and the neighborhood continues. MIT now has the upper hand, gaining support in 1988 from the Cambridge City Council to rezone the 27-acre site for a high-tech development to be known as University Park.[110] The university's advantage, however, has come at great cost and with significant struggle. About one year prior to the rezoning decision the Simplex Steering Committee, the group with which many Cambridgeport activists remained involved over the years, held a "Tent City" weekend celebration of Cambridgeport's united opposition to MIT. What was to be a weekend neighborhood action escalated. Homeless people were invited to the celebration and decided to stay, for a month. It was an extraordinary act of defiance and empowerment for the people of the neighborhood, for the homeless, and for the MIT students who joined them to protest the university's response to the action. Ultimately, an exasperated and threatened MIT sent campus police in to level the tent city and arrested 10 people for trespassing, all of whom had charges against them dismissed or were found not guilty.[111] One month after the rezoning decision a Cambridge rent control hearing examiner found that MIT kept run-down, vacant apartments on the 27-acre site, "flagrantly" violating city laws.[112] Two days later homeless activists were arrested during a sit-in at MIT's administration building.

Some say all for naught. Development has begun at the site. MIT is moving ahead with its plans. And yet, while the neighborhood activists were not victorious, their persistence and militance did win them significant concessions. MIT, for example, has guaranteed that at least a quarter of all new housing on the site will be for people of low and moderate incomes. More than that, the legacy of more than 20 years of struggle in Cambridgeport makes a strong statement to would be developers that neighborhood projects must take into account the concerns of working people or face costly challenges.

In another part of the City of Cambridge, Steve Meacham (discussed in the introduction) continues his radical community organizing. The founder of the Cambridgeport Homeowners and Tenants Association in the early 1970s and an ally of Bill Cavellini and others in the struggle against MIT's expansion, Meacham, like many activists in the late 1970s, turned his attention to labor organizing. He went to work and to organize at the shipyards outside Boston. After years of mixed success there, involved with both union organizing and industrial conversion to nonmilitary uses, he returned to Cambridge to work as an organizer for the Cambridge Economic Opportunity Committee, struggling to stop Cambridge from becoming "a city for rich, white people only."[113] One of the remarkable things he has been able to help organize as an independent activist is an eviction-free zone in Cambridge. There is another eviction-free zone effort not far away in Jamaica Plain, organized by City Life. City Life conducts a similar form of radical, community-oriented, multiracial, class-focused organizing around tenant rights and housing issues. Both eviction-free zone efforts in the Boston area print leaflets, hold meetings, and organize in multiple languages, including Spanish, Creole, and Haitian in addition to English. These organizations challenge the prerogatives of private enterprise, give residents greater control of their community, and work hard to develop "indigenous" organizers and leaders. For them, more struggle, around class and race inequities, not moderation, should be the direction of community organizing.

While the militance and radical politics of these selected efforts in the Boston area is not unique, it is unusual. Throughout the 1980s community organizing strategies were less openly confrontational and less overtly critical of the role of capitalism in undermining community life. This was especially so in more conservative cities and communities. The politics of moderation practiced by IAF is more typical of neopopulism in the 1980s—a period when being labeled "liberal" put you on the far left. Neopopulist organizations were most likely to end up like the South Austin Coalition Community Council in Chicago, the successor to the Alinskyite Organization for a Better Austin (OBA), which while it would prefer to spend more time on "pressure campaigns" finds itself instead occupied with making contributions to its constituents through social service and community development projects.[114]

The Problem of Scarce Resources—Money and People

Saul Alinsky advised that if you follow the money, you will find the institutions that shape our lives. Following the money also reveals the constraints of community organizing. Total IAF resources are about $5 million a year for 28 affiliates, "a pittance by corporate, church, union, or political party standards." The total IAF full-time organizers and support staff number no more than 75. The average annual budget for a local project is about $120,000, and almost all of that goes for staff.[115] ACORN is certainly no better off. The total annual budget, of some $4 million, "is equivalent to three good Safeway supermarkets."[116] This covers a staff of 75 organizers in 25 cities, 15 national staff, and an administrative staff of some 15 people. IAF pays fewer people higher salaries, a middle-class versus working-class wage, but both efforts are bare-bones operations. And the lion's share of funding comes from membership dues, especially in IAF, which taxes member institutions, but also in ACORN, where only about 23 percent comes from gifts and grants.[117]

Funding for all types of grassroots projects may not be in decline. There are too many organizations to know for certain. There are more people involved, given the proliferation of voluntary efforts around new social movement groupings such as women, gay men, people of color, and the environment, as well as all the organizing that occurs around issues such as opposition to neighborhood crime, toxic waste dumps, and ineffective public schools. But there is clearly less money and fewer people available for social action efforts, especially those focused on organizing the poor and working class.

IAF, given its limited resources, cannot do everything well. It cannot stand for the whole, do political education, transform constituents, and win victories against or in cooperation with local government leaders. That is partially why its organizers end up doing a form of interest-group brokerage politics. For IAF, with few resources, brokered actions can have the greatest immediate impact. The same is true for CDC work; CDCs focus on the accomplishment of specific tasks with visible physical results, which, if they are good and lucky, keeps the funds coming.

The other resource issue relates to leadership generation. Community organizing resources include not only funds recruited from membership dues, foundation support, and the like, but, equally important, the skills and energy of members.[118] Through the 1980s most people lost interest in a radical social action agenda. Few gave money or their own time and energy. Fewer made it part of daily political discourse. This is Bill Cavellini's complaint. Funds are sparse, certainly in comparison to the magnitude of the problems faced by organizations. Leadership development is much more difficult in a conservative context, without a social democratic orientation in Washington and without a left-oriented mass movement providing fervor, animus, and a general program. As ACORN's Wade Rathke puts it: there's just too few people organizing. Robert Rivera concurs. As well as IAF does, and as many people as it is able to attract, there remains "a shortage of organizers" based on a larger absence nationwide of movement politics.[119]

The hegemony of business values and individualism has led people away from progressive social action and, if anything, toward New Right opposition to the prior gains of women, gays and lesbians, and African-Americans. Rathke says "it was increasingly difficult to find organizers as young people became yuppies."[120] But it seems that there are middle-class, college-educated recruits, especially for new identity-specific social movements. When they focus on urban/neighborhood problems, however, they are more interested in community development or public school reform and come from a more professional, reformist perspective than a working-class, social movement orientation. It is not surprising then to find that one of the major tasks of the 1980s and 1990s became the recruitment and education of class-conscious, social-justice-minded organizers. As the coordinator of a community health clinic says: "It would be a shame if, after all of the battles with the New Right, we failed to survive because no one cared.

You see, we have not succumbed to the right and all its horrible tricks and attacks. But we cannot continue if we don't get new blood into the movement. That, and not the New Right, is our biggest threat."[121]

Neopopulist organizations are only as strong as the skills and numbers of their organizers. A large percent of organizing may be persistence and will, but you have to find capable people who love the work, find it challenging, are angry at injustice, and understand the work is a marathon, not a sprint.[122] To this end, organizer training schools sprang up nationwide in the 1970s and 1980s, the most distinguished among them being IAF, the Midwest Academy, the Organizing Training Center, the Center for Third World Organizing, Grassroots Leadership, Direct Action and Research Training (DART), the Gamaliel Foundation, and the Pacific Institute for Community Organizing (PICO).

Still, in the 1980s and early 1990s it was not as easy to find left-oriented people as it was during the 1960s and early 1970s, when social movements and a more liberal national political discourse supported the view that being an activist was among the most rewarding and valuable things a person could do with her or his life. In some cases the recruits just stopped coming. In the 1970s ACORN used to get, fresh out of school, master of social work graduates who majored in community organization. But MSWs in the 1980s were interested in more psychotherapeutic/individualistic approaches and better salaries. Generally, throughout the decade few trained as social workers were committed to community organizing careers.

Therefore it is not surprising in an IAF or ACORN or Citizen Action group for the organizers to increasingly step forward to center stage and become political leaders and power brokers rather than try to work themselves out of a job. This may be a natural occurrence over time as people remain in a community or with a single organization. And it is certainly naive to think that Alinsky or his followers simply worked behind the scenes. They were powerful and knowledgeable people who always played key roles. Nicholas Lemann, in his study of black migration to Chicago, tells the story of how at meetings of TWO in the 1960s people would turn en masse to Alinsky organizer Nick Van Hoffmann for ideas and answers. Organizers might say they wanted to let the people decide, but the people wanted to know what the organizer thought, and generally followed. People are much more used to being led than leading. In an era where recruitment is more difficult, resources fewer, social movements quiescent, mass protest disdained, political opportunity structures more resistant, and democracy questioned, community organizers increasingly tend to rely on their own skills and knowledge and become major players themselves. At one level, the diminished support for these and other social action efforts is quite discouraging given the magnitude of the problems. How is it possible to effect progressive change when the odds are stacked so heavily against progressives? In a postmodern, fragmented culture and a complex, highly competitive global economy, it looks as if these efforts do not stand a chance. On another level, however, it is quite extraordinary how much these political activist groups have been able to achieve. Social action organizing remains a good investment, argues Gary Delgado of the Applied Research Center in Oakland, California, certainly much better than CDCs. Compare the $300 million raised in loans and grants around Community Reinvestment Act organizing, on a national investment of less than $1 million, to the $400 million allocated from public and private sources for economic development projects that have had minimal impact, some 40,000 housing starts.[123]

Political activist community organizing efforts provide a great deal of hope, for even without resources and in a very hostile context they have been able to organize constituents, empower individuals and communities, and influence policy. As Gale Cincotta of National People's Action says, "Cities have no hope without community organization. Problems these days are so big, so bad, that you've got to enlist the support of neighborhood people. There's no other way."[124] There are undoubtedly other ways. Community organizing is limited in what it can accomplish. Should more resources become available, in terms of more people or more support, however, the potential for more significant impact remains.

Community Work, Fragmentation, and the Challenge to Neighborhood Organizing

We want to build up a tradition which goes to the roots of where people are, but which at the same time enables them to act in a public way. The political parties are in disarray. The movements have faded away . . . so we feel we have to do it on our own.

—Ernie Cortes, IAF

Low income neighborhoods have been carved up into dozens of separate and isolated constituencies, and experienced activists are burned out and overwhelmed by the challenges which loom on every street corner.

—Bill Traynor, Community Training and Assistance Center

The devastation of the human and natural worlds that marked the 1980s was only possible because the people hurt by it were divided from each other. Whether the 1990s will be a time of continued devastation or an era of creative renewal will largely depend on whether their divisions are overcome.

—Jeremy Brecher and Tim Costello, political commentators

The new voluntarism is nowhere more apparent than in the thousands of community-based social service and advocacy organizations that have sprung up in the past decade. Unlike most community development projects, which are fundamentally economic in orientation, or neopopulist efforts, which see themselves as political, those in the tradition of social work community organizing see their work as fundamentally social or as social and cultural. Food pantries, church-related social ministries, and homeless shelters deliver services to the poor. They provide dinner, a few extra dollars to pay the rent or a light bill, a place to spend the night or longer. AIDS hospices, domestic violence shelters, community centers in the African-American community, and refugee service alliances all deliver services to their constituencies and engage in a culturally based politics of identity. The proliferation of such groups results not only from worsening conditions and federal "load shedding" of responsibility but also from the dramatic emergence of identity-specific movements and issue-based constituencies seeking to meet their own needs, build community capacity, and empower themselves.

While there is not one type of social work community organizing, contemporary efforts have two essential elements: empowerment and service delivery. The empowerment component argues for an integration of private needs and public life. Its roots lie in the feminist movement ("the personal is political") and the development of a feminist practice in social work community organizing during the 1980s and early 1990s. The goal of feminist organizing, according to social work-

ers Lorraine Gutierrez and Edith Lewis, "is the elimination of permanent power hierarchies between all people which can prevent them
from realizing their human potential."[125] At the heart of this practice is
the process of individual and collective empowerment. Raise consciousness about oppression and its causes. Reconceptualize power as
human agency, not simply structural domination. Challenge people
and institutions that deny human needs and undermine human dignity. Give people skills and knowledge to help them "make history."[126]

The central component of social work organizing, however, is the
connection between service delivery and social action. In the best of
the social work tradition, what social worker Cheryl Hyde calls "social
movement agencies," providing social services and engaging in social
action go hand in hand. Social action alone is insufficient, because services "make the organization real and significant to its members."[127]
But because service delivery alone does not address the cause of
social problems, social work community organizing seeks to mobilize
and empower people through the services delivered. Activist social
service academics Ann Withorn and Cheryl Hyde, among others,
understand the tensions inherent in doing both service delivery and
social action. Nevertheless, they object strenuously to the false
dichotomy of social service and political objectives.[128] While service
work has often been seen as an alternative to politics, good service
work includes progressive political activity.[129] Community work
improves social conditions, redistributes power and influence,
strengthens community participation, advances the interests of
oppressed groups, *and* provides needed social services.[130]

This is no easy package to deliver. Social workers Herbert Rubin
and Irene Rubin suggest that organizers face three basic dilemmas.
One is the tension between mass participation and effectiveness,
which is demonstrated in the CDC dilemma of wanting to develop the
community physically, with literally concrete projects, without losing
sight of greater community participation. Another is the tension
between power and dependence. Organizations can get more power
when they increase their membership, establish ties with power brokers, or join coalitions. But, as we have seen with IAF efforts, the
scarce resources or desire for greater impact that drives organizations
to establish ties with those with power creates new restrictions and
obligations. A third dilemma is the tension between empowerment
and service delivery. This is one that the more progressive social work
efforts have always faced. How do you continue to give members more

capacity to solve their problems and simultaneously provide services, whether for victims of rape, homelessness, and AIDS or for public needs like day care, recycling, and adequate health care?[131] This is essentially a matter of emphasis related to resources and tactical choices. It is a dilemma, not an oppositional dualism. Social service delivery is not an alternative to politics. Service is part of politics.

Withorn argues further, for example, that "to be a feminist has meant to engage in service work as much as it has meant to do the things which are normally defined as political."[132] Social service delivery helps meet the needs of residents and addresses community problems while simultaneously addressing the larger structural causes of those conditions. Feminist practice in social work community organizing understands that effective community work proceeds not from held up ideals and lofty political goals but from building relationships with community people around issues *and* specific needs. Set up community-based service approaches to address both economic instability and the needs of the poor for food, clothing, and shelter. Provide services related to job training and the elimination of sexual harassment and discrimination. Offer mental and general health services, services for victims of violence, and rehabilitative services related to substance abuse. Understand that "the needs for service development and political action are intertwined."[133]

Take, for example, organizing around AIDS in cities throughout the nation. Some groups provide traditional medical services through local hospitals or research institutes. Those which see themselves as community organizing efforts, however, blend service and advocacy. They provide counseling, clinics, and hospices for people with AIDS and support for their families. They lobby, advocate, empower, and educate around the AIDS issue and the struggle against homophobia. They organize diverse efforts in the gay community, in which the rate of infection has stabilized largely as a result of the success of such grassroots efforts.

Or consider the problem of homelessness. A wide range of projects concern the urban homeless. Mainstream service delivery programs, usually tied to local government or charities, provide, at best, needed services such as shelter and food. Supporters drop off cans of beans and tuna fish for the disadvantaged or contribute funds to sustain a shelter. Progressive efforts, Joel Blau documents in *The Visible Poor,* deliver services *and* advocate. They fulfill basic needs but also engage in lobbying and advocacy on behalf of the homeless, forge coalitions of homeless-related institutions to leverage for more public funds and attention, and organize the homeless to help themselves and fight back against their oppression.[134]

In the impoverished, primarily African-American community of the Third Ward in Houston, SHAPE Community Center offers a wide array of services with the overall intent of building community through self-help strategies and challenging the causes of economic poverty. Cultural programs for kids and adults build personal and community pride. Social programs that focus on prevention of drug abuse, teen counseling, community safety, parenting education, school reform, and health care help meet desperate community needs. The founders and primary activists at SHAPE, people like Deloyd Parker and social worker Theola Petteway, come out of the civil rights and black power movements. So the programs at SHAPE have a great deal of political content. Parker's nationally recognized, community-based work on drug problems in the community, for example, emphasizes developing community responses without more police intervention, improving social service resources for drug users, and empowering community residents to help them address community problems. The waiting room at SHAPE is filled with political pictures, leaflets, and newspapers. When Nelson Mandela came to Houston in 1992, he spoke at SHAPE. Despite the fact that Houston is more hostile to social action than most cities, at SHAPE services and social action go hand in hand.

At the Good Neighbor Health Care Center in the Fourth Ward, Jeanne Sickman manages an impressive array of preventive and primary health care services, which include a full-time general practice medical doctor, a well-baby clinic, and a prenatal program. The center also houses an optometry clinic associated with the University of Houston, an infant feeding program, and a literacy center. Nevertheless, as social worker Sickman emphasizes, "If I just deliver services and did not begin to get at the causes of needs, I'd go nuts."[135] So she lives in the inner-city, low-income community that surrounds the centers. She brings services to community institutions, like the local elementary school, and seeks to build alliances between the center and other community organizations.

These organizations all practice social action within institutional and societal constraints. Depending on what resources are available, who pays the bills and salaries, how bureaucratic the structure, how conservative the ideology of any agency or community organization, organizers vary in terms of their autonomy, access to power, integration in the community, and constituency support. They all have to balance differing levels of intervention, from personal services to collective advocacy. And yet, despite such constraints, community work efforts that blend social action and social service delivery continue to proliferate as community workers learn that neither is sufficient alone.

Curiously, it is this proliferation that further complicates the task. As mentioned earlier, since the decline of the civil rights and antiwar movements, organizing has fragmented. It occurs around cultural groupings, mostly identities of race, gender, and sexual preference. It occurs around problem issues, such as rape, violence, alcoholism, AIDS, toxic-waste dumping, air and water pollution, drunk driving, and homelessness. It is this decentering of political struggle, away from the core class struggle of the old social movements to a more diverse, polyvocal discourse of the varied new citizen initiatives, that gives current grassroots efforts such potential and such problems. The commitment to diversity encourages each constituency, identity, or issue group to identify its own struggles, develop its own voice, and engage in its own empowerment. Never before have so many groups, heretofore relatively quiescent or silenced, begun to demand signification and power.

The challenge of this diversification is the fragmentation of oppositional efforts into exclusive, often antagonistic, parochial components. "By politicizing the personal," critic L. A. Kauffman writes, "feminists, queers, and people of color have privileged difference over commonality, and have splintered movements of opposition."[136] Urbashih Vaid, executive director of the National Gay and Lesbian Task Force, argues differently. "When gay people work in the labor movement, or the peace movement, or the women's movement we have experiences such as this: 'Well, we support equal rights for gay people but that's not what we're here to talk about—we're here to talk about housing, we're here to talk about peace.' But there are gay and lesbian perspectives on each of these issues. We have experiences of discrimination that are particular, and should be aired in these forums."[137]

To the extent that efforts continue to splinter, however, their chances of developing the power to challenge problems nationally, let alone internationally, dwindle. As more efforts develop, as diversity increases, as struggle is decentered, resources, scarce already, stretch thinner. John Davis notes that neighborhood organizers in Cincinnati's West End found themselves competing with others "for the time and allegiance of a limited pool of potential volunteers, while *all* of the West End's leaders and activists found themselves stretched and scattered to the point of ineffectiveness."[138]

Social theorist Alain Touraine warns further that these efforts, if left totally to their own devices, could open the way for a retreat into a parochial politics of culture, self-help, and identity.[139] In the old social movements, class tended to unite disparate cultural elements around a common program and ideology. In our era, geographic and interest communities, such as neighborhoods and identity groupings, have become the primary arenas of defense and insurgency, of social action. If the current widespread proliferation and persistence of community organizing is to have a significant impact, that is, to truly address the causes of community problems, efforts must move beyond the narrow focus of cultural and single-issue politics. The challenge is to simultaneously encourage diversity at the grassroots, find unity in varied efforts, and tie cultural politics to political economy. Deliver services, build community, empower people and communities as they seek power at levels—the city, state, and nation—beyond their own limited universe.

Those community organizers working closest to the social work tradition have been quick to respond sensitively to the needs of these cultural and issue-based groups. Cultural competence is a major concern in social work community organizing. Attend a conference or participate in a large discussion with a diverse group of social work activists, and it seems that everyone comes at issues or problems from their own identity base. The discussions are vibrant, vigorous, engaged, and challenging. To hear a disabled woman challenge housing professionals for ignoring the disabled or a gay man with AIDS criticize a homeless coalition for its homophobia brings to mind the resistance of earlier social movements. Social work community organizing understands well the legitimacy and importance of these claims. But the dilemma remains. How do organizers achieve larger structural and political changes in a context divided along cultural lines? Cultural sensitivity will help to empower constituencies and improve service delivery, but the concomitant fragmentation deepens already profound divisions.

The worsening conditions of our cities demand a more unified political response. The problems are great, certainly far beyond the ability of single neighborhood organizations to solve. Luther Jones, who worked extensively with EPISO, an IAF group in El Paso, Texas, puts it bluntly: "There are immense problems along the border that El Paso didn't cause and can't control. We can get these people water, but we're not going to solve poverty."[140] The proliferation of community organizations has not stemmed the tide of overall worsening conditions, especially for the poor and people of color. A more unified political response, however, is undercut not only by the neoconservative context but also by the fragmentation of resistance. Because diversity is both a symptom of the fragmentation of resistance as well as a force for the more humane reorganization of society, the challenge of the 1990s and beyond is for groups to learn how to maintain their identity, focus, and constituency *and* work together in progressive organizations that advance social justice.

Chapter Seven

Conclusion: The Nature, Potential, and Prospects of Neighborhood Organizing

We have built clinics in our communities, rebuilt neighborhoods in inner cities, challenged politicians throughout the country, blocked the strip miners and the redliners, won stop signs and bus lines, we have even stopped a war. We need to recognize not only what we are doing wrong and what we still need to do but how much we are doing right.

—Si Kahn, organizer and musician

The first edition of this book argued that it would have been presumptuous to conclude with a general theory of neighborhood organizing, since the field was still in its infancy and just beginning to develop a body of case studies and theoretical materials. One commentator had specifically warned that "any global assumptions about the results of neighborhood organizing programs across all types of communities is inappropriate."[1] The problem was made more difficult by the inclusion in this work of the three dominant approaches to neighborhood organizing: social work, political activist, and neighborhood maintenance. Almost every study of the subject limited itself to a single type of neighborhood organizing. While the three approaches share much, they are sufficiently different so as to make comparisons, let alone general theories, difficult to construct.[2]

The social work approach views the community essentially as a social organism; it focuses on social issues such as building a sense of community, gathering together social service organizations, or lobbying for and delivering social resources. It assumes that the community's problem is basically social disorganization. The organized group is generally working and lower class. The organizer functions either as an "enabler" to help the community gather itself together or as an "advocate" to secure additional services for the community. The strategy is usually gradualist and consensual, which means that organizers assume a common interest between dominant groups and the neighborhood and a willingness of at least some in power to meet community needs. The structure of organizations in this tradition tends to be more formalized and led by professionals trained in schools of social work. Organizations in this tradition vary in their extent of indigenous participation and grassroots leadership, but the professional community worker is almost always the core of the program. He or she provides at least the initial stimulus for the program, and, quite often, the focus and personality of the organization. The social work approach to community work sees itself as a social agency and operates within the general orientation of the social work profession.

Moreover, the social welfare approach reflects its liberal origins in charity work and social engineering. At their best social welfare projects coordinate and deliver needed social services to the poor and working class and complement services with social action. At their worst they are elitist and manipulative, seeking to maintain existing class arrangements by palliating social problems and coopting social disorder. In both instances social welfare neighborhood organizing projects usually serve at the pleasure of liberally oriented officials and foundations. Community workers may seek to do more in the way of neighborhood organizing; they may seek to gain some power for working people and even challenge the causes of poverty and powerlessness that plague their clients. But in general the reformist vision, liberal objectives, consensus strategies, scanty resources and power, and professional orientation characteristic of the social welfare approach militate against developing democratic grassroots projects that, by altering class and power arrangements in their favor, could truly serve the interests and needs of neighborhood residents.

The political activist approach regards the community as a political entity and/or potential power base. It focuses on obtaining, maintaining, or restructuring power. Or, if it does not seek to empower community residents, it is political in that its goal is to develop alternative institutions. The community's problem, as defined by organizers, is the absence of power needed to defend the neighborhood and/or give people more control over their lives. The organized group is generally working and lower class. The organizer's role is first to help the community understand its problem and its potential power and then to mobilize it around this understanding. The strategy of the political activist ranges from consensual to confrontational, but in all cases it is rooted in the presumption of a conflict of interest between the community and those in power. The organization usually has a less professional and less formal structure than groups in the social work tradition, and leaders if not organizers come more often from the neighborhood. Where the organizers focus solely on their own goals of building the organization rather than on meeting community needs and developing meaningful democratic participation, the political activist approach, like its social work counterpart, can take on an externally led and autocratic posture. Where the political activist approach differs most significantly from the social work model is in its class perspective. The social work approach often seeks a class rapprochement based on a "partnership" between upper-class supporters, social welfare professionals, and working- and lower-class neighborhood residents. The political activist type, on the other hand, seeks to promote, and sometimes resist, social change by challenging those in power, most often at the local level but not infrequently at the national level, too.

As Paul Wellstone noted of his experience with an Alinsky-style organization, the Organization for a Better Rice County, "If I had to pick out the most significant thing that has happened since OBRC's inception, it would be the dramatic change in the political consciousness among the poor."[3] The raised political consciousness to which Wellstone refers does not develop in efforts that seek consensus with the powers that be and that seek to limit and manage conflict. People in neighborhood organizing efforts benefit personally and politically from conflict, though in the short run such conflict may be painful and disharmonious. Kathleen McCourt emphasizes in her study of working-class women organizers that participation in assertive, conflict-oriented, community organizations was a politicizing experience in and of itself, regardless of the issues addressed by the women. Participation in such organizations helped members see the implications of their concerns and armed them with new information, greater self-confidence, and pride. In short, conflict empowers people, for even a defeat against what most of the women saw as an "all powerful" power structure was often a psychic victory that led to continued efforts and greater involvement.[4]

But conflict develops more than individual potential. It prevents a neighborhood organization from becoming a static formal organization. It can help it become a dynamic training ground of democracy and political education that by challenging assumptions about power and poverty in poor communities has the potential to alter class balance or provide the breeding ground for such change. In conflict people are forced to examine and confront the political system and to experiment with strategies of resistance and democratic insurgency. Only those adversarial neighborhood organizing efforts that pursue progressive goals, engage in conflict with existing powers, and do not fear principled struggles within their organizations, however, are true training grounds for democracy and its potential for change.

A third tradition, less commonly thought of as neighborhood organizing, focuses on neighborhood maintenance. Here the community is defined as a residential area. The problem is maintaining and improving the neighborhood while opposing external and internal threats to its permanence and commercial value. The organized group is generally upper or middle class. The organizer comes from within the neighborhood and serves as an elected representative and civic leader of the association; the neighborhood residents serve primarily as dues-paying members of the organization. The strategy is generally one of consensus, wherein the association first applies neighborhood peer pressure to resolve problems and, then, if necessary, resorts to political and legal channels. Unlike the political activist approach, which will publicly confront local officials, neighborhood maintenance associations function as traditional interest groups, most often working quietly behind the scenes in cooperation with local officials. The goal is to promote the neighborhood status quo, focusing essentially on maintaining, if not improving, property values. Unlike the social work and political activist approaches, the neighborhood maintenance tradition is most often found in outer-city neighborhoods and suburbs where residents own single-family homes and where they have a vested property interest in protecting their neighborhood. A study of 197 neighborhood homeowner associations in Indianapolis, for example, did not find a single one in lower socioeconomic areas of the city.[5] Affluent neighborhoods have fewer problems obtaining public services or convincing local power brokers of their needs than those neighborhoods where organizers in the social work and political activist traditions are most active. The neighborhood maintenance association, in fact, is usually free of major problems or pressing concerns, except when threatened by forces of commercial development or social change. Whereas the social welfare approach seeks class rapprochement and the political activist type challenges the class in power, the neighborhood maintenance tradition seeks to defend its class interests and maintain the status quo.

Neighborhood improvement associations in affluent communities tend to act more as neighborhood interest groups than as community-oriented organizations. They have limited citizen participation, are led by the more established residents in the neighborhood, pursue political and economic interests by going through established official channels, and in general do little to create or sustain real community life. They may give the neighborhood a stronger voice at city hall, and they may supply or coordinate the delivery of certain services deemed necessary to maintain or improve the neighborhood. But because the primary objective is improving property values, neighborhood improvement associations tend to bind people together only around a limited and material self-interest. To the extent that the fundamental goal is not the maintenance of property values but the promotion of community life or protection of the community against commercial or urban renewal forces, neighborhood improvement associations tend to become more participatory and better grounded in neighborhood life. (See Table 1 in the introduction for a sketch of these three approaches.)

It is an error, however, to paint these traditions into completely exclusive corners. Studying them together is difficult, but not like comparing apples and oranges. In the decade preceding World War I, partly because of the still weak professionalization of social work, the social work and political activist traditions occasionally overlapped in the more progressive settlements. Settlement workers pioneered the social work tradition of community organization, but they also sought at times to mobilize neighborhood residents in political struggle against local political bosses and industrial sweatshops. As Mary Follett, a settlement worker and activist in the community center movement, proclaimed in 1918: "Politics can no longer be an extra-activity of the American people, it must be a means of satisfying our wants. . . . Our proposal is that the people should organize themselves into neighborhood groups to express their daily life, to bring to the surface the needs, desires, and aspirations of that life, that these needs should become the substance of politics, and that neighborhood groups should become the recognized political unit."[6]

In the 1960s the two approaches overlapped again as the decade's political ferment forced them together. Activist organizers and the organizations they were involved with—SNCC, SDS, and a host of other programs spawned by the black struggle and new left protest, for instance—forced those in the social work tradition to reexamine their consensual and social service approach to community organizing. At the same time, the Great Society coopted many activists into a form of community organizing that straddled both traditions but, as exemplified by the Community Action Program, was rooted in the social work approach.[7] The overlapping is also evident in the contemporary social movement agencies discussed in chapter 6.

Less frequent are connections between the politically conservative, neighborhood maintenance tradition and the other two. Nevertheless, many aspects of Alinskyism and the new populism, especially the neighborhood development approach that appeared in Back of the Yards, The Woodlawn Organization, and the Southeast Community Organization in Baltimore, share much in common with improvement association efforts in more affluent neighborhoods. They are fundamentally localist in outlook, consensual, and interested in improving and protecting their neighborhood and securing additional services. In fact, one of the major impacts of the conservative 1980s was to draw the social work and political activist approaches closer to the neighborhood maintenance model.

New Social Movement Theory

Since the writing of the first edition, social theorists have begun to explain better the diversity, global proliferation, and persistence of community organizing as a dominant form of citizen politics. While it may still be good advice to warn against a single general theory of neighborhood organizing, new social movement theorists, for example, have begun to provide a theoretical paradigm for understanding the origins, nature, growth, and potential of contemporary community organizing in the United States and throughout the globe. Admittedly, any social theory, especially a dualistic one like new social movement theory, is too simple and too rigidly time-bound to do justice to the complexities of both history and social movements. Nevertheless, the global proliferation of a shared form of citizen action suggests that an explanation of grassroots activism, applicable from place to place, is in order.

Let us step back first to the "old" social movements. In the early twentieth century, as described in chapters 1 and 2, social democratic movements arose in the United States and Western Europe in response to the excesses of industrial capitalism. These "old" social movements share critical elements.[8] The locus of organizing was the industrial factory. Here activists organized unions around class issues. Their ideology—social democratic or communist—offered a critique of capitalism and proposed a working-class vision of the future. They targeted their employers, the owners of the means of production, and at the same time they got involved in politics, hoping to win state power. Their victories, in the United States and in Western Europe, became the foundation of politics in the West after World War II. As described in chapter 3, between 1946 and the late 1960s organizers built a consensus around economic growth, welfare state expenditures, and U.S. imperial control. The Fair Deal, the New Frontier, and the Great Society programs personified this era, and the CIO is a classic example of old social movement formation.[9]

Many factors led to the decline of the old social movements. The increasing globalization of the world economy undermined the ability of their political representatives to redistribute resources to constituents. As capital flow increasingly superseded state control in the global economy, the welfare state faced increasing fiscal crises. The social democratic state lost support and those associated with it lost credibility. Moreover, the new postindustrial global economy pressured two inherent weaknesses in the old social movements. First, those social movement leaders developed an increasingly parochial and self-serving agenda. Second, the old social movements may have achieved power as the voice for disadvantaged workers, but they also perpetuated the silence of others, such as minorities, women, and the least skilled. Increasingly, previously quiescent groups such as African-Americans, students, and women organized, challenging the social democratic leaders and parties that excluded them last. The opposition—the new social movements—emerged in insurgent grass-roots associations over issues of democratic participation, personal liberty, civil rights, and quality of life. The heirs of the old social movements, liberal and social democratic politicians in the West, hamstrung by a global economy and under attack from the right and segments of the new social movements for their statist politics, seemed to devolve into anachronisms between 1960 and 1990.[10]

The new social movement opposition to the postwar political economy, while emerging at different places at different times, possesses five characteristics that distinguish it from the old social movements.

First, efforts are community based, that is, they arise around communities of interest or geography, not necessarily at the site of production or against the principal owners of capital.[11]

Second, they are transclass groupings of constituencies and cultural identities, such as African-Americans, ethnics, women, gay men, students, ecologists, and peace activists. Labor becomes one, not *the,* constituency group. Class becomes part of, not *the,* identity.[12]

Third, the ideological glue is a neopopulist vision of democracy. New social movements reject authoritarianism: in the government, leadership, party, organization, and relationships.[13] Their organizational form is sufficiently small, loose, and open to be able to "tap local knowledge and resources, to respond to problems rapidly and creatively, and to maintain the flexibility needed in changing circumstances."[14] As noted in chapter 5, some see the new social movements as "nonideological," because they dismiss the old ideologies of capitalism, communism, and nationalism and because they tend to be without a clear critique of the dominant system. But others argue that ideological congruence is their essence. Their neopopulist principles and beliefs are what makes them new.[15]

Fourth, struggle over culture and social identity play a greater role in contemporary community-based movements than in the workplace-based efforts of the past. "After the great working class parties surrendered their remaining sense of radical political purpose with the onset of the cold war," political scientist Steven Bronner writes, "new social movements emerged to reformulate the spirit of resistance in broader cultural terms."[16] Of course, culture and identity—grounded in historical experience, values, social networks, and collective solidarity—have always been central to social movement formation.[17] But as class becomes increasingly fragmented in the postindustrial city and as the workplace declines in significance as the locus of organizing, resistances that emerge increasingly do so around cultural and identity-specific bases.[18]

Fifth, strategies focus on community self-help and empowerment, though the most effective efforts go beyond building community to targeting the public sector. Most community-based organizing seeks independence from the state rather than state power. It relies on a unitary conception of democracy within the community and deemphasizes adversarial democracy, which challenges national, state, and local politics and presupposes conflicting interests.[19] As social work academician James Midgley points out, central to the rationale of community participation is "a reaction against the centralization, bureaucratization, rigidity, and remoteness of the state. The ideology of community participation is sustained by the belief that the power of the state has extended too far, diminishing the freedoms of ordinary people and their rights to control their own affairs."[20] Community building thus becomes the natural focus of new social movement efforts, reflecting the anti-statist, decentralization trends of the postindustrial political economy. The most effective new social movement efforts, however, understand the limits of decentralization and, therefore, target the public sector. They know, at least implicitly, that the sites of production cannot be leveraged as easily or effectively by the new social movements as they could by the old social movements and, equally important, that the state is the entity potentially most responsible for and vulnerable to new social movement claims and constituencies.[21]

This trend plays out a bit differently in other parts of the world. One key difference is that the old social movements in the Third World and Second World were nationalistic and communistic, respectively, not social democratic as in the West.[22] Given their subordinate position in the world economy, the old social movements, in the Third World for example, did not have the power to deliver material security or political liberty. They often became arms of Western imperial control.

In response to Western imperialism and the failure of national elites, community movements mushroomed. Like their counterparts in the West, they are community-based, constituency or identity oriented, neopopulist in ideology, and focused on self-help strategies. But in the Third World community movements put greater emphasis on material needs.[23] Where old social movements achieved distributional victories only for a few, as in the Southern Hemisphere, or where such victories did not include significant minority segments, as in the United States, new social movements struggle to achieve a minimal standard of living and to provide basic services like housing and health care. Where material victories have occurred, primarily among the more affluent in the United States and Western Europe, the social base tends to be the educated middle class.[24] Where basic material needs still remain to be filled in the Third World and among the oppressed and disenfranchised in the West, new social movement efforts include the poor and powerless and interweave the struggle over "postmaterial values" with material objectives.[25]

Let the People Decide serves as both a refutation and substantiation of new social movement theory. Neighborhood organizing is not just a post–World War II phenomenon. That is a major point of this book. In the United States, especially prior to industrialization, people resisted domination and oppression outside of the factory and outside of a class-conscious movement. Social change movements and politics in the United States have long been organized around race, gender, ethnicity, and cultural issues. But new social movement theory argues that with the coming of the Industrial Revolution, the dominant form of resistance became factory organizing. Likewise, with the shift to a global political economy focused on informational and service functions, which began to occur after World War II and accelerated in the late 1960s, resistance and civic response took on a different *dominant* form.

In this light social settlements, the Cincinnati Social Unit Plan, and the efforts of the Communist party, discussed in chapters 1 and 2, serve as community-based antidotes to the idea that all old social movement activity occurred only in the factory or that all community-based efforts occurred after 1945. There is no denying, however, that these pre–World War II neighborhood organizing efforts were very much class oriented and tied to a social democratic or communist ideology. Saul Alinsky, discussed in chapter 2, is the transitional figure in the history of community organizing in the United States between the old and new social movement form. He blended 1930s union-style organizing and politics with a focus on the citizen rather than class, the community rather than the factory, and the espousal, later, of a "nonideological" approach to organizing.[26] SNCC and ERAP, discussed in chapter 4, and the "neo-Alinskyite" efforts discussed in chapters 5 and 6 take us, for better and for worse, away from the older forms of organizing.

Let the People Decide focuses on the dominant form of neighborhood organizing—such as social work, political activist, or neighborhood maintenance—in each historical period since the 1890s. New social movement theory informs this second edition further by suggesting that community organizing itself became a dominant form of democratic politics after World War II and especially since the 1960s.

Lessons from the Past

What does the future hold for neighborhood organizing? There are certainly as many terribly pessimistic visions as there are optimistic ones.[27] All understand that community-based solutions have limits. Some people, like Edward Camacho, the former research director of the Community Renewal Society, are very critical. "The community movement's influence is "overstated," Camacho argues. "You can find many instances where they have lost consistently. It's not that they don't matter. They are a piece of the quilt. . . . But their powers are extremely marginal."[28] Others, like Harry Boyte, once saw community organizing as the basis of a "backyard democracy" and the "free spaces" of a new citizenship. History can offer a valuable perspective on this debate. It provides a powerful collective memory to legitimize and support current efforts. It also renders a body of knowledge to which contemporary resistance can turn for insights, if not direction.

For example, if the working-class insurgency of the 1930s could emerge out of the "new era" of the late 1920s, and if the civil rights revolution could develop out of the reactionary context of the early 1950s, then surely there is the potential for a revived social activism in the 1990s. What we face in terms of a historical parallel, however, may be more akin to the 1890s than the 1930s or 1960s.[29] The close of the last century came on the heels of an acquisitive era, the heart of the Gilded Age, during the emergence of industrial capitalism in the United States. In the decade of the 1890s financiers amassed great fortunes, extolled the virtues of social Darwinism and laissez-faire capitalism, and used government to keep workers in check and support the corporate agenda. The 1890s, however, was a decade of fierce conflict, new party formations (the Populist party), ideological challenges to free-market capitalism, and, ultimately, the laying of the limited reform agenda and progressive politics of both the Progressive and New Deal eras. Such a scenario of ideological and political struggle over previously ignored and festering social and economic problems is likely in the years ahead; such conditions in the 1890s produced the first neighborhood organizing movement.

Whatever the trajectory of activism, neopopulists correctly instruct us to ground it in the daily experience of people, whether in the neighborhood or the workplace, because these "free spaces" serve as the seedbeds of democratic insurgency.[30] Joe Kling and I go further, however, proposing that the historical dialectic of domination and resistance must be understood and fashioned in terms of the interplay between class, community, and the search for new cultural orientations.[31] Not to do so means that constituency-based efforts will remain parochial and of limited impact. They will be manipulated by, instead of challenging, a global capitalist economy that seeks to replace the centralized welfare state with a less responsible, highly decentralized and privatized apparatus.[32] Therefore, perhaps the following lessons from the past can inform strategies for a more progressive and effective organizing practice in the future.

Neighborhood organizing cuts across the political spectrum. While neighborhood organizing is a political act, it is not inherently reactionary, conservative, liberal, or radical, nor is it inherently democratic and inclusive or authoritarian and parochial. It is above all a political method, an approach used widely by various segments of the population to achieve specific goals, serve certain interests, and advance clear or ill-defined political perspectives. Organizations can be creative efforts open to innovation and supportive of progressive struggles as well as defensive responses to external pressures.

In some ways traditional political labels are not entirely satisfactory in a discussion of neighborhood organizing movements, especially since such labels are relative and people's politics are fluid and not neatly categorized. For example, because an organization seeks to defend traditional values and its neighborhood does not make it reactionary or even conservative. Craig Jackson Calhoun, in an important theoretical study of populist insurgency, writes that "traditional cultural values and immediate communal relations are crucial to many radical movements, (a) because these commitments provide populations with the extent of internal social organization necessary to concerted, radical collective action, and (b) because the largely defensive goals of these movements must be radically incompatible with the introduction of modern capitalist-dominated social formations."[33]

Or, put another way, radical organization can develop out of "conservative" communities when these communities confront social changes that threaten communal relations and attachments to family, friends, and customary ways of life, and that leave them nothing to lose. Most traditional communities tend to develop conservative neighborhood organizations. But given certain historical conditions, such locales do become radical to defend what they have. Similarly, successful "radical" organizations—TWO comes to mind first—may become more conservative when they achieve or seek to achieve greater success. As the process of democracy is not static, neither is the politics of a neighborhood organizing project.

Neighborhood organizing movements develop in a historical context that includes yet transcends local community borders. Conditions at the local level directly spawn and nurture neighborhood organizing projects. The organizers, residents, local conditions, and many other factors at the grassroots level combine to forge consistently unique neighborhood organizing experiences. But while neighborhood organizing projects do have a significant origin, nature, and existence of their own at the local level, they are also the products of national and even international political and economic developments. To no small degree, the larger political-economic context often determines the general tenor and success of local efforts.

The national political economy affects neighborhood organizing in surprising ways. Many incorrectly assume, for example, that radical organizing occurs and thrives only during periods of national economic depression, or that conservative neighborhood maintenance groups form and succeed only in periods of national affluence. While such a theory appears accurate for the 1930s and 1950s, it is not appropriate for the early twentieth century or for the 1960s. In the 1960s and early 1970s, for example, a period of national economic prosperity produced profound radical challenges to the contradictions and hypocrisy of an "affluent society." In the late 1970s and 1980s a period of economic decline yielded a conservative response.

Nevertheless, specific conditions at the national and local levels determine opportunities available to groups to press for their own interests. That neighborhood improvement associations have been continuously active since the 1890s testifies to the ability of those people with wealth and power to defend and enhance their position in all eras. Improvement associations, however, are more prominent, more powerful, when during national prosperity there is a national, conservative political sentiment against social change, as there was in the 1920s and 1950s, the two heydays of improvement association activity.

Likewise, the efforts of working-class and poor people's organizations develop best in periods of profound social dislocation when (1) the regulatory power of social institutions break down and (2) sharp economic change occurs producing depressed *or* improved conditions, the former encouraging people to defend themselves, the latter raising their expectations. It is not so much prosperity or depression at the national and local level that leads to radical neighborhood organizing, but rather external pressures on traditional communities and a breakdown of the routines of daily life that make people more receptive to activism and alternative organizations. Disturbances in the larger political economy, however, are necessary to create the conditions in which the powerless move to mass political insurgency.[34]

There is a critical interaction between neighborhood organizing efforts, national politics, and nationwide social movements. The response at the national level to grassroots movements either encourages or represses them. The conservative atmosphere and policies of the 1920s and 1950s supported the creation of suburban protective associations. The liberal leadership of the first decades of the twentieth century and the 1960s encouraged the expansion of social welfare neighborhood organizing projects. Sometimes liberal attempts at cooption led to heightened, rather than defused, radical activity. Where liberal leaders failed to coopt insurgency, however, as in the late 1940s and late 1960s, the government ultimately resorted to repression.[35] This is not to suggest that the national government is an all-powerful arm of the ruling groups in the United States. While it functions mainly in the service of the upper class, the government also serves as a battleground, an arena of conflict, where grassroots groups can pressure the ruling groups for change. The national government is not as formidable, well directed, or monolithic as it once appeared from the grassroots to be.

A critical interaction also occurs between neighborhood organizing projects and nationwide social movements. Generally, neighborhood organizing and other forms of grassroots activity serve as the building blocks of larger social movements. They provide the spaces, organizational skills, and grassroots heritage that can renew itself in political struggle.[36] At the same time, national movements, once established, provide direction and support to local efforts. This was true in the Progressive era, with national movement leaders coming out of local reform campaigns and then, once in power, assisting directly and indirectly liberal efforts at the local level. It was also the case in the civil rights movement, as the movement developed first at the local level, grew to national proportions, and spawned, often unintentionally, the efforts of SNCC, SDS, and the antiwar and black power movements. On occasion, national movements that are detached from local institutions and are organized largely at the national or state level, as was the antiwar movement of the 1960s and 1970s, distract and detract from community organizing efforts. But generally community and national movements of similar political persuasions reinforce each other, and the destruction of one often signals the imminent decline of the other. In the 1980s for example, the rise of the New Right movement dramatically affected community efforts on both the right and left.

Problems besetting neighborhoods demand political organization beyond the neighborhood level.   Small may be beautiful, more manageable, and more feasible for democratic participation, but commonly the neighborhood is neither the site of the causes of its problems nor the site of the power needed to address them. The limited effectiveness of neighborhood organizing since the 1890s demonstrates the existence of powerful forces beyond the local level that are antagonistic to the neighborhood. Sidney Dillick, the author of the first monograph on the history of neighborhood organizing, pointed out over a generation ago "the danger of focusing attention upon neighborhood needs to the neglect of the underlying social forces not necessarily originating in the neighborhood."[37]

Relatedly, what neighborhood organizing movements need, as the experiences of the new left and many other projects since have demonstrated, are ongoing, national political organizations that can provide continuity, direction, and motivation for local efforts and that, in turn, can be guided and reinvigorated by struggles in communities and workplaces at the local level. Without the continuity provided by a federated national organization, neighborhood organizing projects usually start their work anew, in a vacuum, without benefit of historical experience or perspective, and generally must survive on their own, against very powerful forces and odds and without experience and support.

While the need for larger and more powerful organizational forms seems obvious, the history of neighborhood organizing, in general, tends to be one of working alone, not joining with other groups. And that is still the case. In the mindset of most community activists, democratic participation and larger organizational forms are antagonistic.[38] Coalitions and alliances sound reasonable and simple enough, except when you consider that most neopopulist and identity groups, for example the IAF, have little to do with other comparable efforts. Competition for scarce resources as well as differences in politics, culture, and strategy continue to divide them.

This is a central problem for organizing. Strategies must focus on building organizational forms that bring people together—coalitions, alliances, networks, and political parties. Feminist practice in social work proposes that the first steps are ideological. A focus on unity instructs that oppressed people must build solidarity with other oppressed people. In so doing organizers affirm variety and diversity while working "to synthesize and build unity that transcends diversity."[39]

Increasingly, people are building new progressive alliances. Gregory Pierce argues that community organization offers residents and members of church congregations the opportunity to build neighborhood coalitions.[40] No one type of neighborhood organizing is sufficient, he argues. In fact, the more progressive efforts, the better. But these efforts must be able to work together to form community organizations large and powerful enough to confront the causes of problems. Neal Pierce and Carol Steinbach in their study of CDCs concur: "As macro-economic forces erode still further the position of society's poorest, and federal deficits prevent broad national remedies, the local alliances may be the only vehicle for change."[41] Political commentator Barbara Ehrenreich calls for a broad coalition of the middle class and working class to bring about significant social change. Mike Miller of the Organize Training Center argues that "the middle class needs to tell and be told its own story of oppression—the private lives of quiet desperation that so frequently characterize its individualism."[42] Only then will they be able to forge coalitions with other classes and see themselves as part of the common plight, not distanced, alienated yuppies or charity workers.

Of course, it is not easy to build larger organizational forms. It is the hardest type of community organizing work; almost everyone wants to put in as little as possible and get out of it more than they put in.[43] Nevertheless, in communities throughout the nation people organize coalitions, alliances, and networks to enhance their power and potential. They form around neighborhood concerns such as housing, homelessness, poverty, safety, schools, abortion, ecology, and peace, as well as around identity-specific groups such as gays, lesbians, seniors, the handicapped, African-Americans, Latinos, Asian-Americans, and labor.[44] Organizers recognize that building multicultural coalitions and alliances is one of the primary tasks ahead.[45]

Neighborhood organizing requires a gentle balance between organizing, leading, and educating. The best organizer is not so much a leader as a catalyst. "Grassroots organizations must have organizers," Michael Ansara of Mass Fair Share noted, "just as they eventually must be led and controlled by the local people."[46] To the extent that the organizer assumes a controlling leadership role, he or she reinforces ideas and insecurities among neighborhood people of how and why they cannot lead themselves. To the extent that organizing perpetuates the mystique of the great, gifted, self-sacrificing, professional organizer, people shy away from tasks and rely on the organizer. The organizer may accomplish many things, but he or she will not develop indigenous leaders, will not be able to educate people in the process of democracy, will perpetuate interest-group styles of neighborhood organizing, and will not organize a project with any long-term staying power. The best organizers are not the ones who are the most skilled, energetic, or forceful, but rather those who have a sense of both a larger vision and what is possible and combine this with the knowledge, ability, and skills of local people.

But organizers do need to provide leadership. Organizing projects that completely deny the leadership role of the organizer and emphasize letting the people decide are often either dishonest and manipulative or parochial and undirected. James Forman, a SNCC leader, correctly criticized "an ailment known as local-people-itis . . . [which] carried with it the idea that local people could do no wrong, that no one, especially somebody from outside the community, should initiate any kind of action or assume any form of leadership."[47] Organizers bring ideology, skills, experience, and perspective to their work; they owe it to neighborhood people to share this with them openly and honestly. Not to do so will in the long run increase suspicion. The craft is to do so in a democratic manner where organizers see themselves not only as catalysts and guides but also as recipients of the knowledge, experience, and strength of local people and their traditions, where there is a true sense of sharing in a dynamic democratic process.

All formal organizations tend toward oligarchic control, toward organizational maintenance objectives superseding other goals, and toward defusing citizen participation by giving the impression that since an organization already exists to carry the struggle, personal sacrifice for the cause is no longer necessary. Nevertheless, creating powerful organizations, even if they exist only for a few years, is critical to advancing the interests of neighborhood people. While there are no sure cures for the maladies of formal organizations, neighborhood organizations can make important gains in counteracting and preventing them by espousing an ideology and engaging in a practice of organizing that is committed to membership education, democratic process, and long-term objectives.

Political education must be an integral part of neighborhood organizing. Clearly not all organizers can do political education or do it simultaneously with other tasks. Advocating a clear, long-term vision that addresses class imbalances is often impolitic for those engaged in daily organizing activities, especially for leaders of neighborhood organizing projects. What is necessary is a subtle division of labor among organizers, where possible, so that some are able to focus more on organization-building questions and others are more free to address issues of political education. Political education should help people develop the confidence necessary to rely on themselves, win the personal dignity and self-respect basic to participation, and challenge existing authority when necessary. It should not simply teach organization-building skills but must also reveal the roots of people's problems in the workings of the economic and political system.

Moreover, education must be ongoing and tied to a class perspective. If not, most people in neighborhood organizing projects will continue to believe that once those in power are shown the problem and the errors of their ways, either through conflict or consensus tactics, they will support the necessary remedies. Without this, despite continued problems and conflicts, most people will continue to believe that the system, with all its faults, is inherently good, that inadequacies can be corrected, and that racism, sexism, poverty, income inequities, and powerlessness are due to individual mistakes or historical circumstances rather than elements inherent in the social, political, and economic structure. The role of political education, which is an analysis that grows out of people's political experience, is to broaden people's perspective and to give them more information on which they can make more reasoned assessments of the conditions, problems, and alternative solutions they face.[48]

Neighborhood organizing must create a more consciously ideological practice. Most neighborhood organizing projects emphasize the importance of delivering rewards and incentives to keep member interest high and the organization progressing. Alinskyism was based on the assumption that people organize solely for their own economic self-interest. Similarly, neighborhood improvement associations are rooted in maintaining property values, and liberal social welfare programs are geared to offering rewards and incentives in the form of social services. Such material incentives are important, but they are not the glue that keeps neighborhood organizing efforts together. Victories are critical; people see themselves and their power differently after initial successes. But effective neighborhood organizing efforts, especially in lower income areas where the neighborhood organization does not have the resources to deliver rewards for very long, demands more than a reliance on incentives. In order to sustain an organization, especially of the political activist type, and to promote long-range objectives, neighborhood organizing must be built around issues of personal development and an ideology that articulates a sense of purpose extending beyond individual advantage.[49] It must be committed to developing the knowledge, dignity, and self-confidence of community residents. And these people must come to see themselves as part of a larger cause. While traditional interest-group studies on neighborhood organizing emphasized that indigenous people prefer organizations that deliver services and immediate rewards rather than those which are engaged in social change or revolutionary objectives, those political activist organizations that have been most successful over time, whether Unemployed Councils in the 1930s or SNCC in the 1960s, were part of larger social movements and incorporated into their work and into their organizing a class- or race-based vision of something worth fighting for that was larger and more important than simply member self-interest.[50]

Most social welfare and neighborhood improvement association projects make no pretense of developing a mobilizing ideology. Populist neighborhood organizing efforts in the twentieth century have never been able to articulate a vision of society beyond corporate liberalism and the New Deal. Marxist and politically radical neighborhood organizing efforts, from the Unemployed Councils to later projects such as those of the Black Panther party, came closest to articulating a broad ideology that addressed the causes of poverty and powerlessness. But a vision of noncapitalist transformation has to be attentive to such traditional American ideals as equality, self-help, local self-reliance, participatory democracy, group solidarity, cultural pluralism, and grassroots insurgency. Of course, putting forward a clear, long-term vision does not guarantee success. The Populist farmers movement of the late nineteenth century, the CIO organizing drives of the 1930s, and the black power movement of the late 1960s all articulated, to greater or lesser degree, a radical, participatory vision, but were destroyed by external pressures and government repression activated by that vision. Lower-class and working-class neighborhood organizing must develop long-range goals that address imbalances in a class society, an alternative vision of what people are fighting for, and a context for all activity, whether pressuring for a stop sign or an eviction blockage. Otherwise, as has happened repeatedly, victories that win services or rewards will *undermine* the organization by "proving" that the existing system is responsive to poor and working people and, therefore, in no need of fundamental change.

An essential task of the organizer is to help create a progressive oppositional consciousness tied to people's daily lives and to specific demands and policies. Ideological organizing has always been suspect in much of community organizing. Now even critical social theorists doubt the efficacy of ideological constructs. Postmodern theory declares the death of universal ideologies, such as Marxism.[51] Nevertheless, we must seek new unifying narratives of progressive social change, or, at least, more common programs that can draw the decentered politics of our time toward a focal point. Organizations guided by a democratic program and activists skilled at articulating problems and bringing people to deeper levels of understanding about the character of their political-economic world are the only instruments we have to ground insurgency in people's day-to-day lives and move it into larger organizational forms and into more inclusive ideological frameworks. Historian George Rude, for example, argues that all successful transformative social movements include a two-part ideology: a popular, inherent ideology rooted in people's traditions *and* a derived ideology, primarily external, that connects their concerns to forces and events beyond personal experience.[52] Together they form the basis of an ideology of resistance and insurgence that legitimates grievances and mobilizes and sustains participants. Other factors, of course, are critical. But without such consciously ideological leadership and organizations, and the willingness to engage in ideological conflict, the discourse of dominant groups reproduces itself. There is no other way to move people to a set of ideas that critiques the current system, understands the importance of class and community, connects work to place and public to private spheres, and gets people to take risks and transcend what they thought was possible for themselves and their world.

This is a dilemma inherent in all organizing. Democratic social change relies on people's perceived understanding of their grievances. At the same time, to get at the causes of these problems, those very people must come to relate the larger sources of their grievances to objective conditions outside their immediate experience. Current politics lacks this sort of clearly focused ideological cleavage. It is the responsibility of organizers to help create it, because without ideological conflict community mobilization efforts will not advance very far.

Ideological conflict is necessary to combat corporate domination, service cutbacks, racial and gender discrimination, unwanted luxury real estate development, and industrial despoilation. Racial tensions, the belief that women threaten men's jobs, hostility to gay rights, suspicions of affirmative action, the attempt to resolve the menace of environmental pollution by putting the incinerator in the next community, the belief that the rising violence in America can be stopped only by building more prisons, training more police, and owning more guns, the idea that people are allies only as far as their immediate material interests are concerned—these are not convictions that spontaneously disappear as people struggle to control the conditions of their lives. Certain values still must be challenged by organizers if new progressive ones are to develop. Without ideological challenges, those in power continue to set the agenda, and activists continue to respond to it. The danger is that "you become a junior partner, negotiating within a framework already defined by someone else."[53] This kind of opposition may make some things better, but it may also make things only get worse a little more slowly.[54]

Take, for example, the problem of privatization. Increasingly we live in a world where public life and the public sector disappear and private life and the private sector dominate. Organizations must do more than focus on their communities—building community, empowering residents, delivering services. Their work must include an explicit critique of the increasing privatization of problems, policies, programs, and politics in the local and global political economy. New formations and groupings will make community mobilization stronger. But an explicitly oppositional ideology, a progressive vision and critique of the privatized status quo, is necessary if community movements are not to remain bound by the limits of personalized and localized consciousness and if they are to challenge the structural roots and causes of contemporary problems.

The organizer's most valuable skill remains the ability to challenge the accepted vision of things. It lies with the understanding of what is involved in moving people beyond their received notions of how they are related to other cultural and identity-based groups. It rests with the sensitivity that brings people to recognize the ways in which a deep and authentic commitment to "human solidarity, mutual responsibility, and social justice" demands a profound reexamination of the values on which their society, and way of life, is based. Such transformations of consciousness do not emerge without intervention and engagement.

What intellectual, theoretically based content might such an ideology have? The first edition of this book was criticized by some for its lack of a specific ideology. Obviously, the nature of any progressive ideology salient to our times is still very much in the making. Some current visions are greener, others blacker, others still red—though of a social democratic, rather than communist, hue. Any new critique of the present, vision of the future, and strategy to move from one to the other must recognize the importance of linkages between community experience and struggles for the affirmation of identity, on the one hand, and larger class and institutional structures on the other. Barbara Epstein argues that building

a majoritarian movement requires a hegemonic project that is more than the array of particular constituencies and perspectives that now make up the opposition to the power of the right. . . . The labor/liberal alliance of the 30s was organized primarily around issues of economic justice and the distribution of resources. In the late 20th century, any parallel historic bloc will have to be organized around cultural as well as economic issues in order to contest for hegemony. . . . [T]here is still a need for economic restructuring, but the issues of the late 20th century also require a profound transformation of values.[55]

An organizing ideology for our times needs to combine new demands for autonomy and identity with older ones for social justice, production for human needs rather than profit, and a spirit of connectedness and solidarity rather than competition.

The bases for such an ideology can be found in the themes that have been emerging in community organizing and social movements since the end of the 1950s. Concerns for social justice, and the strategies for achieving it, developed out of the new social movements of the past generation, from civil rights through black power, antiwar, women's, Chicano, and neighborhood efforts. Continuing critiques of global capitalism and free enterprise have been sharpened and refined by the insights of neo-Marxist political economy in recent years, the dissection of statist societies carried out by the dissidents of Eastern Europe, and the critiques of global imperialism offered by activists and intellectuals on the left in the Third World. Feminist theory instructs us on the need to build relationships, make connections, and accept responsibility—connecting the public and private, challenging patriarchal and hierarchical forms of domination, and recognizing the importance of solidarity across differences of class, ethnicity, race, and sexual orientation. Finally, following from Alain Touraine and the student movements of the late 1960s, there is the demand for autonomy from technocratic control, stemming from the belief that people have the ability and the right to control their day-to-day lives and feel empowered as both private and public citizens.

Day-to-day organizing, if it is to move beyond the received wisdom of traditional values and cultures, must be informed by this sort of challenging politics grounded in the central social movements and intellectual discourse of our era. Social justice and autonomy for one dominated group is impossible without social justice and autonomy for all. Individual freedom cannot be achieved without sustaining and nurturing connections to the greater whole, be it humanity, nature, or the planet. Local organizing must include not only a critique of global corporate capitalism but a demand for a responsible public, from the grassroots to the state apparatus. To open activists and constituencies to this broader conception is, along with coalition/alliance formation, the primary challenge to organizers in the 1990s.

Ironically, global capitalism destroys community at the same time it forces people back into it as their primary source of defense. Such structural contradictions mobilize opposition and lead, in the short run, to social disorder, spontaneous rebellion, and grassroots organizing around a wide array of issues and concerns. The task for organizers is to tie people's understanding of their grievances to an analysis that expands as well as addresses the problems, constituencies, and communities with which they immediately identify. "Think Global, Act Local," as the Greenpeace slogan goes, is correct. But it is not enough in our shrinking world. We must also begin to think about how to "Act Global" through international organizations, coalitions, alliances, and networks. The challenges are immense. A consciously ideological, grassroots leadership committed to opposing the privatization of life and to building larger organizational forms is essential.

Notes and References

Introduction

1. Karen Paget, "Citizen Organizing: Many Movements, No Majority," *American Prospect* 7 (Summer 1990): 115–16.
2. Richard C. Harwood, *Citizen and Politics: A View from Mainstreet America* (Dayton, Ohio: Kettering Foundation, 1991), 5.
3. Alain Touraine, "An Introduction to the Study of Social Movements," *Social Research* 52 (Winter 1985: 749–87); Immanuel Wallerstein, "Antisystemic Movements: History and Dilemmas," in *Transforming the Revolution: Social Movements and the World-System* ed. S. Amin et al. (New York: Monthly Review Press, 1990); Alberto Melucci, *Nomads of the Present: Social Movements and Individual Needs in Contemporary Society* (Philadelphia: Temple University Press, 1989); Joan Cocks, *The Oppositional Imagination* (London: Routledge, 1989); Manuel Castells, *The City and the Grassroots* (Berkeley: University of California Press, 1983).
4. Jeff Drumtra, "Power to the People," *World View* 4 (Winter 1991–92): 8–13.
5. Alan Durning, "Action at the Grassroots: Fighting Poverty and Environmental Decline," *Worldwatch Paper* 88 (January 1989): 5.
6. Paget, "Citizen Organizing," 116.
7. Stuart Lowe, *Urban Social Movements: The City After Castells* (London: Macmillan, 1986).
8. Durning, "Action at the Grassroots," 6–7.
9. A. G. Frank and M. Fuentes, "Civil Democracy: Social Movements in Recent World History," in *Transforming the Revolution*, ed. Amin et al., 163.

235

10. Robert F. Berkhofer, Jr., "Comment on James A. Henretta, 'Social History as Lived and Written,'" *American Historical Review* 84 (December 1979): 1328.

11. Rachelle B. Warren and Donald I. Warren, *The Neighborhood Organizer's Handbook* (Notre Dame: University of Notre Dame Press, 1977), 96; Suzanne Keller, *The Urban Neighborhood* (New York: Random House, 1968), 128.

12. Sandra Perlman Schoenberg and Patricia L. Rosenbaum, *Neighborhoods That Work: Sources for Viability in the Inner City* (New Brunswick: Rutgers University Press, 1980), p. 2.

13. Scott Green and Ann Lennarson, eds., *The Neighborhood and Ghetto: The Local Area in Large-Scale Society* (New York: Basic Books, 1974), 309.

14. Richard Clay Rich, "The Political Economy of Neighborhood Organization" (Ph.D. diss., Indiana University, 1977), 9.

15. On the issue of the importance of collective memory to resistance movements, see George Lipsitz, *A Life in the Struggle: Ivory Perry and the Culture of Opposition* (Philadelphia: Temple University Press, 1988).

Chapter One

1. For additional information see Douglass Dowd, *The Twisted Dream: Capitalist Development in the United States* (Cambridge: Winthrop Publishers, 1974).

2. James Weinstein, *The Corporate Ideal in the Liberal State: 1900–1918* (Boston: Beacon Press, 1968), and Gabriel Kolko, *The Triumph of Conservatism: A Reinterpretation of American History, 1900–1916* (New York: Free Press, 1963), were among the first works to advance the corporate liberal thesis about progressivism.

3. Anthony M. Platt, *The Child Savers: The Invention of Delinquency* (Chicago: University of Chicago Press, 1969), xxii.

4. Thomas Lee Philpott, *The Slum and the Ghetto: Neighborhood Deterioration and Middle-Class Reform*, Chicago, 1880–1930 (New York: Oxford University Press, 1978), is an impressive critique of the settlement movement.

5. Robert A. Woods, *The Neighborhood in Nation-Building* (New York: Arno Press, 1970), 148–49. See also Roy Lubove, *The Professional Altruist: The Emergence of Social Work as a Career, 1880–1930* (New York: Atheneum, 1969).

6. Woods, *Neighborhood*, 112, 287; Jesse Steiner, "An Appraisal of the Community Movement," *Journal of Social Forces* 7 (March 1929): 334–35; Allen Davis, *Spearheads for Reform: The Social Settlements and the Progressive Movement, 1890–1914* (New York: Oxford University Press, 1967).

7. Woods, *Neighborhood*, 53.

8. Philpott, *Slum and Ghetto* 76–95.

9. John Daniels, *America via the Neighborhood* (New York: Harper, 1920), 218.

10. Philpott, *Slum and Ghetto*, 80–81.

11. Daniels, *America via the Neighborhood*, 220–21.

12. Ibid., 222.

13. Ibid., 223.

14. Because these self-help associations were not fundamentally neighborhood organizations, that is, the residential area was not the primary basis of organization, they are mentioned here only in passing. See the Bibliography for relevant materials.

15. Philpott, *Slum and Ghetto*, 79, 285.

16. Jeffrey Gurock, *When Harlem Was Jewish, 1870–1930* (New York: Columbia University Press, 1979), 94–98.

17. Clinton Childs, *A Year's Experiment in Social Center Organization* (New York: Social Center Committee, 1912), 21.

18. John Collier, "The Dynamics of the Community Movement," *Community Center*, 13 February 1917; John Collier, "Democracy Every Day, III," *Survey* 40 (28 September 1918): 710.

19. From People's Institute MSS, New York Public Library, reprinted in the *New York Times*, 13 October 1918, sec. 4, p. 8.

20. Leroy Bowman, "Community Organization," *American Journal of Sociology* 35 (May 1930): 1008. See also Lubove, *The Professional Altruist*; and Jesse Steiner, *Community Organization: A Study of Its Theory and Current Practice* (Chicago: University of Chicago Press, 1930).

21. Wilbur Phillips, *Adventuring for Democracy* (New York: Social Unit Press, 1940), 59.

22. Anatole Shaffer, "The Cincinnati Social Unit Experiment: 1917–1919," *Social Service Reviews* 45 (June 1971): 161; Patricia Mooney Melvin, "A Cluster of Interlacing Communities: The Cincinnati Social Unit Plan and Neighborhood Organization, 1900–1920," in *Community Organization for Urban Social Change: A*

Historical Perspective, ed. Robert Fisher and Peter Romanofsky (Westport, Conn.: Greenwood Press, 1981), 58–88.

23. Robert A. Woods and Albert J. Kennedy, *The Zone of Emergence*, cited in Melvin, "Cluster of Interlacing Communities," 102–3.

24. Melvin, "Cluster of Interlacing Communities," 103–8.

25. Ibid., 105–11.

26. Ibid., 110–15.

27. Phillips, *Adventuring*, 280–307.

28. Shaffer, "Cincinnati Social Unit Experiment," 169.

29. Phillips, *Adventuring*, 112.

Chapter Two

1. Of course, the more conservative, social welfare approach to neighborhood organizing was alive if not necessarily well in the social settlements and other neighborhood-based social welfare agencies. But the efforts of settlements were more acts of treading water than new and important developments in the history of neighborhood organizing.

2. This overview of the depression and the New Deal relies on many works. Those that come to mind most readily are Frances Fox Piven and Richard Cloward, *Poor People's Movements: Why They Succeed, How They Fail* (New York: Vintage, 1979), especially 44–48, 107–20; Barton Bernstein, "The New Deal: The Conservative Achievements of Liberal Reform," in *Towards a New Past: Dissenting Essays in American History*, ed. Barton Bernstein (New York: Random House, 1967) 263–88; and William Leuchtenberg, *Franklin D. Roosevelt and the New Deal* (New York: Harper Torchbook, 1963).

3. Piven and Cloward, *Poor People's Movements*, 48–49.

4. For more information on the Socialist party's "traditional" and "unimaginative" community organizing see Roy Rosenzweig, "Organizing the Unemployed: The Early Years of the Great Depression, 1929–1933," *Radical America* 10 (July–August 1976): 38–39.

5. Ibid., 39.

6. Piven and Cloward, *Poor People's Movements*, 51.

7. Charles Trout, Boston, *The Great Depression, and the New Deal* (New York: Oxford University Press, 1977), 55–57.

8. Rosenzweig, "Organizing the Unemployed," 41.

9. Steve Nelson, James Barrett, and Rob Ruck, Steve Nelson, *American Radical* (Pittsburgh: University of Pittsburgh Press, 1981), 77–78, 176, 414.

10. See Mark Naison, "Harlem Communists and the Politics of Black Protest," in *Community Organization*, ed. Fisher and Romanofsky, 89–126, for an impressive, brief discussion of party organizing in the black community of Harlem.

11. Ibid., 114–16; Mark Naison to author, 8 April 1982.

12. Mark Naison, "The Communist Party in Harlem, 1928–1936" (Ph.D. diss., Columbia University, 1976), 137. This thesis has since been published under the title Communists in Harlem during the Depression (Urbana: University of Illinois Press, 1983).

13. St. Clair Drake and Horace R. Cayton, *Black Metropolis* (1945; reprint, New York: Harper, 1962), 735.

14. Naison, "Harlem Communists," 88–98.

15. Naison, "The Communist Party in Harlem," 383.

16. Naison, "Harlem Communists," 112; Piven and Cloward, *Poor People's Movements*, 76–79.

17. Rosenzweig, "Organizing the Unemployed," 46.

18. Naison, "Harlem Communists," 109–12.

19. Paul Wellstone, "Notes on Community Organizing," *Journal of Ethnic Studies* 4 (1976): 78; Marion K. Sanders, "The Professional Radical: Conversations with Saul Alinsky," Harper's Magazine 230 (June 1965): 45 especially; and Harry Boyte, *The Backyard Revolution: Understanding the New Citizen Movement* (Philadelphia: Temple University Press, 1980), 49–54.

20. Playboy, March 1972, 72, quoted in Charles F. Levine, "Understanding Alinsky," *American Behavioral Scientist* 17 (November–December, 1973): 280; Harry C. Boyte, "Community Organizing in the 1970s: Seeds of Democratic Revolt," in *Community Organization*, ed. Fisher and Romanofsky, 217–38.

21. Sanders, "Professional Radical" 45; Saul Alinsky interviewed in Studs Terkel, *Hard Times* (New York: Avon, 1970), 358–61; Gurney Breckenfield, "Chicago: Back of the Yards," in *The Human Side of Urban Renewal: A Study of the Attitude Changes Produced by Neighborhood Revitalization*, ed. Martin Millspaugh, Gurney Breckenfield, and Miles Colean (New York: Ives Washburn, 1960), 182–84.

22. Sanders, "Professional Radical," p. 45. Alinsky exaggerated fascist strength in Back of the Yards to overemphasize the success of

his work. On another occasion he noted, for example, that a Benedictine priest who was leading the Coughlinite movement in the neighborhood was frustrated because no one "paid him any attention." Alinsky boasted that he later made the priest the chairman of the neighborhood antifascist committee.

23. Michael P. Connolly, "An Historical Study of Change in Saul D. Alinsky's Community Organization Practice and Theory, 1939–1972" (Ph.D. diss., University of Minnesota, 1976), 91–92.

24. Saul Alinsky, *Reveille for Radicals* (Chicago: University of Chicago Press, 1946), 132–33.

25. Breckenfield, "Chicago: Back of the Yards," 7.

26. Alinsky quoted in Terkel, *Hard Times*, 360.

27. Ibid.

28. Breckenfield, "Chicago: Back of the Yards," 186.

29. Connolly, "Historical Study," 114–24.

30. Alinsky, *Reveille*, 138–46.

31. Connolly, "Historical Study," 122.

32. Breckenfield, "Chicago: Back of the Yards," 210.

33. For this quote and additional materials critical of the "system-confirming" aspects of Alinskyism, see Joan E. Lancourt, *Confront or Concede: The Alinsky Citizen Action Organizations* (Lexington, Mass.: Lexington Books, 1979).

34. Stanley Aronowitz, "Poverty, Politics, and Community Organization," *Studies on the Left* 4 (Summer 1964): 104; Wellstone, "Notes on Community Organizing," 78.

Chapter Three

1. Gabriel Kolko, *Main Currents in Modern American History* (New York: Harper and Row, 1976), 318.

2. Rosenstein quoted in the *New York Times*, 31 January 1953.

3. Stuart Queen, Alfred Carpenter, and David Bailey, *The American City* (Westport, Conn.: Greenwood Press, 1953), 168.

4. See Elmore B. McKee, *The People Act: Stories of How Americans Are Coming Together to Deal with Their Community Problems* (New York: Harper, 1955).

5. American Council for the Community MSS, Social Welfare History Archive, Minneapolis, Minn.

6. Phillip Ryan, "Social Welfare in a Changing World," address to New Hampshire Social Welfare Council, 11 September 1953, National Social Welfare Assembly MSS, Social Welfare History Archive.

7. The agencies included the American Hygiene Association, the Child Welfare League of America, the Committee on Careers in Nursing, the Family Service Association of America, the National Board of the YWCA, the National Catholic Community Service, the National Committee on Social Work in Defense Mobilization, the National Federation of Settlements and Neighborhood Centers, the National League for Nursing, the National Probation and Parole Association, the National Recreation Association, the National Traveler's Aid Association, the National Urban League, and the American Federation of Labor and Congress of Industrial Organizations' Community Services committees.

8. Louis B. Seltzer, *The Nation's Strength* (United Community Defense Services pamphlet, 1953?). For more detailed information on UCDS and "critical defense areas" see Marvin A. Palacek, *Battle of the Bureaucracies* (New York: Vantage Press, 1972), and Reginald Robinson, *Serving the Small Community: The Story of United Community Defense Services* (New York: Association Press, 1959).

9. National Association for Social Welfare MSS, Social Welfare History Archive.

10. United Community Defense Services Minutes, Meeting on Paducah, Kentucky, 31 October 1951, American Social Health Association MSS, Social Welfare History Archive.

11. Elizabeth Wickenden, "Military Defense and Social Welfare," August 1955, National Association of Social Welfare MSS, Social Welfare History Archive.

12. Elizabeth Wickenden, "The Social Factor of National Defense," September 1954, 38, National Federation of Settlements MSS, Social Welfare History Archive.

13. American Social Health Association MSS, Social Welfare History Archive.

14. Ibid.

15. For a good introduction to the history of neighborhood improvement associations see Joseph Arnold, "The Neighborhood and City Hall: The Origin of Neighborhood Associations in Baltimore, 1880–1911," *Journal of Urban History* 6 (November 1979): 3–30.

16. Zane Miller, "The Role and Concept of Neighborhood in American Cities," in *Community Organization*, ed. Fisher and Romanofsky, 8–10.

17. Roderick D. McKenzie, *The Neighborhood: A Study of Local*

Life in Columbus, Ohio (Chicago: University of Chicago Press, 1923), 361–62.

18. Amalie Hofer, *Neighborhood Improvement in and about Chicago, 1909* (Chicago: Newell E. Stiles, 1909), 20.

19. Woodland Heights promotion brochure, 1909, Houston Metropolitan Research Center, Subdivision File.

20. Philpott, *Slum and Ghetto*, 148.

21. Drake and Cayton, *Black Metropolis*, 70, 178–79.

22. Philpott, *Slum and Ghetto*, 181–200; Drake and Cayton, Black Metropolis. 178–87.

23. Truman speech appointing the Committee on Civil Rights, 1946, quoted in Howard Zinn, *A People's History of the United States* (New York: Harper and Row, 1980), 440.

24. Clement E. Vose, *Caucasians Only: The Supreme Court, the NAACP, and the Restrictive Covenant Cases* (Berkeley: University of California Press, 1959), 251.

25. Gunther cited in Don Carleton, "McCarthyism in Houston: The George Ebey Affair," *Southwestern Historical Quarterly* 80 (October 1976): 167.

26. In 1965 the City of Houston was given authorization by the Texas legislature to enforce deed restrictions. The funds of the city legal department, however, are insufficient to handle the task, and thus almost all restriction enforcement remains a "private" matter.

27. Woodland Heights promotional brochure.

28. Southwest Civic Club MSS, Houston Metropolitan Research Center. I also made use of the papers on the Southwest Civic Club written by Kathy Sexton, Cindy Herbert, and others in my urban history course, spring 1981.

29. Robert Bailey, *Radicals in Urban Politics: The Alinsky Approach* (Chicago: University of Chicago Press, 1972), 30, says parapolitical "refers to formal voluntary associations which are not mobilized primarily for political purposes but which may become political when matters of interest to them are being considered by decisionmakers."

30. *Houston Chronicle*, 18 April 1971, sec. 4, p. 1; Jack E. Dodson, "Minority Group Housing in Texas," in *Studies in Housing and Minority Groups: Special Research Reports to the Commission on Race and Housing*, ed. Nathan Glazer and Davis McEntire (Berkeley: University of California Press, 1960), 106. An invaluable study of the transformation of the Riverside area is Barry J. Kaplan, "Race,

Income, and Ethnicity: Residential Change in a Houston Community, 1920–1970," *Houston Review* 3 (Winter 1981): 178–203.

31. Bertram Mann, a past president of the Allied Civic Club, was kind enough to speak with me about and share some of his materials on the history of the ACC.

32. President, Southwest Civic Club, 1970, Southwest Civic Club MSS, Houston Metropolitan Research Center.

Chapter Four

1. By quasi-anarchist I mean that while these organizations did not reject in principle government or laws, their major thrust as left-wing efforts was to reject organizational forms that they felt perpetuated the status quo and kept the poor powerless.

2. See Seymour Melman, *The Permanent War Economy: American Capitalism in Decline* (New York: Touchstone, 1974).

3. See Dowd, *The Twisted Dream*, especially 123 for Business Week quote.

4. Michael Harrington, *The Other America: Poverty in the United States* (Baltimore: Penguin, 1963), 9.

5. Piven and Cloward, *Poor People's Movements, 190–94*; Frances Fox Piven and Richard Cloward, *Regulating the Poor: The Functions of Public Welfare* (New York: Vintage, 1971), 200–205.

6. Bayrd Still, *Urban America* (Boston: Little Brown, 1974), 406–7.

7. Ben B. Seligman, *Permanent Poverty: An American Syndrome* (Chicago: Quadrangle 1968), 41–61.

8. Richard Dalfiume, *Desegregation and the Armed Forces: Fighting on Two Fronts, 1939–53* (Columbia: University of Missouri Press, 1969), 138.

9. Clayborne Carson, Jr., "Toward Freedom and Community: The Evolution of Ideas in the Student Nonviolent Coordinating Committee, 1960–66" (Ph.D. diss., University of California at Los Angeles, 1975), 140, and Winifred Breines, "Community and Organization: The New Left as a Social Movement, 1962–1968" (Ph.D. diss., Brandeis University, 1979), 35. Both of these impressive doctoral dissertations have since been published; see the Bibliography for citations. Projects affiliated with ERAP were located in Cleveland, New Haven, Appalachia, Baltimore, Oakland (California), Boston, Cairo (Illinois), Hazard (Kentucky), Newark, and Chicago.

10. Davis quoted in Breines, "Community and Organization," 51.

11. Bruce Payne, "SNCC: An Overview Two Years Later," in *The New Student Left: An Anthology*, ed. Mitchell Cohen and Dennis Hale (Boston: Beacon Press, 1966), 87.

12. For more information see the excellent anthology by Massimo Teodori, *The New Left: A Documentary History* (New York: Bobbs-Merrill, 1969); and Carson, "Toward Freedom," 302–3.

13. Kenniston quoted in Breines, "Community and Organization," 159–60.

14. Garrett quoted in Carson, "Toward Freedom," 320; ERAP staffer quoted in Sara Evans, *Personal Politics: The Roots of Women's Liberation in the Civil Rights Movement and the New Left* (New York: Vintage, 1980), 136.

15. Breines, "Community and Organization," 66.

16. Richard Rothstein, "A Short History of ERAP," *SDS Bulletin*, 1964, quoted in Breines, "Community and Organization," 54.

17. Garrett quoted in Carson, "Toward Freedom," 320.

18. Charles McLaurin, "Notes on Organizing," in Arthur Dunham MSS, Social Welfare History Archive.

19. Charles McLaurin, "To Overcome Fear," in Arthur Dunham MSS, Social Welfare History Archive.

20. Davis quoted in Breines, "Community and Organization," 55.

21. Teodori, *The New Left*, 130–31.

22. James Weinstein, *Ambiguous Legacy: The Left in American Politics* (New York: New Viewpoints, 1975), especially 132, is harshly critical of the ERAP projects. So are Milton Kotler, *Neighborhood Government: The Local Foundations of Political Life* (New York: Bobbs-Merrill, 1969), and Paul Bullock, "Morality and Tactics in Community Organizing," in *Poverty: Views from the Left*, ed. Jeremy Larner and Irving Howe (New York: William Morrow, 1968), 137–48.

23. Clayborne Carson, Jr., *In Struggle: SNCC and the Black Awakening of the 1960s* (Cambridge: Harvard University Press, 1982), 154.

24. Carl Wittman and Tom Hayden, two of the strongest proponents of this position in SDS, stated it thusly: "The territorial basis of organization should be carefully considered. Not only are economic conditions varying on the regional, state, and municipal level, but political organization may be appropriate on these levels and on the ward and neighborhood level as well. It is clear that solutions to the problems of these areas are only at the national level, however, and it

continually must be kept in mind that such organization is strictly a means to exert pressure nationally and to gain strength for the movement, not an end in itself." See Carl Wittman and Tom Hayden, "An Interracial Movement of the Poor," in The New Student Left, ed. Cohen and Hale, 201.

25. Moody quoted in Breines, "Community and Organization," 68.

26. Bruce Palmer to author, August 1982.

27. Bennett quoted in Carson, *In Struggle*, 182; Evans, Personal Politics, 137.

28. Richard Flacks, "Organizing the Unemployed: The Chicago Project," in The New Student Left, ed. Cohen and Hale, 144. Flacks's article provides an excellent overview of the Chicago JOIN project.

29. Rothstein quoted in Breines, "Community and Organization," 67.

30. Anne Moody, *Coming of Age in Mississippi: An Autobiography* (New York: Dell, 1968), is a most readable and exciting account of her childhood, movement activity, and subsequent "burnout."

31. Ann Neel, "Experimenting with the Black Community: A Case Study in the Sociology of Applied Knowledge" (Ph.D. diss., University of California at Berkeley, 1978), 162.

32. David Austin, "Organizing for Neighborhood Improvement or Social Change? A Descriptive Study of the Action Methods and Action Issues of Black Residents" (Ph.D. diss., Brandeis University, 1969), 48–53; Miller, "Role and Concept of Neighborhood," in *Community Organization,* ed. Fisher and Romanofsky, 22.

33. The act created a number of programs—the Office of Economic Opportunity, Job Corps, Head Start, Volunteers in Service to America (VISTA), and Legal Aid. Each addressed a different aspect of the poverty condition from a different angle, but all kept to the grassroots, citizen action formula of the NIMH and Ford Foundation.

34. Boone quoted in Piven and Cloward, Regulating the Poor, 270; Economic Opportunity Act, 1964, Title II-A, Section 202 (a); Austin, "Organizing," 48–60. The legislation declared that CAAs were to be "developed, conducted, and administered with the maximum feasible participation of residents of the areas and members of the groups served."

35. The following analysis is heavily influenced by my personal experience as a neighborhood representative from 1973 to 1976 on

the Cambridge, Massachusetts, Economic Opportunity Committee; informal discussions with CAP administrators, neighborhood representatives, and community organizers; and, equally important, the work of Frances Fox Piven and Richard Cloward, most notably *Regulating the Poor*, 248–84.

36. Piven and Cloward, *Regulating the Poor*, 236–39.

37. Ibid., 250–56.

38. Paul E. Peterson and J. David Greenstone, "The Mobilization of Low-Income Communities through Community Action," in *A Decade of Federal Antipoverty Programs: Achievements, Failures, and Lessons*, ed. Robert H. Haveman (New York: Academic Press, 1977), 262.

39. Sar Levitan, *The Great Society's Poor Law* (Baltimore: Johns Hopkins University Press, 1969), 113.

40. Shelley quoted in Ralph M. Kramer, *Participation of the Poor: Comparative Community Case Studies in the War on Poverty* (Englewood Cliffs, N.J.: Prentice-Hall, 1969), 25.

41. Austin, "Organizing," 222–23.

42. Kramer, *Participation of the Poor*, 215–38.

43. Peterson and Greenstone, "The Mobilization of Low-Income Communities," emphasizes the program's objective of black incorporation in the political system. See 264–65 for quoted material.

44. On the history of Mobilization for Youth, good introductions are Piven and Cloward, *Regulating the Poor*, 290–95, and Daniel Moynihan, *Maximum Feasible Misunderstanding: Community Action in the War on Poverty* (New York: Free Press, 1969), 38–60.

45. Shriver quoted in Kramer, *Participation of the Poor*, 10.

46. Levitan, *Great Society's Poor Law*, 115.

47. For information on the Green Amendment begin with Levitan, *Great Society's Poor Law*, especially 66–67, 103–4, and Piven and Cloward, *Regulating the Poor*, 268.

48. Levitan, Great Society's Poor Law, 124.

49. James Leiby, *The History of Social Welfare and Social Work in the United States* (New York: Columbia University Press, 1978), 338.

50. Austin, "Organizing," 237.

Chapter Five

1. Robert L. Heilbroner, *Beyond Boom and Crash (New York:* Norton, 1978), 12; Matthew Edel, "The New York Crisis as Economic

History," in *The Fiscal Crisis of American Cities: Essays on the Political Economy of Urban America with Special Reference to New York*, ed. Roger E. Alcaly and David Mermelstein (New York: Vintage Books, 1977), 231.

2. Editorial, *Business Week*, 12 October 1974, cited in Boyte, *The Backyard Revolution*, 15.

3. John Mollenkopf, "Postwar Politics of Urban Development," in *Marxism and the Metropolis*, ed. William K. Tabb and Larry Sawers (New York: Oxford University Press, 1978), 123.

4. Manuel Castells, *The Urban Question: A Marxist Approach* (London: Edward Arnold, 1977), 422, and William Tabb, "The New York City Fiscal Crisis," in *Marxism and the Metropolis*, ed. Tabb and Sawers, 261.

5. Beame quoted in John Mollenkopf, "The Crisis of the Public Sector in America's Cities," in *Fiscal Crisis of American Cities*, ed. Alcaly and Mermelstein, 113.

6. Cincotta quoted in Boyte, *Backyard Revolution*, 33.

7. Walter Guzzardi, Jr., "To Win in Washington," Fortune, 27 March 1978, quoted in Boyte, *Backyard Revolution*, 17.

8. McBride, "A Nation of Neighborhoods."

9. One of the first and certainly strongest proponents of the new populism is Harry Boyte, the author of *Backyard Revolution*. For a helpful taxonomy of 60 new populist organizations see Janice Perlman, "Grassrooting the System," *Social Policy*, September–October 1976, 4–20.

10. Mike Miller, "The 'Ideology' of the Community Organization Movement," 1979, 22–23, working-paper distributed by the Organize Training Center.

11. Boyte, *Backyard Revolution*, xii.

12. Charles Silberman, *Crisis in Black and White* (New York: Random House, 1964), 318, 346–47, 356.

13. Alinsky quoted in Sanders, "Professional Radical, 1970," 38.

14. See John Hall Fish, *Black Power/White Control: The Struggle of The Woodlawn Organization in Chicago* (Princeton: Princeton University Press, 1973).

15. Best examples are community-based, statewide organizations, such as Massachusetts Fair Share and the Ohio Public Interest Campaign; nationally federated, statewide community organizations, such as Association of Community Organizations for Reform Now (ACORN); coalitions of statewide programs, such as Citizen Action;

and loosely organized national coalitions of neighborhood groups, such as National People's Action and the National Association of Neighborhoods.

16. Castells, *Urban Question,* 421–27.

17. Meg Campbell, North Country Institute, Community Organizing Workshop, February 1982; Boyte, *Backyard Revolution,* 64.

18. Rathke quoted in Andrew Kopkind, "ACORN Calling," *Working Papers for a New Society* 3 (Summer 1975): 14.

19. North Country Institute Workshop, "Models of Organizing" discussion. While this is only a generalized model of ACORN's approach, it is one used and taught by organizers who prefer the methods of Ross to those of Alinsky.

20. Kopkind, "ACORN Calling," 15.

21. John Judis, "Playing for Keeps," In *These Times,* 16–29 June 1982, 12–13.

22. Cortes quoted in Boyte, *Backyard Revolution,* 63.

23. Jim Green and Allen Hunter, "Racism and Busing in Boston," *Radical America* 8 (November–December 1974): 1–32.

24. Linda Gordon and Allen Hunter, "Sex, Family, and the New Right: Antifeminism as a Political Force," *Radical America* 11 (November 1977–February 1978): 9–26. For other criticisms of the new populism that question its left orientation, see Frank Ackerman, "The Melting Snowball: Limits of the 'New Populism' in Practice," *Socialist Revolution* 35 (September–October 1977): 113–28, and Mike Davis, "Socialist Renaissance or Populist Mirage? A Reply to Harry Boyte," *Socialist Review* 40–41 (1978): 53–63.

25. Paul Levy, "Unloading the Neighborhood Bandwagon," manuscript in author's possession, 6. Another version was published in *Social Policy* 10 (September 1979): 28–32. Levy's article divides the neighborhood "movement" of the 1970s into three wings: those who see the neighborhood as a power base, a social community, and a political community.

26. Three good sources on SECO's history are Bob Kuttner, "Ethnic Renewal," *New York Times,* 9 May 1976, reprinted in *Neighborhoods in Urban America,* ed. Ronald Bayor (Port Washington, N.Y.: Kennikat Press, 1982), 209–19; Cassidy, *Livable Cities,* pp. 15–20, 98–99; and McBride, "A Nation of Neighborhoods," 3–5.

27. McBride, "A Nation of Neighborhoods," 3.

28. Ibid.

29. Gleason quoted in Cassidy, *Livable Cities*, 98.

30. McBride, "A Nation of Neighborhoods," 3–5; Cassidy, *Livable Cities*, 15–20.

31. For more information on the Pittsburgh experience see Roy Lubove, *Twentieth Century Pittsburgh* (New York: Wiley, 1969), which discusses the interrelation between corporate, city, and neighborhood revitalization.

32. Philip L. Clay, *Neighborhood Renewal: Middle-Class Settlement and Incumbent Upgrading in American Neighborhoods* (Lexington, Mass.: Lexington Books, 1979), is a good, if limited, introduction to the subject of gentrification.

33. Robert Rosenbloom, "The Politics of the Neighborhood Movement," *South Atlantic Urban Studies* 4 (1979): 116.

34. Friedland quoted in Castells, *Urban Question*, 425.

35. Si Kahn, *How People Get Power: Organizing Oppressed Communities for Action* (New York: McGraw-Hill, 1970), 59, and Lawrence Goodwyn, *The Populist Moment: A Short History of Agrarian Revolt in America* (New York: Oxford University Press, 1978), xix.

36. Quoted in Kathleen McCourt, *Working-Class Women and Grass-Roots Politics* (Bloomington: University of Indiana Press, 1977), 182.

37. Heather Booth interviewed in *Social Policy*, May–June 1981, 31.

38. See Evans, *Personal Politics*.

39. Ronald Lawson and Stephen G. Barton, "'Women in the Tenants Movement: A Case History in New York City," *Shelterforce* 7 (1982): 13.

40. McCourt, *Working-Class Women*, 17.

41. Quoted in ibid., 135.

42. Ibid., 183.

Chapter Six

1. Kevin Phillips, *The Politics of Rich and Poor: Wealth and the American Electorate in the Reagan Aftermath* (New York: Harper Collins, 1990), 4.

2. Samuel Bowles, David Gordon, Thomas Weiskopff, *After the Wasteland: A Democratic Economics for the Year 2000* (Armonk, N.Y.: M. E. Sharpe, 1990), 4–5.

3. Bob Kuttner, "The Splitting of America," Boston Globe 18 May 1992, reprinted in *Organizer Mailing* 6 (July 1992): 1.

4. Walter Russell Mead, "Recession Obsession Blurs Economic Decay," *Houston Chronicle*, 21 April 1991, 1E.

5. Phillips, *Politics of Rich and Poor*, 76–79.

6. Robert Reich, *The Next American Frontier: A Provocative Program for Economic Renewal* (New York: Penguin, 1983), 157; Bowles, Gordon, and Weiskopf, After the Wasteland, 5.

7. See Phillips, *Politics of Rich and Poor*; Center on Budget and Policy Priorities, as quoted in "Study of Income Gap Finds Rich Get Richer," *Chicago Tribune*, 24 July 1990, 5.

8. Center on Budget and Policy Priorities, in *Chicago Tribune*, 5.

9. Kuttner, "Splitting of America," in *Organizer Mailing*, 1.

10. Bennett Roth, "Number of Poor Texans Increases by 281,000 in 1991," *Houston Chronicle*, 4 September 1992, 14.

11. Terry Rosenberg, *Poverty in New York City, 1985–1988: The Crisis Continues* (Community Service Society of New York, 1989); James S. Mickelson, ed., Houston's Children 1992 (Houston: Children at Risk, 1992); Ruth Sidel, *Women and Children Last: The Plight of Poor Women in Affluent America* (New York: Penguin, 1986).

12. George Gilder, *Wealth and Poverty* (New York: Bantam Books, 1982), 87–88.

13. Editorial, *New York Times*, 6 May 1992, A18; Charles Tilly, "Down and Out in the City: Examining the Roots of Urban Poverty," *Dollars and Sense*, no. 155 (April 1990): 6.

14. Tom Morganthau, John McCormick, and Marc Levinson, "Are Cities Obsolete?" *Newsweek*, 8 September 1991, 42–44.

15. Bowles, Gordon, and Weisskopf, *After the Wasteland*, suggest that the neoconservative strategy be called a "right-wing" strategy because they see little of value that was conserved by it. I agree. But since the term neoconservative was used in the first edition of this book, I will continue to use it.

16. See, for example, Cheryl Hyde, "The Ideational System of Social Movement Agencies: An Examination of Feminist Health Centers," in *Human Services as Complex Organizations*, ed. Yeheskel Hasenfeld, (Newbury Park, Calif.: Sage Publishers, 1992).

17. See Edward Banfield, *The Unheavenly City* (Boston: Little Brown, 1968); Charles Murray, *Losing Ground: American Social Policy, 1950–1980* (New York: Basic Books, 1984).

18. Cockburn quoted in Keith Matis, "Panelists Accuse Journalists of Strangling the Truth," *Daily Cougar* (22 March 1991), 8.

19. Sam Bass Warner, Jr., *The Private City: Philadelphia in Three Periods of Growth* (Philadelphia: University of Pennsylvania Press, 1968), x–xi.

20. An earlier version of some of this material appeared in Robert Fisher, "Organizing in the Private City: The Case of Houston, Texas," in *Black Dixie*, ed. Howard Beeth and Cary Wintz, (College Station: Texas A&M University Press, 1992), 253–77.

21. William Schambra, "Conservatives, Liberals, and the Principles of 'Public Life,'" *Public Life* 2 (March 1991): 6. Also see Stuart M. Butler, "The Enterprise Zone: Capitalism in the Inner City," Special Report #21 (Grove City, Pa.: Public Policy Education Fund, 1982), 4. The first chapter in Randall Fitzgerald, *When Government Goes Private: Successful Alternatives to Public Services* (New York: Universe Books, 1988), is entitled "Giving Power Back to the People."

22. Gale Cincotta, "The Next Move," *Disclosure*, no. 127 (March–April 1992): 2.

23. Paul Starr, *The Limits of Privatization* (Washington, D.C.: Economic Policy Institute, 1987), 11.

24. Norman Fainstein and Susan Fainstein, "Regime Strategies, Communal Resistance, and Economic Forces," in *Restructuring the City*, ed. Susan Fainstein et al., (New York: Longman, 1983), 241.

25. Jeffrey R. Henig, "Collective Reponses to the Urban Crisis: Ideology and Mobilization," in ed. M. Gottdiener, *Cities in Stress* (Beverly Hills, Calif.: Sage, 1986), 233.

26. C. Wright Mills, *The Sociological Imagination* (New York: Oxford University Press, 1959).

27. R. Emmett Tyrell, Jr. quoted in Barbara Ehrenreich, "The New Right Attack on Social Welfare," in *The Mean Season: The Attack on the Welfare State*, ed. Fred Block et al. (New York: Pantheon, 1987), 167.

28. For a fuller argument, see Fisher, "Organizing in the Private City."

29. Jennifer Wolch, *The Shadow State: Government and Voluntary Sector in Transition* (New York: Foundation Center, 1990), 209.

30. Gary Delgado et. al., "An Examination and Assessment of Organizational Activity," report commissioned by the Levi Strauss Foundation, Project Change, 1993.

31. William Schambra, "Progressive Liberalism and American Community," *Public Interest* 80 (Summer 1985): 31–48.

32. Stuart Butler, "The Enterprise Zone: Capitalism in the Inner

City," *Special Report #21* (Grove City, Pa: Public Policy Education Fund, 1982), 4.

33. Craig Calhoun, *The Question of Class Struggle* (Chicago: University of Chicago Press, 1982).

34. Wolch, *Shadow State*, 4.

35. Ibid., 7–8.

36. Trapp quoted in Jeffrey L. Katz, "Neighborhood Politics: A Changing World," *Governing* 4 (November 1990): 49.

37. Robert Rivera, phone interview with author, 10 May 1993.

38. John R. Logan and Todd Swanstrom, eds., *Beyond the City Limits: Urban Policy and Economic Restructuring in Comparative Perspective* (Philadelphia: Temple University Press, 1990), 37.

39. John Emmeus Davis, *Contested Ground: Collective Action and the Urban Neighborhood*, (Ithaca, N.Y.: Cornell University Press, 1991), 4–5. A similar argument is made in John Logan and Harvey Molotch, *Urban Fortunes: The Political Economy of Place* (Berkeley: University of California, 1987).

40. Davis, *Contested Ground*, 7.

41. Renee Berger, *Against All Odds: The Achievements of Community-Based Development Organizations* (Washington, D.C.: National Congress for Community Economic Development, 1989), 4.

42. Neal R. Peirce and Carol F. Steinbach, *Enterprising Communities: Community-Based Development in America, 1990* (Washington, D.C.: Council for Community-Based Development, 1990), 15–16.

43. Mott quoted in Neil R. Pierce and Carol F. Steinbach, *Corrective Capitalism: The Rise of America's Community Development Corporations* (New York: Ford Foundation, 1987), 26.

44. Pierce and Steinbach, *Corrective Capitalism*, 30.

45. Benjamin Marquez, "Mexican American Community Development Corporations and the Limits of Directed Capitalism," *Economic Development Quarterly* 7 (August 1993): 287–95.

46. SECO, "Twentieth Anniversary Report," *Southeast Review* Baltimore, 1991, 2.

47. Ibid., 4–7.

48. Christopher Gunn and Hazel Dayton Gunn, *Reclaiming Capital: Democratic Initiatives and Community Development* (Ithaca, N.Y.: Cornell University Press, 1990), 92–94.

49. Krumholz quoted in Katz, "Neighborhood Politics," 49.

50. Berger, *Against All Odds*, 5–8; Pierce and Steinbach, *Enterprising Communities*, 8.

51. Avis Vidal, *Rebuilding Communities: A National Study of Urban Community Development Corporations* (New York: Community Development Research Center, 1992).

52. Ibid., 53.

53. Ibid.; New School for Social Research study cited in Pierce and Steinbach, *Enterprising Communities*, 49.

54. *Expanding Horizons: Foundation Grant Support of Community-Based Development*, A Research Report of the Council for Community-Based Development, Washington, D.C., April 1989, 11.

55. Pierce and Steinbach, *Enterprising Communities*, 11.

56. Franklin A. Thomas, foreword to Pierce and Steinbach, *Corrective Capitalism*, 5.

57. Dick Flacks, "The Revolution of Citizenship," *Social Policy* 21 (1990): 48–49.

58. Marquez, "Mexican American Community Development," 11.

59. Bill Traynor, "Community Development and Community Organizing," *Shelterforce*, March/April 1993, 4.

60. W. Dennis Keating, "The Emergence of Community Development Corporations," *Shelterforce*, February/March/April 1989, 11.

61. Marquez, "Mexican American Community Development," 8–9.

62. Ronald Shiffman and Susan Motley, "Comprehensive and Integrative Planning for Community Development," New School for Social Research, New York, March 1990.

63. Schiffman and Motley, "Comprehensive and Integrative Planning," 16.

64. Steven Kest, "Proposal for General Support of the ACORN Organizing Project," grant proposal, 1991, 4.

65. Ibid.

66. Ibid., 8.

67. "Chicago Warms to Acorn Housing," *Homesteader: A Publication of the Acorn Community Land Association*, Winter 1991, 1.

68. Wade Rathke, lecture at University of Houston Graduate School of Social Work, 8 April 1991.

69. Schiffman and Motley, "Comprehensive and Integrative Planning," 4, 11.

70. John McKnight and John Kreutzman, "Community Organizing in the 80's: Toward a Post-Alinsky Agenda," *Social Policy* 14 (Winter 1984): 17.

71. Letter from Mike Eichler to author, 30 March 1993.

72. Mike Eichler, lecture at the University of Houston Graduate School of Social Work, 15 November 1990.

73. Katz, "Neighborhood Politics" 49.

74. Jack Rothman, *Three Models of Community Organization Practice*, National Conference on Social Welfare, Social Work Practice, 1968 (New York: Columbia University Press, 1968).

75. Vidal, *Rebuilding Communities*, documents the dramatic shift of CDCs in a five-year period away from a style of "confrontation" to one of "cooperation."

76. Letter from Mike Eichler to author, 30 March 1993.

77. Jane Mansbridge, *Beyond Adversary Democracy* (New York: Basic Books, 1980), 3. Also see Hannah Pitkin and S. Shumer, "On Participation," *Democracy* 2 (Fall 1982): 46.

78. See, for example, John T. Cumbler, *A Social History of Economic Decline: Business Politics, and Work in Trenton* (New Brunswick: Rutgers University Press, 1989).

79. Paget, "Citizen Organizing"; Herbert Rubin and Irene Rubin, *Community Organizing and Development*, 2d ed. (New York: Macmillan, 1992).

80. Robert Fisher and Joseph Kling, eds., *Mobilizing the Community: Local Politics in a Global Era* (Newbury Park, Calif.: Sage, 1993).

81. M. W. Newman and Lillian Williams, "People Power: Chicago's Real Clout," *Chicago Sun-Times*, 6 April 1990, 12.

82. Shel Trapp, "Dynamics of Organizing," *Disclosure*, March–April 1992, 2.

83. Interview with Bill Cavellini, Cambridge, Massachusetts, 6 August 1991.

84. Ernie Cortes quoted in Harry Boyte, *Commonwealth: A Return to Citizen Politics* (New York: Free Press, 1989), 191, 21.

85. Peter Applebome, "Changing Texas Politics at Its Roots," *New York Times*, 31 May 1988, A16.

86. Mary Beth Rogers, *Cold Anger: A Story of Faith and Power Politics* (Denton: North Texas State University Press, 1990), 2.

87. John Moyer memo cited in Boyte, *Commonwealth*, 189, 7.

88. See Robert Fisher and Joseph Kling, "Leading the People: Two Approaches to the Role of Ideology in Community Organizing," *Radical America* 21 (1987): 31–45.

89. Gregory Pierce, *Activism that Makes Sense: Congregations and Community Organization* (New York: Paulist Press, 1984), 37–38; Boyte, Commonwealth, 90–95.

90. On "inherent" and "derived" ideology see George Rude,

Ideology and Popular Protest (New York: Pantheon, 1980). For an evaluation of how it relates to Alinsky organizing, see Fisher and Kling, "Leading the People."

91. Bernard Crick, *In Defense of Politics* (Chicago: University of Chicago Press, 1972).

92. Carl Boggs, *Social Movements and Political Power: Emerging Forms of Radicalism in the West* (Philadelphia: Temple University Press, 1986), especially 26–27, would see both as forms of the strategy of "corporatism," characterized by an absence of political conflict, an institutionalized framework of bargaining among the state, business, labor, and other organized groups, and a broadly defined consensus of ideological moderation.

93. Mike Miller, "Saul Alinsky and the Democratic Spirit," *Christianity and Crisis* 52 (25 May 1992), copy sent to author, no page numbers. Miller asks, sarcastically, if "the next book [will] be Reveille for Moderates", as distinct from Alinsky's two books, *Reveille for Radicals* and *Rules for Radicals*.

94. "Standing for the Whole," Industrial Areas Foundation statement, 1990.

95. Boyte, *Commonwealth*, 131.

96. From *Organizing for Texas Families and Congregations,* quoted in "Texas IAF Network: Vision, Values, and Action," ed. Pearl Ceasar, a brochure published by the Texas IAF Network, 1990, 13.

97. Boyte, *Commonwealth*, especially chapters 6 and 7, offers a thoughtful, if uncritical, analysis of IAF organizing.

98. Robert Rivera lecture, University of Houston Graduate School of Social Work, 18 April 1991. On IAF in New York, see Samuel Freedman, *Upon This Rock* (New York: HarperCollins, 1994).

99. Bill Moyers, introduction to Rogers, *Cold Anger*, i.

100. "Standing for the Whole."

101. Rogers, *Cold Anger*, 194–95.

102. "Standing for the Whole."

103. Miller, "Saul Alinsky and the Democratic Spirit."

104. See Boyte, *Commonwealth*, 122.

105. Miller, "Saul Alinsky and the Democratic Spirit."

106. Ernie Cortes quoted in Rogers, *Cold Anger*, 198.

107. Steve Max, "The Politics of Majorities," *Social Policy* 21 (Summer 1990): 52.

108. Jeremy Brecher and Tim Costello, *Building Bridges: The Emerging Grassroots Coalition of Labor and Community* (New York: Monthly Review Press, 1990).

109. See, for example, Valerie Lehr, "The Difficulty of Leaving "Home": Gay and Lesbian Organizing to Confront AIDS," in *Mobilizing the Community*, ed. Fisher and Kling.

110. J. Barry Mothhes, "Council Approves Major Rezoning of Simplex Site," *Cambridge Chronicle*, 14 January 1988.

111. Thomas Huang and Harold Stern, "Four in 'Tent City' Trial Are Not Guilty," *Tech*, 20 January 1988.

112. Diego Ribadeneira and Alexander Reid, "Homeless Activists Arrested at MIT," *Boston Globe*, 26 February 1988, 18.

113. [Cambridge] Eviction-free Zone Committee leaflet.

114. Katz, "Neighborhood Politics," 51–52.

115. Boyte, *Commonwealth*, 141.

116. Wade Rathke interview with author, New Orleans, 16 March 1991.

117. Steven Kest, "Proposal for General Support of the ACORN Organizing Project," grant proposal, 1991, 11–12.

118. Abraham Wandersman, Richard C. Rich, and John Prestby, "Keeping Community Organizations Alive" *Citizen Participation*, Fall 1985, 16.

119. Robert Rivera lecture at the University of Houston, Graduate School of Social Work, 18 April 1991.

120. Dan Russell, "Roots of a Social Justice Movement," in *Twenty for the Many*, ACORN Twentieth Anniversary Convention Pamphlet, 1990, 15.

121. Cheryl Hyde, "Commitment to Social Change: Voices from the Feminist Movement," 1, draft in possession of author, to be published in *Advances in Community Organization and Social Administration*, ed. Ray MacNair and William Buffum (Binghamton, N.Y.: Haworth, forthcoming).

122. Wade Rathke interview with author, New Orleans, 16 March 1991.

123. Gary Delgado, "Activism in Communities of Color," unpublished paper, March 1992.

124. Gale Cincotta, quoted in Lillian Williams, "Cincotta's Grass Roots Blossom," Chicago *Sun-Times*, (8 April 1990), 13.

125. Lorraine Guitierrez and Edith Lewis, "A Feminist Perspective on Organizing with Women of Color," in *Community Organizing in a Diverse Society*, ed. Felix Rivera and John L. Erlich (Boston: Allyn and Bacon, 1992), 116.

126. Gutierrez and Lewis, "Feminist Perspective," 116; Stephen

Rose lecture, University of Houston, Graduate School of Social Work, Future's Conference, May 1993.

127. Cheryl Hyde, "The Ideational System of Social Movement Agencies: An Examination of Feminist Health Centers," in *Human Services as Complex Organizations*, ed. Yeheskel Hasenfeld (Newbury Park, Calif.: Sage Publishers, 1992), 122; Herbert J. Rubin and Irene Rubin, *Community Organizing and Development* (Columbus, Ohio: Merrill Publishing, 1986), 56.

128. Ann Withorn, *Serving the People: Social Services and Social Change* (New York: Columbia University Press, 1984); Cheryl Hyde, "A Feminist Model for Macro-Practice: Promises and Problems," *Administration in Social Work* 13 (1989), especially p. 173. See also Burghardt, *The Other Side of Organizing*, and Stuart Rees, *Achieving Power: Practice and Policy in Social Welfare* (Sydney: Allen and Unwin, 1991).

129. Harry Boyte, "Populist Politics," *American Prospect*, June 1991; draft in author's possession.

130. Ecklein, *Community Organizers*, 4.

131. Rubin and Rubin, *Community Organizing and Development*, 50–59.

132. Withorn, *Serving the People*, cited in Gutierrez and Lewis, "Feminist Perspective," 117.

133. Marie Weil, "Women, Community, and Organizing," in *Feminist Visions for Social Work*, ed. Nan Van Den Bergh and Lynn B. Cooper (Silver Springs, Md.: NASW, 1986), 205.

134. Joel Blau, *The Visible Poor: Homelessness in the United States* (New York: Oxford University Press, 1992).

135. Jean Sickman lecture, University of Houston, Graduate School of Social Work, 23 April 1992.

136. L. A. Kauffman, "The Left Attacks Identity Politics," *Village Voice*, 30 June 1992, 20.

137. Urvashi Vaid, "An Interview with Urvashi Vaid," Democratic Left 19 (1991), cited in Valerie Lehr, "The Difficulty of Leaving 'Home': Gay and Lesbian Organizing to Confront Aids," in Fisher and Kling, *Mobilizing the Community*, 256.

138. Davis, *Contested Ground*, 164.

139. Alain Touraine, "An Introduction to the Study of Social Movements," *Social Research* 52 (Winter 1985): 780.

140. Jones, quoted in Benjamin Marquez, "Organizing the

Mexican-American Community in Texas: The Legacy of Saul Alinsky," *Policy Studies Review* 9 (Winter 1990): 355–73.

Chapter Seven

1. Austin, "Organizing," 320.

2. An earlier version of the following typology appeared first in Robert Fisher, "Community Organizing in Historical Perspective: A Typology," *Houston Review* 4 (Summer 1982): 75–89. For another typology see Jack Rothman, "Three Models of Community Organization Practice," in *Strategies of Community Organization: A Book of Readings*, ed. Fred Cox et al. (Itasca, Ill.: F. E. Peacock, 1979), 25–45.

3. Paul Wellstone, *How The Rural Poor Got Power* (Amherst: University of Massachusetts Press, 1978), 204.

4. McCourt, *Working-Class Women*, 100.

5. Rich, "Political Economy of Neighborhood Organization."

6. Mary P. Follett, *The New State: Group Organization the Solution of Popular Government* (New York: Longmans, Green and Company, 1918), 189–92.

7. Charles Grosser, *New Directions in Community Organization: From Enabling to Advocacy* (New York: Praeger, 1972), and Jeffrey Galper, *The Politics of Social Services* (Englewood Cliffs, N.J.: Prentice-Hall, 1975), reflect changes in the social work profession during the late 1960s and early 1970s.

8. Barbara Epstein, "Rethinking Social Movement Theory," *Socialist Review* 90 (January–March 1990), 35–66; Anthony Scott, *Ideology and the New Social Movements* (London: Unwin Hyman, 1990); Robert Fisher, "Organizing in the Modern Metropolis," *Journal of Urban History* 18 (1992): 222–37.

9. Claus Offe, "Challenging the Boundaries of Institutional Politics: Social Movements since the 1960s," in *Changing Boundaries of the Political: Essays on the Evolving Balance between the State and Society, Public and Private in Europe*, ed. C. Maier, (Cambridge: Cambridge University Press, 1987).

10. Richard Flacks, "The Revolution of Citizenship," *Social Policy* 21 (1990): 37–50.

11. Offe, "Challenging the Boundaries."

12. Jeremy Brecher and Tim Costello, *Building Bridges: The Emerging Grassroots Coalition of Labor and Community* (New York:

Monthly Review Press, 1990); Fisher, "Organizing in the Modern Metropolis."

13. Samir Amin, "The Social Movements in the Periphery," in *Transforming the Revolution*, ed. S. Amin et al.

14. Durning, "Action at the Grassroots," 6–7.

15. R. Dalton and M. Kuechler, eds., *Challenging the Political Order: New Social and Political Movements in Western Democracies* (New York: Oxford University Press, 1990); Offe, *Challenging the Boundaries*; Harry Boyte and Frank Riessman, *The New Populism* (Philadephia: Temple University Press, 1986); Robert Fisher and Joseph Kling, "Leading the People: Two Approaches to the Role of Ideology in Community Organizing," *Radical America* 21 (1988): 31–46; Harry Boyte, Heather Booth, and Steve Max, *Citizen Action and the New American Populism* (Philadelphia: Temple University Press, 1986).

16. S. E. Bronner, *Socialism Unbound* (New York: Routledge, 1990), 161.

17. Herbert Gutman, *Work, Culture, and Society in Industrializing America* (New York: Vintage, 1977); E. P. Thompson, *The Making of the English Working Class* (New York: Vintage, 1963).

18. Touraine, "Introduction to the Study of Social Movements"; Robert Fisher and Joseph Kling, "Popular Mobilization in the 1990s: Prospects for the New Social Movements," *New Politics* 3 (1991): 71–84.

19. Mansbridge, *Beyond Adversary Democracy*, 3.

20. James Midgley, *Community Participation, Social Development, and the State* (London: Methuen, 1986), 4.

21. Fisher, "Organizing in the Metropolis." For a related argument see Frances Fox Piven and Richard Cloward, *The New Class War: Reagan's Attack on the Welfare State and Its Consequences* (New York: Pantheon, 1982).

22. Wallerstein, "Antisystemic Movements."

23. Frank and Fuentes, "Civic Democracy."

24. Peter Merkl, "How New the Brave New World: New Social Movements in West Germany," *German Studies Review* 10 (February 1987): 125–47.

25. The analysis of old social movements and new social movements has appeared in various versions in a number of my articles during the past few years. The material here borrowed heavily from Robert Fisher, "Grassroots Organizing Worldwide," in Fisher and

Kling, Mobilizing the Community, and Robert Fisher, "Organizing in the Modern Metropolis," *Journal of Urban History* 18 (February 1992): 222–37.

26. Chapter 3 discusses reactionary, nonprogressive uses of the neighborhood, an important element but one that new social movement theory, tied to a leftist "oppositional" imagination, does not address.

27. Mark Gottdeiner, *The Decline of Urban Politics* (Newbury Park, Calif.: Sage Publications, 1987); Boyte, *Backyard Revolution*.

28. Camacho quoted in Newman and Williams, "People Power," 14.

29. This conclusion rests heavily on a series of articles, especially Fisher and Kling, "Popular Mobilization in the 1990s: Prospects for the New Social Movements," *New Politics* 3 (1991): 71–84, and an edited book, *Mobilizing the Community*, that Joe Kling and I have worked on together since 1988.

30. Boyte, *Backyard Revolution*; Sara Evans and Harry Boyte, *Free Spaces: The Sources of Democratic Change in America* (New York: Harper and Row, 1986); Wellstone, *How the Poor Got Power*; Craig Calhoun, "The Radicalism of Tradition: Community Strength or Venerable Disguise and Borrowed Language?" *American Journal of Sociology* 88 (March 1983): 886–914.

31. See Fisher and Kling, *Mobilizing the Community*.

32. For the potential in community efforts to replicate as well as challenge power relations, see Margit Mayer, "Restructuring and Opposition in West German Cities," in *Global Cities*, ed. M. P. Smith and J. Feagin, (New York: Basil Blackwell, 1987), and Margit Mayer, "The Career of Urban Social Movements in West Germany," in Fisher and Kling, eds., *Mobilizing the Community*.

33. Craig Jackson Calhoun, "The Radicalism of Tradition," *American Journal of Sociology* 88 (March 1983): 886–914.

34. Piven and Cloward, *Poor People's Movements*, 7.

35. Carson, *In Struggle*, carefully details how the government harassed and repressed the black power movement after 1965.

36. Wellstone, *How the Rural Poor Got Power*, 218.

37. Sidney Dillick, *Community Organization for Neighborhood Development: Past and Present* (New York: William Morrow, 1953), 69.

38. See, for example, Midgley, *Community Participation*; Fisher, "Organizing in the Private City"; Susan Fainstein and Norman

Fainstein, "Participation in New York and London: Community and Market under Capitalism," in Fisher and Kling, *Mobilizing the Community.*

39. Marie Weil, "Women, Community, and Organizing," 202–3. Weil adds other components to feminist practice. First, consciousness raising and praxis give people the opportunity to "reflect on, reexperience, identify, and analyze the social stereotypes and environmental forces that have impeded their development" and help build both individual and collective strength. Second, the personal is political, which means being sensitive to the ways that "systemic factors result in problematic personal conditions" and recognizing that how people choose to live their daily lives is political as well. Third, organizers emphasize and work for structural change—in organizations, institutions, and society at large—to eliminate racism, sexism, homophobia, classism, and other forms of oppression. The material taken from Weil's women-centered practice has been adapted to a more universal feminist practice.

40. Pierce, *Activism that Makes Sense*, 57.

41. Pierce and Steinbach, *Enterprising Communities*, 61.

42. Mike Miller, "Questions for Community Organizing," unpublished paper, (May 1991), 20. This paper appeared in an abbreviated version as Miller, "Saul Alinsky and the Democratic Spirit."

43. Burghardt, *The Other Side of Organizing.*

44. Jeremy Brecher and Tim Costello, "Community Labor Coalitions," *Z Magazine*, April 1990, 79; Ann Withorn, "A Future Worth Campaigning For," Radical America 23 (Summer 1991): 1–13.

45. Gary Delgado, "Activism in Communities of Color," unpublished paper, March 1992.

46. Michael Ansara, "The People's First: An Organizer's Notebook," *Working Papers for a New Society* 2 (Winter 1975): 36.

47. Forman quoted in Carson, *In Struggle*, 156.

48. See Chafe, *Civilities and Civil Order*, 350, for a description of how this consciousness developed and was challenged in the civil rights movement in Greensboro, North Carolina.

49. Wellstone, *How the Rural Poor Got Power*, pp. 200–215.

50. Arthur Hillman and Frank Seever, "Elements of Neighborhood Organization," in *Strategies*, ed. Cox et al., 284.

51. See, for example, J. F. Lyotard, *The Postmodern Condition: A Report on Knowledge* (Minneapolis: University of Minnesota Press, 1979).

52. Rude, *Ideology and Popular Protest*, 28–29.
53. Miller, "Saul Alinsky and the Democratic Spirit."
54. Bruce Palmer, personal comment to author, 15 May 1993.
55. Epstein, "Rethinking Social Movement Theory," 61.

Bibliographic Essay

What follows is a selected list of what I have found to be the most useful readings in the history of neighborhood organizing. The bibliography is intentionally brief, and includes, for the most part, only the most accessible published materials. For additional references to materials on neighborhood organizing, national political economy, and urban history used in this study, consult the Notes and References.

Historical Overviews and Theories of Neighborhood Organizing

Most of the materials with a historical perspective on neighborhood organizing are written by social work academics. The only book-length surveys of the history of neighborhood organization are Sidney Dillick, *Community Organization for Neighborhood Development: Past and Present* (New York: William Morrow, 1953), which traces the history of community organization for social welfare from the late nineteenth century through the early 1950s; *Community Organization for Urban Social Change: A Historical Perspective,* edited by Robert Fisher and Peter Romanofsky (Westport, Conn.: Greenwood Press, 1981); and, most recently, *American Community Organizations: A Historical Dictionary* edited by Patricia Mooney Melvin (Westport, Conn.: Greenwood Press, 1986). Monna Heath and Arthur Dunham, *Trends in Community Organization: A Study of Papers on Community Organization Published by the National Conference on Social Welfare, 1874–1960* (Chicago: University of Chicago Social Service Monographs, 1963), is an excellent overview and analysis of articles written by community workers and academics. Good brief surveys of the history of community organization are Meyer Schwartz, "Community Organization," in *Encyclopedia of Social Work* (New York: National Association of Social Workers, 1965), 179–89; Howard W. Hallman, "The Neighborhood as an Organizational Unit: A Historical Perspective," in *Neighborhood Control in the 1970s,* edited by George Frederickson (New York: Chandler Publishing Co., 1973), 7–16; Fred Cox and Charles Garvin, "Community Organization Practice: 1865–1973," in *Strategies of Community Organization,* edited by Fred Cox *et al.* (Itasca, Ill.: F. E. Peacock, 1974), 39–58; Arthur Dunham, *The New Community Organization* (New York: Thomas Y. Crowell, 1970), chapter 4; and Steve Burghardt, "Community-Based Social Action," in *Encyclopedia of Social Work Eighteenth Edition* edited by Anne Minahan *et. al.* (Silver Spring, Mass.: National Association of Social Workers, 1987), 292–99. Robert Fisher, "Community Organizing in Historical Perspective: A Typology," *Houston Review* 4 (Summer 1982): 75–88, elaborates on the typology presented in the conclusion of this book. Milton Kotler, *Neighborhood Government: The Local Foundations of Political Life* (New York: Bobbs-Merrill, 1969), provides some materials on the historical origins of neighborhoods and on different approaches to neighborhood organizing. Jeffrey H. Galper, *The Politics of Social Services* (Englewood Cliffs, N.J.: Prentice-Hall, 1975), is a leftist critique that includes some interesting criticisms about community organization as practiced by members of the social work profession. Surprisingly little has been written on community organization by historians interested in the history of social welfare. Even the overviews of social welfare history, such as James Leiby, *The History of Social Welfare and Social Work in the United States* (New York: Columbia University Press, 1978), devote but a few pages to the subject.

General studies of neighborhood organizing that approach the subject from different perspectives are David J. O'Brien, *Neighborhood Organization and Interest-Group Processes* (Princeton: Princeton University Press, 1975); Rachelle B. Warren and Donald I. Warren, *Neighborhood Organizers Handbook* (Notre Dame: University of Notre Dame Press, 1977); Steve Burghardt, *The Other Side of Organizing* (Cambridge: Schenkman, 1982); and Jeffrey R. Henig, *Neighborhood Mobilization: Redevelopment and Response* (New Brunswick: Rutgers, 1982). More recent critical analyses of the limits of community organizing as a strategy for urban regeneration include Karen Paget, "Citizen Organizing: Many Movements, No Majority," *American*

Prospect 7 (Summer 1990); Mark Gottdiener, *The Decline of Urban Politics* (Newbury Park, Calif.: Sage Publications, 1987); *The Dilemmas of Activism: Class, Community, and the Politics of Local Mobilization,* edited by Joseph Kling and Prudence Posner (Philadelphia: Temple University Press, 1990).

Social Welfare Neighborhood Organizing before 1929

The liberal reformers of the years 1890–1920 were as prolific as they were optimistic. The first account in the genre was Stanton Coit, *Neighborhood Guild: An Instrument of Social Reform* (London: Sonnenshein, 1891). Other excellent examples include Jane Addams *Twenty Years at Hull House with Autobiographical Notes* (New York: Macmillan, 1910); Lillian Wald, *The House on Henry Street* (New York: Henry Holt and Co., 1915); and Robert A. Woods, *The Neighborhood in Nation-Building* (New York: Arno Press, 1970). During and after World War I, some even stronger statements were written on the need for community organizing, the best examples of which are Mary Parker Follett, *The New State: Group Organization the Solution of Popular Government* (New York: Longmans, Green, 1918), and John Daniels, *America Via the Neighborhood* (New York: Harper and Bros., 1920).

For recent literature covering this early history of community organizing see Neil Betten and Michael Austin, *The Roots of Community Organizing 1917–1939* (Philadelphia: Temple University Press, 1990); and Patricia Mooney Melvin, *The Organic City: Urban Definition and Neighborhood Organization, 1880–1920* (Lexington: University of Kentucky Press, 1987).

American historians have written widely about the activities of settlement workers, but, until recently, rarely from the perspective of the reformers as community organizers. On the social settlements, see Thomas Lee Philpott, *The Slum and the Ghetto: Neighborhood Deterioration and Middle-Class Reform in Chicago, 1880–1930* (New York: Oxford University Press, 1978); Mina Carson, *Settlement Folk* (Chicago: University of Chicago Press, 1990); Elisabeth Lasch-Quinn, *Black Neighbors: Race and the Limits of Reform in the American Settlement House Movement, 1890–1945* (Chapel Hill: University of North Carolina Press, 1993); Rivlen Shpak Lissak, *Pluralism and Progressives: Hull House and the New Immigrants, 1890–1919* (Chicago: University of Chicago, 1989); and Judith Trolander,

Professionalism and Social Change: From the Settlement House Movement to Neighborhood Centers, 1886 to the Present (New York: Columbia University Press, 1987). On community centers, begin with Robert Fisher, "Community Organizing and Citizen Participation: The Efforts of the People's Institute, 1910–1920," *Social Service Review* 51 (September 1977): 474–90.

The 1920s witnessed the continued advocacy of the neighborhood unit and the professionalization of community organization as a sub-discipline within the field of social work. The first texts on community organization were written by Edward Lindeman, *The Community* (New York: Association Press, 1921), and Jesse Steiner, *Community Organization: A Study of its Theory and Current Practice* (Chicago: University of Chicago Press, 1925). One of the best community studies of the period, with a focus on the role of neighborhood organizing efforts, is Harvey W. Zorbaugh, *The Gold Coast and the Slum: A Sociological Study of Chicago's Near North Side* (Chicago: University of Chicago Press, 1929). Wilbur Phillips, *Adventuring for Democracy* (New York: Social Unit Press, 1940), is the autobiography of the founder of the block organizing social unit plan. For secondary sources, see Patricia Mooney Melvin, "A Cluster of Interlacing Communities: The Cincinnati Social Unit Plan and Neighborhood Organization, 1900–1920," in *Community Organization,* edited by Fisher and Romanofsky, 59–88, and Anatole Shaffer, "The Cincinnati Social Unit Experiment, 1917–1919," *Social Service Review* 45 (June 1971): 159–72. Roy Lubove, *The Professional Altruist: The Emergence of Social Work as a Career* (New York: Atheneum, 1965), includes some information about the origins and professionalization of the field of community organization. For an analysis of the ideology of community organization in the 1920s and 1930s, see Michael J. Austin and Neil Betten, "Intellectual Origins of Community Organization, 1920–1939," *Social Service Review* 51 (March 1977): 155–70.

On community life and ethnic associations in working-class neighborhoods that are not specifically neighborhood organizing projects but that serve as important reminders of the alternatives to the settlements and community centers that immigrants used and controlled, see Jeffrey Gurock, *When Harlem Was Jewish* (New York: Columbia University Press, 1979); Emory Tolbert, *The UNIA and Black Los Angeles: Ideology and Community in the American Garvey Movement* (Los Angeles: UCLA Center for Afro-American Studies, 1980); John

Bodnar, *Immigration and Industrialization: Ethnicity in An American Mill Town, 1870–1940* (Pittsburgh: Pittsburgh University Press, 1977); and Josef Barton, *Peasants and Strangers: Italians, Rumanians, and Slovaks in an American City, 1890–1950* (Cambridge: Harvard University Press, 1975).

On the changing conception of neighborhoods in American history and the importance of local history, see Zane Miller, "The Role and Concept of Neighborhood in American Cities," in *Community Organization,* edited by Fisher and Romanofsky 3–32; *Neighborhoods in Urban America,* edited by Ronald Bayor (Port Washington NY: Kennikat Press, 1982); Henry Bedford, *Trouble Downtown: The Local Context of Twentieth Century America* (New York: Harcourt, Brace, 1978); and Thomas Bender, *Community and Social Change in America* (New Brunswick: Rutgers University Press, 1978).

Radical Neighborhood Organizing, 1929–1946

Surprisingly little has been written about decentralized neighborhood organizing efforts during the Great Depression. While the period abounded with organizing efforts on both the right and the left, most organizations, especially after 1933, had a national basis or orientation. Economic problems that the nation and the world faced did not seem to lend themselves to solutions at the neighborhood level.

For information on the Unemployed Council efforts during the 1930s, start with Mark Naison, "Harlem Communists and the Politics of Black Protest," in *Community Organization,* edited by Fisher and Romanofsky, 89–126, and Mark Naison, *Communists in Harlem During the Depression* (Urbana: University of Illinois Press, 1983). Also of significant help are Steve Nelson, James K. Barrett, and Rob Ruck, *Steve Nelson, American Radical* (Pittsburgh: University of Pittsburgh Press, 1981), an autobiography of a Communist party and Unemployed Council leader; Roy Rosenzweig, "Organizing the Unemployed: The Early Years of the Great Depression, 1929–1933," *Radical America* 10 (July–August 1976): 37–60; and Frances Fox Piven and Richard Cloward, *Poor People's Movements: Why They Succeed, How They Fail* (New York: Pantheon, 1977). For some recent perspectives on communist organizing, see Robin D. G. Kelley, *Hammer and Hoe: Alabama Communists during the Great Depression* (Chapel Hill: University of North Carolina Press, 1990); Joshua B. Freeman, *In*

Transit: The Transport Workers Union in New York City, 1933–1966
(Oxford University Press, 1989); and Leon Fink and Brian Greenberg,
*Upheaval in the Quiet Zone: A History of Hospital Workers' Union Local
1199* (University of Illinois Press, 1989).

On the early efforts of Saul Alinsky and the Alinsky method, the
most helpful works are Saul D. Alinsky, *Reveille for Radicals* (Chicago:
University of Chicago Press; 1946); Saul D. Alinsky, *Rules for Radicals*
(New York: Random House, 1971); Michael P. Connolly, "An
Historical Study of Change in Saul D. Alinsky's Community
Organization Practice and Theory, 1939–1972" (Ph.D. diss., University
of Minnesota School of Social Work, 1976); and Marion K. Sanders,
The Professional Radical: Conversations with Saul Alinsky (Evanston,
Ill.: Harper and Row, 1965). Good critiques of the Alinsky method are
Robert Bailey, Jr., *Radicals in Urban Politics: The Alinsky Approach*
(Chicago: University of Chicago Press, 1974); Paul Wellstone, "Notes
on Community Organizing," *Journal of Ethnic Studies* 4 (1976): 73–89;
Joan E. Lancourt, *Confront or Concede: The Alinsky Citizen-Action
Organizations* (Lexington, Mass.: Lexington Books, 1979); Stanley
Aronowitz, "Poverty, Politics, and Community Organization," *Studies
on the Left* 4 (Summer 1964): 102–5; and Frank Reissman, *Strategies
against Poverty* (New York: Random House, 1969). Gurney
Breckenfield, "Chicago: Back of the Yards," in *The Human Side of
Urban Renewal,* edited by Martin Millspaugh, Gurney Breckenfield,
and Miles Colean, (New York: Ives Washburn, 1960), is a descriptive
study of the Back of the Yards Neighborhood Council. On the Back of
the Yards see two recent studies: Thomas J. Yablonsky, *Pride in the
Jungle* (Baltimore: Johns Hopkins University Press, 1993), and Robert
Slayton, *Back of the Yards* (Chicago: University of Chicago, 1986). For
the best insight into Alinsky, especially his early work, see the recent
biography by Sanford D. Horwitt, *Let Them Call Me Rebel: Saul
Alinksy—His Life and Legacy* (New York: Alfred A. Knopf, 1990).

For related information on the history of the tenant organizing
movement, see Joseph Spencer, "Tenant Organization and Housing
Reform in New York City: The Citywide Tenants Council, 1936–1943,"
in *Community Organization,* edited by Fisher and Romanofsky,
127–56; Ronald Lawson and Stephen G. Barton, "Women in the
Tenants Movement: A Case History in New York City" *Shelterforce* 7
(1982); *The Tenant Movement in New York City, 1904–1984,* edited by
Ronald Lawson, with the assistance of Mark Naison, (Rutgers
University Press, 1986).

Conservative Neighborhood Organizing, 1946–1960

The years during and directly after World War II witnessed a reemergence of interest in the social work profession in the neighborhood as an organizing unit and in the possibilities of community organizing. A number of now classic monographs on community organizing were published in the decade or so after the war. Most notable are H. Wayne McMillen, *Community Organization for Social Welfare* (Chicago: University of Chicago Press, 1945); Clarence King, *Organizing for Community Action* (New York: Harper, 1948); James Dahir, *The Neighborhood Unit Plan: Its Spread and Acceptance* (New York: Russell Sage Foundation, 1947); Arthur Hillman, *Community Organization and Planning* (New York: Macmillan, 1950); Murray G. Ross, *Community Organization and Planning* (New York: Harper and Bros., 1955); and *Community Organization in Action: Basic Literature and Critical Comments,* edited by Ernest B. Harper and Arthur Dunham (New York: Associated Press, 1959).

For examples of how the Cold War affected the practice of community organization, see Elmore McKee, *The People Act: Stories of How Americans Are Coming Together to Deal with Their Community Problems* (New York: Harper and Bros., 1955); Marvin Palacek, *Battle of the Bureaucracies* (New York: Vantage Press, 1972); and Reginald Robinson, *Serving the Small Community: The Story of the United Community Defense Services* (New York: Associated Press, 1954).

On international community development projects, begin with Charles E. Hendry, "Community Development," in *Encyclopedia of Social Work,* 1965, 170–77; Arthur Dunham, *Community Development—Rural and Urban* (New York: International Conference of Social Work, 1962); and Marshall B. Clinard, *Slums and Community Development: Experiments in Self-Help* (New York: Free Press, 1966), which includes material on projects in India.

For information on neighborhood improvement association activity before 1946, I relied heavily on the following sources: Joseph Arnold, "The Neighborhood and City Hall: The Origins of Neighborhood Associations in Baltimore, 1880–1911," *Journal of Urban History* 6 (November 1979): 3–30; Roderick D. McKenzie, *The Neighborhood: A Study of Local Life in Columbus, Ohio* (Chicago: University of Chicago Press, 1923); St. Clair Drake and Horace R. Cayton, *Black Metropolis* (New York: Harper, 1962); and Clement Vose, *Caucasians Only: The Supreme Court, the NAACP, and the Restrictive Covenant Cases*

(Berkeley: University of California Press, 1959). On more recent conservative uses of neighborhood associations and what is now known as the NIMBY (not in my back yard) phenomenon, see Sidney Plotkin, *Keep Out: The Struggle for Land Use Control* (Berkeley: University of California Press, 1987).

For information on the civic club movement in Houston I used, almost exclusively, primary sources made available to me by the Southwest Civic Club, additional materials at the Houston Metropolitan Research Center, and personal interviews. For two very different materials on neighborhood improvement association activity in other cities, see Mario Cuomo, *Forest Hills Diary: The Crisis of Low-Income Housing* (New York: Random House, 1974); and Mike Davis, *City of Quartz* (New York: Vintage, 1992), especially chapter 3.

The Neighborhood Organizing "Revolution" of the 1960s

The literature on the neighborhood organizing "revolution" is abundant. A good place to start is any of the numerous social-work-oriented anthologies that survey recent theory and practice. See, for example, *Strategies of Community Organization: A Book of Readings Fourth Edition,* edited by Fred Cox *et al.* (Itasca, Ill.: F. E. Peacock, 1987); and *Readings in Community Organization Practice,* edited by Ralph Kramer and Harry Specht (Englewood Cliffs, N.J.: Prentice-Hall, 1983). For an invaluable codification of the social science literature related to community organizing and to other areas of social action during the years 1964–70, see Jack Rothman, *Planning and Organizing for Social Change: Action Principles from Social Science Research* (New York: Columbia University Press, 1974). Many of the books on the history of community organizing written in the past two decades are still available in paperback and often contain excellent bibliographies.

On civil rights and new left organizing efforts I used William Chafe, *Civilities and Civil Rights: Greensboro, North Carolina, and the Black Struggle for Freedom* (New York: Oxford University Press, 1980); Clayborne Carson, Jr., *In Struggle: SNCC and the Black Awakening of the 1960s* (Cambridge: Harvard University Press, 1982), a most impressive study of shifting organizing methodologies and of SNCC in general; Wini Breines, *Community and Organization in the New Left, 1962–1968: The Great Refusal* (New York: Praeger, 1982), which developed from her excellent dissertation cited often in this study; and Sara Evans, *Personal Politics: The Roots of Women's Liberation in the*

Civil Rights Movement and the New Left (New York: Random House, 1979), which gives an insider's view of the process of community organizing in the 1960s and 1970s and of the role of women in new left organizing projects. For two good collections of primary sources, see *The New Student Left: An Anthology,* edited by Mitchell Cohen and Dennis Hale (Boston: Beacon Press, 1966); and Massimo Teodori, *The New Left: A Documentary History* (New York: Bobbs-Merrill, 1969).

In recent years, the collective memory of the movements of the 1960s has been sustained in a literature written by former participants and other commentators. It is much too large and impressive to do justice here. For some representative works see James Miller, *Democracy is in the Streets* (New York: Touchstone, 1987); Doug McAdams, *Freedom Summer* (Bristol, Pa.: Open University Press, 1988); Taylor Branch, *Parting the Waters: America in the King Years, 1954–1963* (New York: Touchstone, 1988); Mary King, *Freedom Song: A Personal Story of the 1960s Civil Rights Movement* (New York: William Morrow, 1987); Todd Gitlin, *The Sixties: Years of Hope, Days of Rage* (New York: Bantam, 1987); Jo Ann Robinson, *The Montgomery Bus Boycott and the Women Who Started It* (Knoxville: University of Tennessee Press, 1987); Richard Flacks, *Making History: The American Left and the American Mind* (New York: Columbia University Press, 1988); Jack Whalen and Richard Flacks, *Beyond the Barricades: The Sixties Generation Grows Up* (Philadelphia: Temple University Press, 1989); and Henry Hampton and Steve Fayer, eds., *Voices of Freedom: An Oral History of the Civil Rights Movement from the 1950s through the 1980s* (New York: Bantam, 1990), a companion volume to the extraordinary film series *Eyes on the Prize* and *Eyes on the Prize II.*

A voluminous literature exists on the origins and practice of the antipoverty community action programs of the early 1960s. See Peter Marris and Martin Rein, *Dilemmas of Social Reform: Poverty and Community Action in the United States* (New York: Atherton, 1967); Ralph Kramer, *Participation of the Poor: Comparative Case Studies in the War on Poverty* (Englewood Cliffs, N.J.: Prentice-Hall, 1969); Frances Fox Piven and Richard Cloward, *Regulating the Poor: The Functions of Public Welfare* (New York: Vintage Books, 1971); Sar Levitan, *The Great Society's Poor Law* (Baltimore: Johns Hopkins University Press, 1969); and Paul E. Peterson and David J. Greenstone, "The Mobilization of Low-Income Communities through Community Action," in *A Decade of Federal Antipoverty Programs:*

Achievements, Failures, and Lessons, edited by Robert Haveman (New York: Academic Press, 1977), 241–78.

For recent neoconservative reinterpretation of the War on Poverty, a hot topic in the 1980s as neoconservatives sought to dismantle and delegitimize social democratic programs, see Charles Murray, *Losing Ground: American Social Policy, 1950–1980* (New York: Basic Books, 1984). For a critique of the neoconservative perspective see Frances Fox Piven and Richard Cloward, *The New Class War: Reagan's Attack on the Welfare State and Its Consequences* (New York: Pantheon, 1985), and Fred Block et. al, *The Mean Season: The Attack on the Welfare State* (New York: Pantheon, 1987). For a more "neoliberal" position, see Nicholas Lemann, *The Promised Land: The Great Black Migration and How It Changed America* (New York: Vintage, 1991).

For leftist criticisms of community organizing during these years, see Katherine Coit, "Local Action, Not Citizen Participation," in *Marxism and the Metropolis: New Perspectives in Urban Political Economy,* edited by William K. Tabb and Larry Sawers (New York: Oxford University Press, 1978), 297–311; John Cowley *et al., Community or Class Struggle* (New York: Stage 1 Publishers, 1977); and Charles F. Grosser, *New Directions in Community Organization: From Enabling to Advocacy* (New York: Praeger, 1972).

For additional materials on the wide variety of neighborhood resistance and community control efforts that flourished in the late 1960s and early 1970s, see Alan Lupo, Frank Colcord, and Edmund Fowler, *Rites of Way: The Politics of Transportation in Boston and the U.S. City* (Boston: Little, Brown, 1971), which chronicles highway resistance efforts; *Confrontation at Ocean-Hill Brownsville,* edited by Maurice Berube and Marilyn Gittell (New York: Praeger, 1969), which details this prominent struggle for community control of schools in New York City; and J. Clarence Davies, *Neighborhood Groups and Urban Renewal* (New York: Columbia University Press, 1966), which describes urban renewal resistance.

The New Populism of the 1970s and 1980s

On changes in cities and neighborhoods in the last two decades, see Larry Bennett, *Fragments of Cities: The New American Downtowns and Neighborhoods* (Columbus: Ohio State University, 1990); *Beyond the City Limits: Urban Policy and Economic Restructuring in Comparative Perspective,* edited by John R. Logan and Todd Swanstrom

(Philadelphia: Temple University Press, 1990); David Harvey, *Studies in the History and Theory of Capitalist Urbanization* (Baltimore, Md.: Johns Hopkins University Press, 1985); John Mollenkopf, *The Contested City* (Princeton: Princeton University Press, 1983); *The Capitalist City: Global Restructuring and Community Politics,* edited by Michael Peter Smith and Joe Feagin (Oxford: Basil Blackwell, 1987); Susan S. Fainstein and Norman I. Fainstein, "Economic Restructuring and the Rise of Urban Social Movements," *Urban Affairs Quarterly* 21 (December 1985); and Todd Swanstrom *The Crisis of Growth Politics: Cleveland, Kucinich, and the Challenge of Urban Populism* (Philadelphia: Temple University Press, 1985).

An excellent source on the recent proliferation of voluntarism in the United States is Jennifer Wolch *The Shadow State: Government and Voluntary Sector in Transition* (New York: Foundation Center, 1990). On the phenomenon worldwide, see Alan Durning, "Action at the Grassroots: Fighting Poverty and Environmental Decline," *Worldwatch Paper 88* (January 1989): 1–70; *Mobilizing the Community: Local Politics in a Global Era,* edited by Robert Fisher and Joseph Kling (Newbury Park, Calif.: Sage, 1993); *Transforming the Revolution: Social Movements and the World-System,* edited by Samir Amin *et al.* (New York: Monthly Review Press, 1989); and the excellent essay by Stuart Corbridge, "Third World Development," *Progress in Human Geography* 15 (1991): 311–21. For case studies of grassroots organizing in other nations, see Arthur Bonner, *Averting the Apocalypse: Social Movements in India Today* (Durham: Duke University Press, 1990); Daniel Lehmann, *Democracy and Development in Latin America: Economics, Politics, and Religion in the Postwar Period* (Cambridge: Polity Press, 1990); Stuart Lowe, *Urban Social Movements: The City After Castells* (London: Macmillan, 1986); *Social Movements and the State in Latin America,* edited by David Slater (Holland: Foris Publications, 1985).

For historical and theoretical perspectives on pre-twentieth-century populism, see Lawrence Goodwyn, *The Populist Moment: A Short History of Agrarian Revolt in America* (New York: Oxford University Press, 1978); Bruce Palmer, *"Man over Money": The Southern Populist Critique of American Capitalism* (Chapel Hill: University of North Carolina Press, 1980); Craig Jackson Calhoun, *The Question of Class Struggle* (Chicago: University of Chicago Press, 1982), and his "The Radicalism of Tradition: Community Strength or Venerable Disguise and Borrowed Language?," *American Journal of Sociology* 88 (March

1983): 886–914. On the Alinsky roots of the new populism, see Harry C. Boyte, *The Backyard Revolution: Understanding the New Citizen Movement* (Philadelphia: Temple University Press, 1980). On Alinsky efforts with The Woodlawn Organization, begin with John Hall Fish, *Black Power/White Control: The Struggle of The Woodlawn Organization in Chicago* (Princeton: Princeton University Press, 1973). Lancourt, *Confront or Concede,* and Janice Perlman, "Grassrooting the System," *Social Policy* 7 (September–October 1976): 4–20, are excellent introductions to Alinsky and new populist organizing projects, respectively.

For information on neo-Alinsky organizing I relied heavily on interviews, organizer training workshops, organizational literature, and the expanding scholarship on the subject. See Boyte, *Backyard Revolution;* Si Kahn, *Organizing: A Guide for Grassroots Leaders* (New York: McGraw-Hill, 1982), and his *How People Get Power: Organizing Oppressed Communities for Action* (New York: McGraw-Hill, 1970); Michael Ansara, "The People's First: An Organizer's Notebook," *Working Papers for a New Society* 2 (Winter 1975): 26–38; Robert Rosenbloom, "The Politics of the Neighborhood Movement," *South Atlantic Urban Studies* 4 (1979): 103–20; Paul Wellstone, *How the Rural Poor Got Power: Narrative of a Grass-Roots Organizer* (Amherst: University of Massachusetts Press, 1978); and Linda Gordon and Allen Hunter, "Sex, Family, and the New Right: Anti-feminism as a Political Force," *Radical America* 11 (November 1977–February 1978): 9–26. On busing in Boston, J. Anthony Lukas, *Common Ground: A Turbulent Decade in the Lives of Three American Families* (New York: Vintage, 1985), is most readable.

For recent texts on neo-Alinsky organizing, see Gary Delgado, *Organizing the Movement: The Roots and Growth of ACORN* (Philadelphia: Temple University Press, 1986); ed., *After Alinsky: Community Organizing in Illinois,* edited by Peg Knoepfle (Springfield, Ill.: Illinois Issues, 1990); Harry Boyte, *Commonwealth: A Return to Citizen Politics* (New York: Free Press, 1989); *The New Populism: The Politics of Empowerment,* edited by Harry Boyte and Frank Reissman (Philadelphia: Temple University Press, 1986); Kim Bobo, Jackie Kendall, and Steve Max, *Organizing for Social Change: A Manual for Social Activists in the 1990s* (Washington, D.C.: Seven Locks Press, 1991); Mary Beth Rogers, *Cold Anger: A Story of Faith and Power Politics* (Denton: University of North Texas Press, 1990); and Gregory

Pierce, *Activism That Makes Sense: Congregations and Community Organization* (New York: Paulist Press, 1984).

The literature on the new community development is finally emerging. For early treatments, see Robert Cassidy, *Livable Cities: A Grass-Roots Guide to Rebuilding Urban America* (New York: Holt, Rinehart, and Winston, 1980); Phillip L. Clay, *Neighborhood Renewal: Middle Class Resettlement and Incumbent Upgrading in American Neighborhoods* (Lexington, Mass.: Lexington Books, 1979); and Harry Edward Berndt, *New Rulers in the Ghetto: The Community Development Corporation and Urban Poverty* (Westport, Conn.: Greenwood Press, 1977). More recent studies on community development and on CDCs more specifically include Christopher Gunn and Hazel Dayton Gunn, *Reclaiming Capital: Democratic Initiatives and Community Development* (Ithaca: Cornell University Press, 1991); Avis Vidal, *Rebuilding Communities: A National Study of Urban Community Development Corporations* (New York: Community Development Research Center, 1992); Neil Pierce and Carol Steinbach, *Enterprising Communities: Community-Based Development in America, 1990* (Washington, D.C.: Council for Community-Based Development, 1990); Neil Pierce and Carol Steinbach, *Corrective Capitalism: The Rise of America's Community Development Corporations* (New York: Ford Foundation, 1987); Benjamin Marquez, "Mexican American Community Development Corporations and the Limits of Directed Capitalism," *Economic Development Quarterly* 7 (August 1993), 287–95; W. Dennis Keating, "The Emergence of Community Development Corporations," *Shelterforce,* February/March/April 1989, 8–11, 14.

On other trends in the new populism of the 1970s, specifically the "neighborhood alternative institutions and technology" perspective, not discussed in this book, see David Morris and Karl Hess, *Neighborhood Power: The New Localism* (Boston: Beacon Press, 1975); *Coops, Communes, and Collectives: Experiments in Social Change in the 1960s and 1970s,* edited by John Case and Rosemary Taylor (New York: Pantheon, 1979). For materials on the positive impact of the new populism among working-class women, see Kathleen McCourt, *Working-Class Women and Grass-Roots Politics* (Bloomington: Indiana University Press, 1977).

For books on the social work approach to social action, see Ann Withorn, *Serving the People: Social Services and Social Change* (New

276		*Let the People Decide*

York: Columbia University Press, 1984); Stuart Rees, *Achieving Power: Practice and Policy in Social Welfare* (North Sydney, Australia: Allen and Unwin, 1991); *Not for Women Only: Social Work Practice for a Feminist Future,* edited by Mary Bricker-Jenkins and Nancy Hooyman (Silver Springs, Md.: NASW, 1986); John Erlich and Felix Rivera, *Community Organizing in a Diverse Society* (Boston: Allyn and Bacon, 1992).

For social work texts on community organizing, reflecting both social action and social service delivery functions, see Steve Burghardt, *The Other Side of Organizing* (Cambridge, Mass.: Schenkman, 1982); Herbert Rubin and Irene Rubin, *Community Organizing and Development Second Edition* (New York: Macmillan, 1992); eds., *Strategies of Community Organization,* 4th ed., edited by Fred M. Cox *et al.* (Itasca, Ill.: F. E. Peacock, 1987); Joan Ecklein, *Community Organizers* (New York: John Wiley and Sons, 1984); Lee Staples, *Roots to Power: A Manual for Grassroots Organizing* (New York: Praeger, 1984); and James Midgley *et al., Community Participation, Social Development, and the State* (New York: Methuen, 1986).

On coalition development, see, for starters, Jeremy Brecher and Tim Costello, *Building Bridges: The Emerging Grassroots Coalition of Labor and Community* (New York: Monthly Review Press, 1990); Sheila Collins, *The Rainbow Challenge* (New York: Monthly Review Press, 1986); and C. Spretnak and F. Capra, *Green Politics* (London: Grafton, 1985). On the difficulty of coalition development, see Barbara Epstein, *Political Protest and Cultural Revolution: Nonviolent Direct Action in the 1970s and 1980s* (Berkeley: University of California Press, 1991).

On privatization, see, for example, the excellent studies by Paul Starr, *The Limits of Privatization* (Washington, D.C.: Economic Policy Institute, 1987); Timothy Barnekov, Robin Boyle, and Daniel Rich, *Privatism and Urban Policy in Britain and the United States* (New York: Oxford University Press, 1989); Robin Hambleton, "Urban Government Under Thatcher and Reagan," *Urban Affairs Quarterly* 24 (March 1989): 359–88; and Jeffrey Henig, Chris Hamnett, and Harvey Feigenbaum, "The Politics of Privatization: A Comparative Perspective," *Governance: An International Journal of Policy and Administration* 1 (October 1988): 442–68. For perspectives more enamored of privatization, see the books by E. S. Savas, former assistant secretary of Housing and Urban Development in the Reagan years, *Privatization: The Key to Better Government* (Chatham, N.J.: Chatham House Publishers, 1987), and Randall Fitzgerald, *When Government Goes Private: Successful Alternatives to Public Services* (New York: Universe Books, 1988). On the challenge of privatization to community organizers, see Robert Fisher, "Organizing in the Private City: The Case of Houston, Texas," in *Black Dixie: Afro-Texan History and Culture in Houston,* edited by Howard Beeth and Cary Wintz (College Station: Texas A&M, 1992), 253–76.

For an introduction to recent work on social movement theory, including resource mobilization theory, see Aldon Morris, *The Origins of the Civil Rights Movement* (New York: Free Press, 1984); Doug McAdam, *Political Process and the Development of Black Insurgency* (Chicago: University of Chicago Press, 1982); James L. Wood and Maurice Jackson, *Social Movements: Development, Participation, and Dynamics* (Belmont, Calif.: Wadsworth Publishing, 1982). On new social movement theory, see Alain Touraine, *The Voice and the Eye: An Analysis of Social Movements,* translated by Alan Duff (London: Cambridge University Press, 1981); Alain Touraine, "An Introduction to the Study of Social Movements," *Social Research* 52 (Winter 1985); Manuel Castells, *The City and the Grassroots* (Berkeley: University of California Press, 1983); Alberto Melucci, *Nomads of the Present: Social Movements and Individual Needs in Contemporary Society* (Philadelphia: Temple University Press, 1989); Carl Boggs, *Social Movements and Political Power: Emerging Forms of Radicalism in the West* (Philadelphia: Temple University Press, 1982); *Challenging the Political Order: New Social and Political Movements in Western Democracies,* edited by Russel J. Dalton and Manfred Kuechler (New York: Oxford University Press, 1990); and *Mobilizing the Community: Local Politics in a Global Era,* edited by Robert Fisher and Joseph Kling (Newbury Park, Calif.: Sage Publishers, 1993). For a criticism of new social movement theory see Anthony Scott, *Ideology and the New Social Movements* (London: Unwin Hyman, 1990).

On the issue of ideological community organizing, see George Rude, *Ideology and Popular Protest* (New York: Pantheon, 1980); Robert Fisher and Joseph Kling, "Leading the People: Two Approaches to the Role of Ideology in Community Organizing," *Radical America* 21, no. 4 (January–February, 1987); Bob Fisher and Joe Kling, "Popular Mobilization in the 1990s: Prospects for the New Social Movements," *New Politics* 3 (Winter 1991): 71–84. Also see George Lipsitz, *A Life in the Struggle: Ivory Perry and the Culture of*

278 Let the People Decide

Opposition (Philadelphia: Temple University Press, 1988), for a discussion of indigenous leaders—"organic intellectuals"—as critical forces in the organizing process. See also Sara Evans and Harry Boyte, *Free Spaces: The Sources of Democratic Change in America* (New York: Harper and Row, 1986), for an emphasis on "free spaces" as the critical basis for grassroots resistance. For a broader interpretation of the nature and frequency of resistance, see James Scott, *Domination and the Arts of Resistance* (New Haven: Yale University Press, 1990).

On feminist theory, political economy, and community organizing most helpful were Jean Baker Miller, *Toward A New Psychology of Women* (Boston: Beacon Press, 1986); Sara Evans, *Personal Politics;* Ruth Sidel, *Women and Children Last: The Plight of Poor Women in Affluent America* (New York: Penguin, 1986); Angela Davis, *Women, Race, and Class* (New York: Random House, 1981); Bell Hooks, *Ain't I a Woman: Black Women and Feminism* (Boston: South End, 1981); Caroline Ramazanoglu, *Feminism and the Contradictions of Oppression* (New York: Routledge, 1989); Lorraine Gutierrez, "Working with women of color: An empowerment perspective," *Social Work* 35 (1990), 149–54; Cheryl Hyde, "A feminist model for macro practice: Promises and problems," *Administration in Social Work* 13 (1989), 145–181; and Marie Weil, "Women, community, and organizing," in *Feminist Visions for Social Work,* edited by Nan Van DenBergh & Linda Cooper (Silver Springs, Maryland: National Association of Social Workers, 1986), 187–210.

Index

League of United Latin American Cities
(LULAC), 177
Legal Services, 128
"Let the people decide," xvi, 43, 54–55,
107, 108, 154, 156
Lewis, Edith, 204
Lewis, John L., 64
Little Rock, Arkansas, organizing in,
151–52
Localism, as focus for organizing, 9, 111,
144, 146, 157
Logan, John (and Todd Swanstrom):
Beyond the City Limits, 180
Long, Huey, 36
Los Angeles, 40, 88

Majoritarian strategy, of organizing, 140,
146, 148
Malcolm X, 99, 120, 122
Manpower, 128
March, Herb, 58, 59
Marcus Avenue Improvement
Association, 86. *See also Shelley v.
Kraemer*
Mass Fair Share, 152, 153, 226
Max, Steve, 140, 196
McCarthyism, 69
McCourt, Kathleen, 165, 212
McDowell, Mary, 12
McKee, Elmore, 71–72
McLaurin, Charles, 110–11
Meacham, Steve, xiv, 198
Meegan, Joseph, 58, 59–61, 63
Metropolitan Organization, The (TMO),
xiii, 147
Mexican-American communities,
147
MidAmerican Institute, 146
Midgley, James, 218
Midwest Academy, 140, 196, 201
Mikulski, Barbara, 159
Militancy, in organizing, 33–65, 99, 103–7,
127–28, 152
Military Keynesianism. *See*
Keynesianism, military
Miller, Mike, 139, 194, 225
Milwaukee, Wisconsin, Socialist govern-
ment in, 25

Mission Community Organization
(MCO), 140
Mississippi Freedom Democratic Paty,
115
Mobilization for Youth (New York), 119,
126
Moderation, strategy of, 194–96, 199
Mohawk-Brighton (Cincinnati), 24, 27,
29, 31
Monongahela Valley, 187–88
Montgomery bus boycott (1957), 105
Moody, Kim, 115
Muste, A. J., 37

National Association for the
Advancement of Colored People
(NAACP), 85, 105, 177
National Association of Manufacturers, 4
National Association of Real Estate
Boards (NAREB), 84
National budget deficit, 134
National Civic Federation, 6
National Commission on Neighborhoods,
138
National Community Center Association
(NCAA), 19
National Federation of Settlements, 70
National Gay and Lesbian Task Force,
207
National Industrial Recovery Act (NIRA),
35
National Institute of Mental Health
(NIMH), 119–21
National Labor Relations Act (Wagner
Act), xviii, 36, 37, 47, 123, 129
National People's Action, xiii, 137, 153,
174, 186, 191, 202
National political economy: effect of on
local organizing, xviii, 4, 5; failure of
settlement houses to challenge, 10,
14; pump priming, 34–36. *See also*
Great Society projects, New Deal
National Recreation Association, 76
National Social Unit Organization
(NSUO), 26, 28
National Social Welfare Assembly, 73
National Welfare Rights Organization
(NWRO), 130, 140, 147–48

The Author

Robert Fisher is a professor at the Graduate School of Social Work, University of Houston, where he is also chair of political social work. He is the author of numerous articles on community organizing, urban policy, and social history and is, most recently, coeditor of *Mobilizing the Community: Local Politics in the Era of the Global City.*